Pauline Nostitz

Travels of Doctor and Madame Helfer in Syria, Mesopotamia,

Burmah and Other Lands

Vol. 2

Pauline Nostitz

Travels of Doctor and Madame Helfer in Syria, Mesopotamia, Burmah and Other Lands
Vol. 2

ISBN/EAN: 9783337246167

Printed in Europe, USA, Canada, Australia, Japan

Cover: Foto ©Andreas Hilbeck / pixelio.de

More available books at **www.hansebooks.com**

DOCTOR AND MADAME HELFER'S TRAVELS

VOL. II.

LONDON: PRINTED BY
SPOTTISWOODE AND CO., NEW-STREET SQUARE
AND PARLIAMENT STREET

TRAVELS

OF

DOCTOR AND MADAME HELFER

IN

SYRIA, MESOPOTAMIA, BURMAH

AND OTHER LANDS

NARRATED BY PAULINE, COUNTESS NOSTITZ (FORMERLY MADAME HELFER), AND RENDERED INTO ENGLISH BY MRS GEORGE STURGE

IN TWO VOLUMES

VOL. II.

LONDON
RICHARD BENTLEY & SON, NEW BURLINGTON STREET
Publishers in Ordinary to Her Majesty the Queen
1878

CONTENTS

OF

THE SECOND VOLUME.

CHAPTER	PAGE
I. From Bushire to Calcutta	1
II. Residence in Calcutta	23
III. Moulmein, and Expedition on the River Saluen	62
IV. Expedition to the Three Pagodas	125
V. On the River Tenasserim	192
VI. The Plantation at Mergui	207
VII. Helfer's Voyages in the Archipelago, and his Death	226
VIII. Continuation of the Plantation at Mergui	249
IX. The Health Resort, Darjeeling	257
X. In Egypt	269
XI. In London	281
XII. At the Court of Prussia	288
XIII. My Parental Home	298
XIV. In Bohemia	317
XV. The End of the Plantation	329
XVI. Prague and Vienna	336
XVII. Conclusion	343

SYRIA AND BRITISH BURMAH.

CHAPTER I.

FROM BUSHIRE TO CALCUTTA.

WITH eyes fixed on the shore to which we were bidding farewell, we left the roadstead of Bushire. There was no waving of handkerchiefs, no outward sign that friends were parting, probably for ever, but we gazed until our forms were no longer distinguishable to each other in the misty distance. Our thoughts then turned from the past to the future. This parting was like a repetition of the time when, full of undefined hopes and expectations, we left our native shores at Trieste. Helfer had then, however, a certain definite aim before him, in his intention of practising as a physician at Smyrna, but among Hindoos and Englishmen in India he had not even this. In the one case it was precluded by the system of caste, in the other, by the scarcely less decided prejudice of the English against any doctors but their own.

What awaited us in our new destination, how we should begin our life there, what the future might have in store for us, was veiled in impenetrable obscurity. Nevertheless, Helfer's face wore an expression of profound satisfaction, his eye sparkled in the certainty that the dreams of his youth were about to be realised. He imagined himself wandering amongst palm groves, finding a mine of treasures for his natural history collections; he was full of hope.

A favouring breeze rapidly brought us near the coasts of Arabia, and as we glided peacefully along, the captain beguiled the time with dreadful stories of the pirates, who had not long before infested these seas.

With the comfortable feeling of present security we listened to his tales without alarm; we were nearing the once dreaded coast of Omam, the haunt of the most savage Arab tribes, who were daring pirates, ruled the whole coast of the Persian Gulf as far as the Indian Ocean, and made navigation dangerous. As Wahabees they carried on their unhallowed traffic with special cruelty, actuated not only by rapacity but by religious fanaticism. They never accepted nor granted pardon, least of all to Europeans; they used to bind their prisoners to the gun-carriages, and coolly cut their throats, saying prayers the while. Large merchantmen were attacked by them, and even an English man-of-war, until, in 1821, the allied troops of the East India Company and the Imam of Muscat, whose existence was threatened by these independent tribes, routed them out of their haunts on the coast and the scattered islands, and, after a fierce struggle, destroyed their strongholds, and put an end to the nuisance for ever.

To our regret, the captain cast anchor a few miles off the harbour of Muscat, but he told us that a boat should be at our service. He would only permit us to land, however, on the solemn promise that we would come on board in the evening, for it endangered the lives of Europeans to spend a night on shore at this season. Exaggerated as we thought these precautions, we had to submit, and congratulated ourselves on being able to pay even so fleeting a visit to this interesting country. In the course of the next day, a boat, manned by powerful rowers, took us into the romantic bay of Muscat; it is a semi-circular inlet in the hills, on the coast, surrounded by bare and frowning cliffs, from 300 to 400 feet high; on their craggy heights there are ruins of forts and towers, dating from the time of the Portuguese dominion, long useless and inaccessible, inhabited only by hawks and sea-swallows. The cliffs are rent by clefts and fissures, into which daylight never penetrates. Large caves invite the visitor to seek shelter in them from the burning sun, but if he lingers long in them he is sure to incur the penalty of severe illness, or even death, so that our boatmen had strict orders not to permit us to land in any of them, much as we should have liked to explore them. They took us to the house of the British Consul, a wealthy Jewish merchant. Three Englishmen having succumbed to the climate within a short time, the Government had entrusted a native with this important post.

We were received, in a most obliging manner, by a tall and dignified man, with fine, curly hair and beard, clad in a long black robe. He could make himself understood in English, and the preliminary salutations over, he offered us an escort from his retinue of servants to explore the town, which we at once accepted.

Picturesque as it looks at a distance, rising in terraces at the foot of beetling crags, the interior, as in nearly all large oriental towns, is a labyrinth of dirty and narrow lanes. A very few handsome buildings tower above the roofs of the houses, such as the Imam's palace, which is a former Portuguese church transformed, and the Portuguese cathedral, still standing, though in a dilapidated state, and used as a warehouse. Besides these there is nothing to attract the eye but a pair of airy minarets, the consul's residence, and a few other buildings. They are shaded by isolated groups of palm trees, which, with a few spots, watered and cultivated outside the walls, are the only green things to be seen round Muscat. Not a tree nor shrub, not even a blade of grass relieves the eye.

But the maritime power which the harbour has to show is imposing; it is the key of the Persian Gulf, which it commands, and in European hands it would be a second Gibraltar. We were surprised by the forest of masts in the bay. Flags of all nations, and numerous native ones, fluttered in the breeze. These vessels supply the bazaar with all the necessaries of life in the greatest profusion: corn, meat, vegetables, fruit, fish, roasted locusts, a favourite article of food here, and every luxury of the European, Indian, and Chinese markets, the most *recherché* stuffs, spices, perfumes, precious stones, and many other costly wares, a striking contrast to the gloomy, dirty, narrow lanes of the bazaar. The booths, covered with lightly woven palm branches, afford protection from the sun, but let in the rain, turning the unpaved ground into mud.

The suburbs, which are extensive, consist of huts made of mats, and, during the rainy season, they are a mere swamp, peopled by nomadic Arabs and Abyssinian slaves. The townsfolk, on the contrary, are a medley of Arabs, Persians, Indians, Syrians, and even Kurds and Affghans, escaping from despotism at home, or attracted to the place as an emporium of trade. Then the intermarriages with negresses from Zanzibar and Habesh give rise to a singular variety of physiognomy, although to a European eye, not accustomed to the nicer shades of difference, all seem to have a character in common.

We were treated, without exception, with the utmost respect, though our light complexions and hair must have made us conspicuous; we were annoyed neither by curiosity nor Mussulman fanaticism like that of the Persians, who, though they pride themselves on their refined manners, would, but for timely aid, have driven me into the sea.

The most ancient and remarkable foreigners who have settled here are Indians of the Bangan caste, who come mostly from Scinde, Cutch, and Gujerat, and are permitted to live according to their own laws. By successful speculation they frequently attain great wealth and consideration, are employed by the Imam as agents and farmers of taxes, contrive to make themselves indispensable to him, and the dignity of the English consulate has often been conferred on one of their number.

They enjoy equal rights with the Moslems, extending even to revenge for bloodshed, which is only allowed to an Arab for the murder of one of his family. They are permitted to retain their custom of burning the dead, and to keep the sacred oxen in honour of their deities, and the number in the temple precincts sometimes amounts to 200. They do not bring their women here, abstain from intercourse with the natives, and live in voluntary celibacy, until they return home with their acquired wealth, often after an absence of fifteen or twenty years. These most cunning of all tradespeople, the Jews of the East, have a peculiar method of making themselves bankrupt, very advantageous to themselves, if not very honourable. They kindle a light in their shop in broad daylight, stand quietly by it, declare themselves insolvent, and await the result. When their creditors assemble they are soundly abused and thrashed, to the delight of the multitude. This may be done more than once, and is not considered derogatory to their honour, nor does it affect their business at a distance, and when the chastisement is over they at once make a fresh start.

The Imam of Muscat was spoken of as one of the most remarkable rulers in the East, an ideal of an oriental prince, combining justice, bravery, and courage with patriarchal simplicity, and he was said to be liberal and generous to Europeans.

No one in his extensive dominions was persecuted on account of his religion; he was very tolerant of other faiths, although, as the holy head of his sect, the Imam has to set an example to his people by strict observance of their religious usages. He must punctually perform the daily ablutions and devotions, wear the simplest attire, and no jewels, neither smoke tobacco, nor drink coffee, nor any spirituous drink, and he must himself make a pilgrimage to Mecca to present rich gifts to the shrine. Simple in his manners, he permitted everyone free access to him; even a beggar might approach him and sit down in his presence.

The war against the Wahabee pirates, the common foes of the Imam and the Indian Government, had given occasion to an alliance between the two states, which had been cemented by costly presents and mutual assurances of friendship.

Fatigue and the great heat induced me to seek rest and shelter in the consul's house, while Helfer, relying on the power he had acquired of making himself understood in Arabic, continued his walk alone.

I was welcomed by the lady of the house with many ceremonious prostrations; she was a stately dame, dressed in thick silks, adorned with the usual gold chains, bracelets, and pearl buckles, and enveloped in a large, white, gold embroidered veil. She threw it aside on my entrance, disclosing traces of great beauty, now fast disappearing under increasing *embonpoint*. With friendly nods she gave me her hand and led me to the divan. Unfortunately she knew no more English than I did Arabic, so that our communications were confined to looks and signs. But a remedy was at hand. In our boat there was an English sailor boy, who could speak sufficient Arabic to help us out. He was fetched, in order to gratify the lady's curiosity, which was much excited by my strange appearance. After they had conversed for a time, and the usual refreshments, sherbet and glico, had been handed, by two negro boys in rich costumes, she asked me whether I should like to pay a visit to the Imam's ladies, who had a great liking for Europeans, and would be much pleased to see a European lady, the greatest rarity here. She described the princess as being superior in knowledge and refinement to all the ladies of the country, perhaps to any other Mussulman lady. The proposal was therefore highly agreeable to me, though I said how much I regretted that we should not be able to understand one another. She considered for a few moments, with her eyes fixed on the English boy, who had performed his task of interpreter admirably.

'How old are you?' she asked.—'Twelve.' 'You can't be so much, you are so little. You are just ten, do you hear? Mind that, if you are asked.'

'We will take him with us to the palace,' she said; 'he cannot be more than ten, and at that age he has free access to the ladies' apartments.'

His dress, which was more than simple, appeared to occasion her some concern. But she had a resource for this difficulty also, and ordered one of her pages, who was about the same size, to array him in his clothes. This order went sorely against the negro. He gnashed his teeth and contemptuously scanned the boy, whom he perhaps took for a future rival, from head to foot, and did not stir, until a commanding look from his mistress informed him that no opposition would be tolerated, whereupon, with a humble prostration, he crossed his arms, and went slowly towards the door, followed by the sailor boy, who was much diverted by his helpless rage. But the door was scarcely closed when we heard a piercing scream. The negro had laid hold of the boy by his ears and hair, and thus dragged him along, and though he had lustily defended himself he was still smarting with the pain. The appearance of the mistress with angry mien and threats at once restored peace. Again humbly prostrating himself the refractory page now accomplished the metamorphosis of his foe, who soon reappeared, transformed out of knowledge. He had on loose red trousers drawn in at the ankles; over these a flying white muslin coat, fastened with a red girdle round the hips, while a large red shawl was bound turban fashion round his temples, beneath which flowed his long, rough, flaxen hair. For some reason or other, perhaps because he thought it beautiful, he had never allowed his hair to be cut. He stood at the door, looking rather sheepish, conscious of the comical figure he cut, while his rival regarded him with a look of triumph, as much as to say: '*I* don't look like that.'

We then mounted the asses which had meanwhile been brought round. The consul's wife, wrapped in a thick veil, bestrode hers like a man, while I rode in the same way, unveiled, by her side, in my Mamaluke garb, and our little interpreter followed with the rest of the attendants. After a short ride we reached the palace, where our visit had been announced. A wooden staircase, rather dark and not over clean, led to the upper floor of the ancient building, the lower apartments of which were wide open. We passed through several empty rooms before we reached a spacious apartment, in which there was quite an assemblage of women. There was great variety in their age, appearance, and costume, as there was also among the children with them; I reckoned that altogether there were over a hundred persons. They were the Imam's concubines, and attendants of his legitimate wife and the princesses. On our entrance they all rose and ranged themselves on one side to allow us to pass.

Our rapid passage through the room allowed me no time to observe them. At the further end, a large door was opened by one of the women, which led into the interior of the harem, the apartment of the Imam's lawful wife. Here there were four ladies, his mother, wife, daughter, and one of his sisters. The former was in the dark unadorned dress appropriate to a widow; she had thrown aside her veil, and sat erect upon raised cushions a little apart from the other ladies, whom she appeared to rule.

The Imam's wife, on the contrary, glittered in all the usual oriental splendour. Dressed in the most costly silks, richly embroidered in gold and silver, with ornaments of emeralds, pearls, and rubies, she was seated upon bright coloured cushions, interwoven with silver thread, spread upon handsome carpets. Her daughter, a girl of from twelve to fifteen, lay by her side, her delicate limbs only covered by a transparent crape like material, of a reddish purple colour, permitting one to admire the proportions of her slender form; but her face, as well as those of the others, was concealed by a wire mask, like a stone-breaker's spectacles, covering forehead, nose, and cheeks, down to the mouth, with oval openings for the eyes, the black edges of which enhanced the effect of their dark colour. These masks, ornamented with jewels of every hue, seemed to be not only intended to conceal the features, but to be articles of the toilet, considered to increase the beauty of the wearers, as the glittering gems formed an excellent foil to their black hair and dark complexions.

There was a large, bronze, four post bedstead in the room, with crimson velvet hangings, and the posts were specimens of artistic work. The Imam's wife said, pointing to it with evident pride: 'It is a present from Queen Victoria, ruler of England, my dear sister!' So the royal fellowship among sovereigns extends even to this remote corner of the world. The lady spoke further of the friendly relations between her husband and her Britannic Majesty, and said that she had presented him with a beautiful fire-ship. The queen mother was hemming a pocket handkerchief, and seeing me looking at it she showed it to me, and asked if she was doing it properly; she said that she had learnt to sew from European ladies, and was very fond of it. This was the first and only time that I ever saw an Asiatic lady employing herself in needle work. A eunuch came in before long and respectfully laid a letter at her feet. She hastily opened it, and told me that it was from the Imam, who, being absent in the wars, had sent her an account of his achievements. It seemed to please her very much to have this opportunity of displaying her superior talents. Costly fruits and preserves were afterwards served for us on crystal plates. The ladies then all withdrew into an adjoining apartment. I thought this very strange, but was told that it was the custom, in order that the visitor may eat as much as he likes. This is certainly a delicate trait of hospitality in countries where the stranger may travel all day through burning deserts, hungry and thirsty, and must eat prospectively. I thought of our ride to Baghdad, and the preliminary meal of the Aniza Arabs, before they felt able to appear as guests at our table, on board the *Euphrates*, without compromising their dignity. Hunger is a bad master of the ceremonies.

When the ladies reappeared, our metamorphosed sailor boy was looking wistfully at the dainties before him. The princesses invited him to help himself, but glancing at his girdle, which was not so easy as his sailor's jacket, he said: 'My belly is so full,' which, being interpreted into Arabic, caused a smile to play on the delicate ladies' lips. They invited him to stow away as much as he could in his ample trousers; he did not require pressing, and soon stuffed them so full that his head and arms appeared to grow out of two elephant's legs, and he looked droll enough.

I had observed that the ladies often regarded me with abashed looks, and after looking me in the face cast down their eyes. On inquiry I learned that my uncovered face was as repulsive to them as the sight of a naked person would be to us. They begged to be allowed to put me on a mask, and after an attendant had tied on a very ornamental one, they all exclaimed: 'Tahip, Tahip!' (beautiful, beautiful!)

For the second time I made the humiliating discovery that appreciation of my beauty did not depend on my personal charms but entirely on my toilet. Is it so very different in Europe, the home *par excellence* of the arts and æsthetics? Is not many a belle there too, only admired when half disfigured by some absurd fashion? The curious thing here was the careful concealment of the face, while the figure was so insufficiently covered with transparent crape.

I was told that this custom is very strictly observed, and that the sight of an uncovered female face is most painful, even to women themselves. A mother does not even see her daughter's face uncovered after her twelfth year; her husband only has the right of lifting her mask.

After many questions and reciprocal communications, in which the princesses showed more intelligence and cultivation than any Mussulman women I had met with, or even the Asiatic Christians, I took leave of them, giving them back the beautiful mask with regret, for I should have liked to have it as a keepsake.

According to promise, we returned on board in the evening, and the next morning a transport of horses was shipped. It was interesting to watch the process. Even the most fiery of them lost their spirit when they missed their firm footing on land; they stood trembling on the planks, and patiently allowed the girdles to be buckled on, by which, on a given signal, they were suddenly hoisted up into the vessel and let down into the hold.

One only lost his equanimity; he struggled with all his might, and knocked his head so hard against a beam that it killed him on the spot. The horses were packed as closely as possible, and prevented from lying down during the whole voyage by two herculean blacks. They told me that this was necessary, as with the rolling motion of the vessel they would be unable to get upon their legs again. No one but these negroes could stand the atmosphere. I tried to see for myself how they fared down there, but hastily retreated, the heat and steam would soon have stifled me.

There is not much that is pleasant to tell of a six weeks' voyage in a sailing vessel in Indian seas during the monsoon, when one storm, with fearful thunder and lightning, quickly succeeds another. I, especially, with my invincible tendency to sea-sickness, soon almost ceased to live a conscious life. Little cared I for the towering waves, with their crests of foam, the sporting dolphins, the flying-fish which fell on deck, and were considered a prize for food, nor the phosphoric lights which followed our track; not even a water spout from the nostrils of a whale near could excite my interest. I did not revive till land was signalled, and soon after we approached the pilot ship in the harbour, and took a pilot to guide our craft up the Hoogly to Calcutta—one of the most dangerous of voyages.

Even the most experienced seaman does not venture up this river without a pilot. From the moment when he comes on board he takes the entire command, and the captain, relieved of responsibility, after sleepless nights and toilsome days, mixes like a gentleman at leisure among his passengers.

In order to supply all vessels with pilots, a large ship lies at anchor far out in the bay. But it does not serve this purpose alone; it is fitted up for the reception of invalids, who come here to be cured, by sea-sickness (for the vessel only rocks the more from being anchored), of enlargement of the liver, the disease produced by living in the plains of Bengal. Horrible remedy—worse than the disease!

Helfer aroused me out of my lethargy with the exclamation: 'The palms of India bend their crowns to greet us,' and led me to the prow of the vessel. There were no palms to be seen, however, nothing but an immense volume of water rushing towards us from the river. The low shores, only just within sight, were covered with brushwood, among which the waters extended. We were in the empire of the Ganges, the largest river of Asia, which pours every instant 500,000 cubic feet of sweet, wholesome water, to the sea, spreads more blessings around than any other, and is held sacred by the inhabitants of its shores. The majestic stream flows from the head of the divine Siva, the sustainer of the universe, enthroned in the Himalayan heights, through the god's curly hair and beard; for it is thus that the myth represents the obstacles which mountain and forest present to its course. In order to denote the animal world which lurks in the forest regions, watered by the river, the god is represented, clad in an elephant's skin, riding upon a tiger, and encircled by serpents. This is very appropriate to the teeming animal life of the Ganges territory; the shores of the river are inhabited by millions of living things, from the insect, almost invisible to the naked eye, to the huge elephant, while its waters teem with creatures, which, though they fall a prey to the crocodiles, breed anew in inexhaustible number and variety.

Although the increasing population has for centuries disputed, with partial success, the possession of its fertile shores with wild beasts, in other parts, where the conformation of the ground or the climate is ill-adapted for human habitation, as in the Sunderbunds, where the Ganges, divided into many arms, empties itself into the sea, they still hold undisputed sway.

It swarms with monkeys, buffaloes, wild boars, gazelles, and every species of game; they swim in herds through the channels from island to island. The huge untamable rhinosceros flounders about in the mire of the forest thickets, unmolested and shunned by man. The woods are enlivened by flocks of birds, with brilliant plumage, and luminous insects, in the water and on the tops of the trees, light up the darkness of night. Thousands of glittering glowworms cling in rows to the slender stems of the marsh palm, which, swayed to and fro by the faintest breeze, look like diamond bouquets, more brilliant than any that ever adorned crowned head.

Reptiles crawl in the long grass. Here the large handsomely marked serpent, there the inconspicuous, but all the more dangerous cobra capella. Butterflies and beetles of every hue swarm in myriads. The royal Bengal tiger is the monarch of this varied animal world, and is here particularly fierce.

Various schemes have been set on foot by the English Government to open the Delta of the Ganges to cultivation, but they have all hitherto been frustrated by obstacles of every kind. The swampy nature of the soil for ten months of the year, the exhalations from the luxuriant vegetation and animal matter, fill the air with miasma, which the human constitution cannot withstand. Only the despised and unhappy race of the Molunghies, salt-makers, who are lower than the pariahs, are condemned to live in the islands of the Sunderbunds, or to fall a prey to wild beasts. The life of these people is, perhaps, the most melancholy on earth. Condemned to their occupation by their caste, they cannot escape it, the son must succeed his father in it. They cannot even save themselves by flight, for whenever escape is not rendered impossible by forests or impassable morasses, guards are placed to intercept it on the sandy tongues of land, stretching far into the sea, on which the Molunghies boil the crystals left by the incrustations of the retreating sea water in large salt pans.

Defenceless as they are, at the sight of the tiger lurking among the reeds, they fly to their caves dug in the sand, from which, however, the bloodthirsty beast not seldom drags forth his victim, though he generally attacks his prey from some safe ambush.

To such cruel subjection, avarice and religious delusions are capable of condemning a whole race of men.

Though not Hindoos, we moistened our foreheads and eyes with the sacred water of the Ganges, but we could not bring ourselves to drink the health-giving draught. It is too much adulterated for European lips.

The rising tide and a favouring wind bore us quickly up the stream; the river gradually narrowed, and we neared the shores, clothed by impenetrable forests, to which fruit gardens succeeded, shaded by the handsome crowns of the cocoa-nut palm. What a contrast to the Syrian deserts, the burning shores of the Persian Gulf, and the bare, dark cliffs of the coasts of Arabia. How refreshing was this verdure, which we had so long sighed for, to heart and eye.

A little boat brought alongside the first Hindoos, and the first tropical fruits, bananas, mangoes, and ananas, all the more welcome after a six weeks' voyage. I took the rowers for women—their delicate, almost weakly forms, their rounded arms and necks, small hands and feet, their regular features, and the mild expression of their beardless faces, their long, black hair, tied in a Grecian knot behind, made them look so like them. They wore nothing but a white cloth round the hips, but their velvety, spotless skin and nut-brown hue makes them look much less repulsive than would be the case with whites. They were Bengalese from the plains, genuine representatives of the mild but weak people who seem born to servitude and willingly submit to it.

The shores gradually closed in; bamboo huts were seen, surrounded by fruit gardens, and half hidden by the gigantic banana leaves.

After reaching the botanic garden on the right shore, we had the first glimpse of Calcutta, seven miles off.

By degrees we could distinguish the palatial buildings of the Europeans, and the masts of numberless ships tossing in the broad stream.

On August 20, on a hot afternoon, we cast anchor on the right shore opposite the city. We had a great wish not to land in the European quarter, but amongst the Hindoo population, and although the captain had seriously warned us against leaving the vessel without his knowledge, and had promised to find us suitable accommodation in the town, we took advantage of the bustle on board, and the preoccupation of captain and crew, to get into a native boat and hasten to shore.

I shall never forget my husband's beaming face when he really set foot on the soil of India, and his eye glanced over the exotic vegetation, among which he hoped soon to search for hidden treasures. His eye roamed above, below, and around, as if he longed to take it in all at once. I believe he would have bent his knees and given vent to his excitement in words of thankfulness, if we had not been surrounded by so many curious human beings. This restored his composure, and without concerning ourselves about them, as we did not understand a word of their language, we continued our stroll in and out through the leafy alleys in which their neat dwellings were placed. The huts of bamboo and lattice work lay hidden in thick foliage; the entrances protected by porches supported by slender poles, and the floors, raised a few steps, were covered with clean mats.

Many of the men were stretched on them comfortably smoking their chibouks, making fishing nets, or baskets, or were engaged in some other light occupation. The women were wrapped in dazzling white shawls, leaving the right arm and breast bare, and the face only partly veiled, so that we could admire their graceful forms and delicate hands and feet. They are not oppressed slaves, like other Asiatic women, condemned to hard and servile work; their lives are free from care or hardship. They were sitting at ease, or squatting on their heels, with naked little nurslings on their laps, while the elder children played near, or lay with their heads on their mothers' breasts.

Their placid countenances showed no trace of passionate affection. When they turned their fine eyes upon us their pleading looks seemed to say: 'Do not disturb our peace, it is the highest bliss of which we are capable.'

We continued our stroll for an hour, which seemed but a few minutes, among these abodes of peace, and yielded ourselves to their soothing influence. We scarcely felt the sun's rays; the Syrian steppes had steeled us against them, and the humid air, fragrant with vegetable odours, so dangerous to Europeans, was refreshing to us, and we inhaled full draughts of it, after the dry atmosphere, of which we had had more than enough.

But we had to retrace our steps, and return to the vessel in the boat that was waiting. Here anything but a peaceful reception awaited us; before we had ascended the ladder the captain's harsh voice greeted us with: 'Are you mad, Doctor, to go walking about at this season of the year, and this time of day? Do you and your lady want to get a sunstroke, to say the least, just as you have arrived at Calcutta?' and he muttered between his teeth, 'I should have thought as a doctor you would have had more sense.' But we were in such good spirits that we only smiled at his wrath, which anyhow betokened hearty goodwill, and of this we had had many proofs before, and we tried to calm him. Somewhat softened, he added: 'I will take you into a place of safety as soon as possible, for I don't want to have the responsibility of such imprudent passengers any longer.'

A boat was in readiness to take us to the other shore. We bade a laconic but hearty good-bye to the good captain, who had given us a letter of introduction to a lady at Calcutta, which he said would ensure us a kind reception. We were soon ready, for we were not encumbered with household goods, as at Smyrna. Our whole possessions, besides our worthy selves in rather weather-beaten costumes, consisted of a small portmanteau, containing some linen. Thus scantily equipped were we about to enter one of the most populous and, certainly, the most luxurious of cities, where money was not counted but measured.

Our boatmen steered dexterously through the crowd of ships of all nations, all sizes and shapes. Large ships, men-of-war, light brigs, and bulky merchantmen; clumsy Chinese junks, alongside of the swift Indian clippers, which carry opium to China; Arabian and Japanese vessels, native coasters, and river boats, all attracted by the lucrative trade of the free port of Calcutta. All were engrossed in their own affairs without troubling themselves about those of their neighbours, as if the world existed for the sake of their particular interests alone.

On the broad steps of the ghauts, the landing stairs, which men and women descend for their daily ablutions in the sacred river, regardless of the crocodiles lying in wait for their prey, we were received by a crowd of officious and noisy people, proving that this placid race could be bustling and active when there were a few annas to be earned.

We entered two palanquins that were standing ready, and were conveyed, at about the pace of a gentle trot, to the elegant quarter of the city. The only opening does not allow you to see out much in the reclining posture you assume; but we comforted ourselves that we should often walk this way, and just as it was getting dark we reached the house of Mrs. Wilson. She welcomed us as expected guests, and showed us into a room all in readiness, which, after what we had been used to, seemed like a really sumptuous apartment, though according to Anglo-Indian ideas it was anything but elegant or comfortable. Privations have their use; they teach us to value a moderate amount of comfort more highly.

We did not incline to join the distinguished society in the house, for as such it had been represented to us, that evening, but asked to have tea served in our own room, and retired early to rest, full of recollections of the past and vague visions of the future.

CHAPTER II.

RESIDENCE IN CALCUTTA.

THE bright morning sun awakened us out of refreshing sleep, such as I had never enjoyed at sea, and it must have been rather late, as the sun does not emerge very early from the morning mists.

We dressed quickly, and as carefully as our wardrobe permitted, and waited for the breakfast bell. There was a knock at the door, and Mrs. Wilson herself appeared; she had scarcely seen us in the dusk the evening before, and had come to take us to breakfast. She glanced in amazement from one to the other, and said: 'I expected to see Mrs. Helfer.' 'You were not mistaken,' I answered; 'I am Mrs. Helfer.' 'But,' she went on with some concern, 'in this costume!' My strange appearance, which had not before occurred to me, and the rigid propriety of English ladies, fell heavy on my heart. We had found the Mamaluke dress so very convenient and comfortable, and had become so used to it, that it had not occurred to us to change it, but we now at once perceived the necessity of Europeanising ourselves, and I informed the lady of our intention.

'Come at once then,' she said; 'I will take you to a *modiste's* near, where you will find the newest fashions from London and Paris'; and without waiting for an answer, as if she could not endure the sight of my dress for a moment, she ordered palanquins to take me to the *modiste's*, and Helfer to a tailor, for he too had to change his dress.

We soon arrived at a splendid shop, furnished with all the most tasteful and elegant requisites for a lady's toilet. I cast my eyes about for the simplest and most modest dresses; but as I also required linen, the proprietress took us up into her bedroom, and ordered piles of things to be brought up. These ladies now undertook to metamorphose me; while the one with contemptuous looks took off my clothes, the other measured and tried on, and chose out what she thought most suitable. I submitted passively to the inevitable, and had leisure to take a view of the room. The furniture was of mahogany and silk; there was a four post bedstead, elegantly carved, with hangings trimmed with heavy silk fringe, and the various washing and toilet apparatus were of silver; and this was the bedroom of a *marchande de modes!*

When I considered the percentage the unfortunate customers must have to pay for all this grandeur, and thought of my slender purse, I began to be alarmed, and begged them to be content with a simple dress, as I had not sufficient cash about me to pay.

'*Pay!*' said my hostess, 'and have money about you! Nobody does that. Only natives count and handle money!' I afterwards learnt to understand these words well enough, but they were quite a puzzle to me then. They went on selecting and laying aside such articles as they thought proper, until they made quite a heap, and then proceeded to dress me.

First of all I was laced up in stiff stays, which English ladies never dispense with, even in the greatest heat; they were to bring my figure, which was somewhat fallen abroad, into shape again. It was vain to protest, they pulled them tighter and tighter, until I was nearly suffocated. The rest was soon accomplished, and I beheld myself in the glass in a light blue flounced muslin. Then the fez and turban had to be taken off, and my hair, which had not been cut for some time, fell down in a thick and shapeless mass. Brushing and combing were of no use, it would not assume the form which was in vogue; it was too short to plait, and too stiff to curl, so there was nothing for it but to confine it with a band, and put it under a cap. An elegant *négligé* head-dress was therefore perched on my head, but the obstreperous hair would not keep in place. To myself I looked perfectly ridiculous, but the *modiste* was charmed with her wares and my appearance.

Thus metamorphosed I was carried back to the house, where Helfer, whose transformation had not taken so long, was waiting for me in his coat. We could not help laughing outright as we looked at each other, so strange and unbecoming did our dress appear. It was a good while before I could transform myself into a lady again, and become a match for the English women, with whom I now had to associate.

At the breakfast table we found a company of 'distinguished' ladies, who, although they had lost the bloom of youth, were all honoured with the title of

'Miss.' They were all very smartly dressed, if not in very good taste, and very anxious to make themselves agreeable to their neighbours, the gentlemen, who evidently belonged to the seafaring class, and to appreciate their jokes and anecdotes. At the head of the table was a jolly, weather-beaten captain, who played the part of host, and was obviously desirous, by undisguised winks and nods, to fan some of the tender flames which seemed to be struggling into life. He devoted his attentions to the daughter of the house, who received them not ungraciously, but with a good deal of affectation.

I felt rather ill at ease in this society, composed of such strange elements, but afterwards received an explanation of it. It seems that a considerable number of English ladies, who have given up hope of marriage in their own country, emigrate to India, where their countrymen, who go out early in life in the service of the East India Company, are cut off in remote stations from all intercourse with Europeans, and have no opportunity of finding wives. These gentlemen await the arrival of the ships with these fair emigrants with no little impatience, often go out to meet them, begin their courting on board, and frequently return engaged.

The scarcity of European ladies in India has produced the evil result that Englishmen of all classes live in concubinage with native women. Strange to say, these women are held in the greatest contempt by their own people, though it cannot arise from principles of morality, as, according to our notions, marriage among the Indians is nothing but concubinage. Every man takes as many wives as he likes, and frequently makes a lucrative trade out of it, particularly when a man of a high caste takes a wife from a wealthy family of a lower one, and makes the parents pay for the honour he does them. He does not even trouble himself to take his wife home, but leaves her with her relations, and repeating the transaction as often as possible, he goes from one wife to another, and lives an easy life of it.

This contempt among the Indians for the women who live with Europeans, arises from their prejudice against men without caste, and extends to their descendants. They despise these half-castes, as they are called, still more than their white fathers. It is a still more curious fact that nature behaves like a step-mother to the offspring of these mixed marriages. Although both parents belong to the Caucasian race, although the English have many personal advantages, and the Indian women are often beautiful, their children are generally very plain. They are quick of apprehension, learn easily, but seldom thoroughly, and are wanting in perseverance. From their mothers they seem to inherit nothing but an evil trait, a tendency to deceit. This is deeply rooted in the native character, and obscures their otherwise good and amiable qualities. In spite of the careful education which the children of these mixed marriages receive in an institution not far from Calcutta, the results are not very satisfactory. The knowledge of their origin, the degradation of their mothers, and their own ambiguous position, destroys their self-esteem, the germ of all other virtues. Of course there are many happy exceptions, and early removal of the children from home, and a careful education in Europe, seem most calculated to produce them.

When I went into our room again I found the parcels of clothing already there. I could not take any pleasure in the finery, but searched for the bill, which I knew must be enormous, but could not find it. Supposing that our hostess must have it, I sent to ask her. She came herself, much surprised at the inquiry. 'I have not received any account,' she said, 'and could not pay it if I had, for I have no money in the house. Your sircar will pay for you!' 'My sircar!' Who could this generous person be? But our eyes were soon to be opened on this point as well as on many others.

The enormous wealth of the English in Calcutta, the high salaries of even the lower officials, the absence of a working class of Europeans, and especially the rigid rules of caste among the Indian population, which makes every occupation only accessible to certain classes; the difficulty of unravelling the labyrinth of the native business transactions, and of following them in all their cunning machinations—all this has induced the Europeans to adopt the custom of the higher classes of natives, and to employ certain agents, the sircars, in all money transactions. They are not paid servants, on the contrary they deposit a sum as caution money; they conduct all the money transactions of their employers, make all purchases, and pay all household expenses. For this they receive considerable advances from the wealthy bankers, and from the officials, an assignment of their income. They keep a precise debit and credit account, and their gains consist of the profit they make of the money that passes through their hands.

The custom of having no money in the house, the aversion even to handling coin, is carried so far, that you never pay even for articles bought in the house, nor for a glass of iced water at a confectioner's, but write down the sum on a piece of paper, and underneath, 'Sircar to pay.' Everybody's sircar is well known, and is a sufficient guarantee to the vendors. The holders of these invoices call upon him once a month, and receive payment. It seldom happens that a sircar misappropriates the money entrusted to him, or that a European abuses his credit. Calcutta is not the place for idle tourists and swindlers; business and gain only, on a large scale, are carried on here.

Who was to be our sircar? And where were the funds to come from wherewith to entrust him for providing for our wants? These were pressing questions, and lay heavily upon our hearts, but our white skin, and the boundless credit it secures for its possessors, came to our aid. A man was soon found, who, having just set up in business, was content with small gains, willingly gave us his services, and made advances until we could receive remittances from home.

Our good spirits, nature's most valuable gift to man for his journey through life, confidence in ourselves, and in our ability to work, prevented our feeling in the least downhearted, though we did not yet know how to set about the worship of the golden calf which, in this modern Babel, more than anywhere else, is the end and aim of all endeavours. We had but one single letter of introduction to Calcutta, a few lines from Colonel Chesney to a Major Hutchinson, whom he had but once met, at the bedside of a common friend. This slight acquaintance, so insufficient for the introduction of strangers, was our one slender means of obtaining access to Anglo-Indian society. Anyone better acquainted with English exclusiveness would scarcely have ventured to avail himself of it; but we had made acquaintance with the English character under its most agreeable aspect, and so Helfer resolved to call on Major Hutchinson. He was in the service of the East India Company, as director of the cannon foundry at Cassipoor, and lived in a charming villa four miles and a half above the city, on the banks of the Hoogly.

The Major received him with some surprise and embarrassment, as is so often the case with the English on coming in contact with foreigners. But this soon gave way to lively interest in what Helfer told him about the Euphrates Expedition, which was of so much importance to Anglo-Indians. He was introduced to Mrs. Hutchinson, who made timid but rather solicitous inquiries about me. It appeared that our travels, under circumstances so peculiar, and involving so many hardships, had made her doubt whether I was a European or a person of colour, and she was anxious to assure herself on the point before committing herself. Finally, Helfer was most politely told, on taking leave, that Mrs. Hutchinson would not fail to call on Mrs. Helfer; this we took for a civil speech and nothing more. We were all the more surprised therefore when, the next morning, Mrs. Hutchinson was announced.

Her appearance was soft and gentle as moonlight on a summer night. Her complexion was of the most ethereal transparence, and pale as marble, an effect of long residence in the tropics. She had a sweet melancholy expression, and was in mourning for her youngest child, so that it was impossible not to feel attracted to her.

She was obviously embarrassed at first, and a slight flush suffused her cheeks. Scanning me with a timid, yet scrutinising glance, she hoped she did not intrude upon me. She had come to see that I was comfortably accommodated in this strange land, and whether she could be of any service to me. She had already won my heart, and my thanks were all the warmer and more sincere. As we sat together on the sofa we carried on a confidential conversation, in which she listened with eager interest to my unreserved communications, as to the objects of our journey and our adventures, while she told me about her quiet domestic life among a numerous family, and of her deep grief for the loss of her child, adding that she would soon be under the painful necessity of parting with her other children, and of sending them to England. On rising to take leave she said with modest, but earnest entreaty: 'Do not return my call, but allow me to send the carriage for you both to-morrow, and bearers to bring your luggage to our house.'

Seeing my look of surprise and indecision, she went

on to say; 'You are not so well accommodated as you ought to be, and it is our custom here to entertain people who are introduced to us, and to provide for their comfort. It will give me the greatest pleasure to see you at my house for as long as it is agreeable to you to stay.' And, as if she wished to remove any painful feeling of obligation, she added, with tears in her eyes: 'Your company will be a real pleasure to me in parting with my dear children. Pray do me this favour.'

I do *her* a favour when she was offering a place in her family circle to homeless wanderers like ourselves! Who could have refused? I should have liked to throw my arms round her neck and kiss her, but that would have been un-English. A pressure of the hand suffices to express the deepest feelings with the Britons, who are so unjustly called cold, and a warm grasp expressed my heartfelt thanks. The next morning we went to this hospitable house, received a hearty welcome, and were conducted to rooms prepared for us.

How neat and nice all the appointments were; how carefully every comfort was provided for, how refreshing the coolness and dim light caused by the half closed jalousies. But I was still more touched and delighted with the goodness of the lady of the house. I felt so much sympathy with, and sisterly attraction to her gentle nature, after being so long deprived of the society of educated women. What a sudden change had taken place in our circumstances, and how delightful it was, after our arduous and perilous travels, all at once to meet with a reception like this in a haven of peace and comfort, without merit or effort of our own.

I gave myself up freely to these pleasant influences and the increasing attraction between myself and Mrs. Hutchinson. It soon ripened into a friendship which lasted far beyond our stay of some months in their house, and after the return of both of us to Europe.

The house, a charming villa in the Italian style, was in the midst of a well-wooded park, such as only tropical Nature can produce, while the attachment of the owners to their native land had enriched and adorned it with products of more northern zones as far as it was practicable. European plants, such as oranges, figs, and almonds, only become acclimatised after several generations; the peach seldom thrives, the vine languishes and does not produce good fruit.

Numerous climbing plants, with fragrant blossoms, whose luxuriant foliage was impenetrable by the sun, were trained to form shady alleys which wound amongst the brilliant parterres. Arbours and tents invited to repose, for there is but little inclination for exercise, and means of rest and comfort are necessities.

One of these alleys led down to the river on whose banks a splendid banyan tree extended its shade far and wide. This tree, of which no European hothouse can give any idea, because space can never be found for it, for it might shelter 10,000 men under its branches, is far more striking to strangers than the cocoa-nut palm, with its superb crown; of this some idea, however imperfect, can be formed.

The banyan, Buddha tree (*Ficus religiosa*) does not consist of one trunk, but of a forest of trees, which are constantly rooting their fibres in the earth. These grow into stems, which, in their turn, plant new scions in the earth to afford fresh support and increased circumference to the mother trunk. Thus it stands, to all appearance, without beginning or end—a contradiction to the laws pervading all other organisms of the animal or vegetable world, and, as it never entirely dies, it is a symbol of eternal rejuvenescence.

It is perfectly intelligible that Indian natural philosophy, pantheism, should attribute divine characteristics to this tree, so unique in its nature and magnificence. In the sacred books of the Brahmins the banyan tree is represented, in a style at once chaste and sublime, as the symbol of the all-pervading, reproductive powers of Nature. Priestly decrees exalt the veneration of it into a dogma; the people place images of the gods upon its branches, erect their chapels, pagodas, and altars under them, and there they make their offerings. All Hindoo penitents, even Mussulman Fakirs, and the naked philosophers known as gymnosophists, mentioned in the earliest Indian history, choose this tree as their place of expiation. The far purer doctrine of the Buddhists beholds in the twofold nature of its roots and branches, directed both towards earth and heaven, a symbol of the physical and spiritual nature of man; and the Burman legend makes Buddha receive his divine nature beneath the shade of the banyan tree. Sitting cross-legged and motionless for eight days, at the foot of this monarch of the vegetable kingdom, absorbed in contemplation of expiation, he conquered his foes, ascended the eternal throne, attained sovereign power, and became an inexhaustible fountain of life to others.

After fatiguing walks we often found rest and coolness beneath its shade; but we observed that it was generally avoided by the inmates of the house, and resolved to discover the reason. As we were walking one day close to the river, a wave washed up a horribly disfigured human face, a second disclosed two arms. Other portions of bodies followed, suggesting the idea of a heap of corpses. We hastened to mention it at the house, but it was received with perfect indifference, as an everyday occurrence; only a servant, whose business it was, was sent with a long bamboo cane to clear the shore, and to push the bodies, which had met with some obstruction, back into the river. We then observed that numerous birds, apparently sitting on the water, were driven away by his approach. They were mostly vultures, standing on the corpses, and devouring their prey as they floated down.

The religious rite of burial in the sacred waters of the Ganges is not confined to corpses; the ashes of bodies that have been burnt are also consigned to it. And not the dead alone; the living either voluntarily, or under compulsion from their relatives, find a grave in the river. We were witnesses of an instance of this ourselves a few days afterwards, when, after collecting insects in the foam left by the receding tide, we were resting under a banyan tree, and observed a human being sitting close to the river. It was an old man with silver hair, leaning against the trunk of a tree; his eyes were fixed on the setting sun, he did not observe our approach, and seemed quite unconscious of everything around him. He was sitting so close to the edge of the water, that the rising tide would carry him away in a few minutes. Helfer, who had diligently studied Hindoostanee on the voyage from Muscat, roused the old man out of his lethargy, called his attention to his danger, and tried to get him away, but he refused his aid with disgust, reproached him with his officious interference, and said in a feeble voice: 'My sons have brought me here that I may find my end in the sacred waters. Begone! leave me undisturbed and undefiled in my last moments.'

Religious fanaticism often leads to this mode of putting an end to life, but as often it is want of means of support. The old people, when no longer able to earn anything, being a burden to their children, partly of their own free will, and partly under compulsion, seek death in the waters of the Ganges.

The repulsive custom of making the beautiful river a place of burial spoiled the pleasure of roaming along its shady shores. But during the great festivals, when the Hindoos put lights upon its waves all along its course, and let them float down the stream, they are very attractive. Everyone desires that his light shall shine bright and clear, and, if possible, reach the sea; so that the river is covered with boats of all sizes, from a nutshell to those of considerable dimensions, filled with burning tapers, and at night it is turned into a stream of fire which makes the stars look pale.

In accordance with the requirements of the climate, the massive walls of the house were pierced with numerous openings closed with jalousies. It was in the form of a rotunda, and was lighted from above;

all round the upper storey was a verandah which prevented the sun's rays from penetrating into the rooms. The lower floor was used for store rooms, kitchens, baths, and other offices, and all the living and sleeping rooms were in the upper storey, having an opening to the verandah, by which a great draught could be produced which would be most unhealthy in Europe. The coolness produced by this and the punkah was so great that at first I had to get used to it, and was often obliged to move out of the current of air.

You rise at daybreak, mount the horses ready for you, and take a ride in the twilight, for the sake of exercise. The sun has scarcely risen, when the riders seek the shelter of their houses as if they were fleeing from the Evil One. It is said that the rays of the rising sun are more unpleasant than his perpendicular beams at mid-day, because they strike the whole body sideways. We were steeled against the heat, and it produced no unpleasant effects; but I became more susceptible to it afterwards.

In the evening comes a drive on the Corso, where the elegant world assembles in carriages or on horseback, but never on foot. European feet never touch the ground, partly because the white gentlemen love their ease too well, and partly because they think it beneath their dignity. The carriage is accompanied by two servants, who lead the horses and keep pace with them. For the novice it is a distressing sight—you feel sure that the runners must be over-exerting themselves; but it is a mistake, for once, when I made my runner sit behind instead, he came next morning to give warning, because, as he said, he had been disgraced.

At the close of the day, or rather as night sets in, dinner, the centre of English social life, is served. Taciturn by nature, and unskilled in light and pleasant chat, an English company assembled for conversation alone is apt to fall into painful pauses, and at dinner these are filled by the clatter of knives and forks. Dinners, therefore, at Calcutta were the order of the day, and were served with all possible luxury and comfort. Behind the chairs of the guests stand their servants (kitmojara), two or three of whom accompany their master to the host's house. This phalanx of attendants has a very imposing effect.

Although pretty well acquainted with the rigid forms of English society, the funereal air assumed on drinking wine together was quite incomprehensible—I might say repulsive—to me. The ceremony might have been taken for an affair of state, or an expression of condolence rather than as a matter of courtesy and sociability. Above all things, I was puzzled to know why gentlemen only were asked, and resolved one day to get an explanation, and perhaps to create a little joke in the solemn company; so I raised my glass, and bowed to a gentleman whom I knew very well, saying 'To your health!'

I was prepared for some surprise, but the effect far surpassed my expectations. A bolt out of the blue falling upon the table could hardly have produced a greater effect. Everyone started on his chair, nervous people nearly fainted, an Oh! and Ah! escaped from several lips, while I, the author of the mischief, could hardly muster sufficient gravity to apologise for my ignorance of English customs. When people's minds were somewhat calmed, a conversation arose about foreign usages and fashions, which gave me an opportunity of lashing some other absurd but rigidly-observed customs, and thus it was turned out of the every-day channel, for which I afterwards received the thanks of the company.

Towards the end of the meal the hookah is brought to the gentlemen—a smoking apparatus of the most elaborate kind. From a broad foot of dark metal inlaid with silver, rises a pipe two feet long wound round with coloured silks and gold thread, with a silver knob at the end of the size of a goose's egg. A second pipe branches out from the middle of the first, to which a tube, from four to six feet long, with a silver mouthpiece is fixed. The compound to be smoked consists of tobacco scalded, dried, and pounded, with which bananas, peaches, rose-water, and sundry spices are mixed. It is made into a ball, and placed in the knob, upon which another ball is placed made of pounded charcoal mixed with rose-water; this is ignited, and the smoker inhales in long deep draughts the vapour of the glowing ball, which is cooled in passing through the tube and the water in the vessel below.

As the uniform burning of the compound is necessary to its perfection, gentlemen of importance always have a servant on purpose to attend to the hookah, called a hookah-badar, behind the apparatus, who keeps it in order with a silver staff, and protects it from too much draught by a low screen.

The flavour of the vapour depends upon the preparation of the compound, which it is the business of the hookah-badar to mix; he must be well initiated into the mysteries of his art, and is paid and prized in proportion to his skill. Bolt upright and with solemn air, without moving a muscle of his face, he stands behind the apparatus as long as his master smokes—often several hours.

Even the ladies do not disdain to take a few whiffs of the aromatic hookah. Thus the English potentates transform themselves into Indian nabobs, and adopt the manners and prejudices of the natives; they, however, certainly adopt some good Asiatic characteristics also —hospitality, for instance.

It is difficult to distinguish the one you want from among the multitude of servants. Although they are known by their costume being more or less rich, by their mode of twisting a turban, by their girdle, and especially by the tattooing of their faces with yellow, it requires study to know a bearer from a waiter, a water-carrier from a tailor, a driver from a sweeper, a steward from a hookah-badar, &c., not to mention all the under-servants of the offices and kitchen; dignity forbids the lady of the house ever to enter these.

There are but two female servants—the ayah, lady's maid, and the meterain, her assistant. All the other work, even the washing and getting-up of ladies' clothes, is done by men.

The separation of work is so rigidly observed that no servant will ever do a thing that belongs to another. I once handed a cup that I had been using to a sweeper.

He started, and put his hands behind his back. The man whose office it was to do really dirty work considered it pollution to handle a cup that my lips had touched!

A foreigner who wishes to secure peace and order in his establishment can only do so by entrusting the entire management of it to an efficient house steward, by submitting to all his arrangements, giving up all his European notions, and never himself interfering with his thirty-two servants. This sounds pleasant enough, but it is not so easy to get accustomed to so idle a life. It takes time, and the enervating effect of the climate. As guests in Major Hutchinson's house, we had only nine personal attendants, but at first some collisions arose through our ignorance of the usages and the deeply-rooted caste prejudices which prevail even amongst humane and enlightened Europeans.

Helfer had sought in vain for an assistant in his pursuits as a naturalist; not one of the poor men sitting about doing nothing could be prevailed upon, even for good pay, to help catch and kill the creatures.

One day he caught sight of a remarkably handsome youth; his scanty clothing enabled you to admire his well-proportioned figure and his spotless nut-brown skin. He did not, like the rest, turn with disgust from Helfer's pursuits, but looked attentively on, and was willing to help. Delighted with his find, Helfer at once took him as his assistant, and as we wanted another waiter, and the youth was as handy as he was good-looking, we decided to promote him to be our khitmatgar, had a handsome suit made for him, such as is worn by these servants, with turban and girdle, and felt quite proud of him as he stood behind our chairs.

But our satisfaction was of short duration. All the servants ran away in a fright as soon as they saw him. No one would touch a thing that he had touched. They had at once recognised him as a pariah of no caste, and even to breathe the same air was pollution. And not the servants alone; even the excellent and kind-hearted master of the house confessed that the presence of this outcast, neat and good-looking as he was, was disagreeable to him, and that he could not tolerate him in his house.

It is difficult for people fresh from Europe to understand these things, but you learn it in time, and even adopt the prejudice yourself. As the outcast might not enter the house, it resulted in Helfer's using an unoccupied pavilion outside for a work-room, greatly to the satisfaction of all the inmates, who had observed his proceedings in capturing, killing, and impaling insects with no little horror.

The Europeans are no less objects of contempt to the Indians than other castes among themselves. After a walk I stepped one day into a poor, but clean-looking Hindoo hut, and asked for some water. A jar was at once handed to me—one of those vessels of porous clay which are set in a current of air to cool. I quaffed the cooling draught, and handed the half-emptied jar with thanks back to the man. He took it, but at once threw it on the ground and broke it to pieces.

There was I, in virtue of my white skin, one of the few who rule over millions, and yet the poorest dweller in a hut considered himself polluted by sharing anything with me. Deep in thought, and with downcast eyes, I stole away.

Still this caste system is not without its humorous aspects. The daily march of the tailor colony into Calcutta is a most diverting sight.

The caste of the Dirji, divided into men's and women's tailors, forms the exclusive population of a place two miles off. Every establishment, in default of female sempstresses, has a dirji for ladies' and another for gentlemen's clothes. The tailors come at nine o'clock to their employers' houses, and have to come across the open plain between Fort William and the city. The short time they allow themselves for their walk obliges them to make great haste, and one sees this army of figures, as thin as whipping-posts, their faultless white muslin dress fluttering in the breeze, approaching the city in a line with giant strides, and all keeping time. If one did not know that they are armed only with needles, scissors, and thimbles, one might tremble for the city.

Arrived at their destination, they sit cross-legged on a clean mat, with a jar of water by their sides, the only thing they taste all day. Four o'clock is their hour of release, and they hasten home in the same way, and take a scanty meal of a handful of rice.

In their work they are patterns of precision and accuracy, only you must take care not to trust anything to their common sense. I once gave my tailor a piece of a beautiful material to make a dress, giving him an old one for a pattern, in which there was a large patch in the front breadth. Having full confidence in my tailor's skill, I left him to himself without looking after him. What was my horror when the man brought me the dress, and with triumphant air showed me how artistically he had put the patch, like the one in the pattern, into the hole he had cut in the new material!

We did not share the fear of the English of taking exercise in the open air, and it is certainly the cause of many of their complaints. It is not to be denied that the effect of the sun's rays is dangerous to Europeans at certain seasons and at some hours of the day, but the entire absence of sunlight, being shut up in darkened and artificially-cooled rooms, and the indolent repose in which the ladies indulge, is far more injurious. The death-like paleness which makes them look like marble is one of the effects of it. We, on the contrary, being used to a great deal of exercise, and steeled against the heat, kept up our usual habits, and made excursions in a carriage, in palanquins, and even on foot, in the neighbourhood of Cassipoor, and sometimes as far as Calcutta.

The nearest way was along the river, and past the place appointed for burning dead bodies. We did not often go that way—the smell was too disgusting, as well as the little heaps of ashes, like molehills, on the sooty ground; and worst of all were the vultures, the only living creatures which had selected this spot, dedicated to the dead, for their abode. They often stood in flocks, insatiable yet lazy-looking, round the smouldering remains of human corpses. They evidently considered themselves masters of the situation, and, protected by the inviolability secured by popular superstition, they gave place to no one, and did not stir an inch if you went near them. More repulsive creatures I have never seen.

From this point the city begins; first come the huts of the poorest Hindoos, made of clay and bamboo, but they are neat, and, under the shade of giant banana leaves, or embosomed in shady fruit gardens, they appeared to me far more picturesque than the houses of the middle-class Mussulmans, which come next; they are built of dark-coloured bricks, with narrow doors and windows, and a high wall protects them from curious eyes.

The streets in this quarter get narrower and narrower, and the unpaved and unwatered soil more dusty; but the wares in the bazaars become richer and more varied too, and the crowds of people of all grades and in every costume, brought together by the traffic, become denser and more noisy.

Mollahs, finishing off their prayers with a howl, naked Fakirs who try to secure heaven after death and gifts on earth by horrible self-torture, martyrs with an iron hook through the skin of their backs, on which they swing themselves to death, all mingled together; and amidst the crowd stalks the sacred bull, conscious of his inviolability. The multitude respectfully makes way for him; to lay hands on him is a crime greater than murder.

Funerals proceed slowly to the place of burning, followed by howling women and a wailing widow, who, even if she never loved her husband, is inconsolable, because she may no longer observe the old custom of burning herself alive on his funeral pile, so hard is the lot of widows.

In the house of a distinguished Indian I once saw, not far from a company of well-dressed women, a bundle of dark blue stuff in a remote corner, which, on a closer inspection, proved to be alive. They told me she was a widow who had been detected as she was about to burn herself. Her relatives made her unveil herself, and show me how her face, arms, and breast were disfigured by burns.

The funeral pile, in a remote district, on which she was sitting with her husband's body, was already ignited, and tongues of flame were shooting up, when police officers interfered with the ceremony, took the woman away by force, and returned her, inconsolable, to her family.

During the time of the popular festivals it is not advisable for Europeans to walk the streets, though the sepoys do their best to keep order. Juggernaut, the god with no legs and stumps for arms, whom, according to the legend, Vishnu, the god-maker, left unfinished, because he was disturbed in his work, is then drawn on a huge car, under a golden canopy, through the streets, and the fanatical people throw themselves under the heavy wheels on purpose to be crushed by them.

The British Government, with wise moderation in respect to the deeply-rooted religious prejudices of the people, never interferes with their worship. In two cases only has it asserted its authority—in the abolition of sutteeism, and the attempt to ameliorate the condition of widows by permitting them to marry again; and it has, as far as possible, exterminated the Thugs, a sect whose method of serving their god, Durga-Kali, was by strangling their enemies.

Among all the representations of deities, that of Durga-Kali is the most hideous. She is a black woman with four arms; one hand grasps a sword, another a giant's head, while the other two are extended in an attitude either of threatening or blessing. She wears two corpses for earrings, and a necklace made of skulls, reaching to the knees; her tongue, of a blood red colour, hangs out of her mouth, below her chin; a girdle of giant hands encircles her body, her hair reaches down to her heels, her eyes are bloodshot, and her eyebrows bloody. She stands with one foot on the breast, the other on the thigh of her husband, the giant Sira, in memory of the war she waged with, and the victory she won over the giants for the gods.

The enemies of the gods in human form spring from the drops of blood of the giant she beheaded. To kill them by shedding their blood would only add to their numbers, as a new race springs from every drop; Durga-Kali, therefore, enjoined upon the secret league who have bound themselves to exterminate the enemies of the gods, to kill them only by strangling or hanging. This secret league carries on its murderous trade according to certain marks, which the posterity of the blood of the giants are said to bear, or actuated by the booty they hope to gain. Its members keep company with their chosen victims under pretext of friendly service, until a favourable moment occurs for throwing a peculiar kind of noose round their necks and throttling them. Singularly enough, they consider white men to have been created later, and therefore to be exempt from the laws of their league, and do not attack them.

As before stated, this sect, as far as it is possible in this extensive empire, has been exterminated, but other customs still exist which have degenerated into murderous fanaticism.

The mouths of sick persons on their exclaiming 'Oribali'—I call upon God—are still filled with the mud of the sacred Ganges to consecrate them to death by suffocation. He who lives in spite of it is cast out by the gods, and therefore by men also. The unfortunate man loses his caste, and seeks an asylum in the village of the Risen from the Dead, on the island of Cassembagar in the Ganges, which is held peculiarly sacred.

In the neighbourhood of Calcutta there are troops of hanumans, long-tailed monkeys, which are considered to be princes metamorphosed in the transmigration of souls, and therefore inviolable. Their audacity is amazing. Troops of them run through the gardens, and over the roofs of the houses, and do much mischief. But the natives do not dare to molest them, and when once some English officers drove them to the river they had some difficulty in escaping from the fanatical rage of the mob.

Thus priestly dogmas, ambition, and self-aggrandisement, have turned pure pantheism into a frightful caricature by personifying as deities the forces of Nature, the processes of which are nowhere so obvious as they are here, and infinitely multiplying them. The number of gods is reckoned at 330,000,000.

Thus in a land of boundless wealth which seems adapted to be the very home of prosperity, the priests have for ages bound in rigid fetters a numerous, tractable, and finely-formed race of men, possessing high mental gifts, and fully capable of receiving all the blessings of civilisation; they have destroyed every sentiment of self-esteem, and so utterly stifled all idea of the sanctity of truth that lying and bearing false witness have become deeply ingrained vices, while they have reserved to themselves all earthly prosperity and the hope of future bliss.

But even here the dawn of civilisation is approaching. Great tracts of country, formerly mere swamps, have been rendered habitable by European culture; wild beasts which once held sway over fruitful territories, and attacked the natives in their agricultural operations, have been exterminated or driven back into the jungles; British legislation affords a security of person and property never enjoyed before; and by the dissemination of knowledge in public schools, without being carried away by zeal for conversion, the English will bring the natives to a knowledge of their errors, and train them for the pursuit of light and truth. May this glorious mission be recognised, and be crowned with success!

Helfer had diligently pursued his researches, and made collections in the neighbourhoods of Cassipoor and Calcutta; but these parts having been thoroughly explored before, did not offer much that was new and interesting. He had by no means lost sight of his desire to explore regions as yet unvisited by Europeans. But the difficulties and great expense of travelling in the interior of Asia made such an undertaking on his own account impracticable. His aim now, therefore, was to awaken the interest of influential men for natural history, in the hope that he might possibly obtain a commission under Government to undertake some exploring expedition.

He was most kindly assisted in his objects by our host, who was a man of cultivated and scientific tastes. He introduced Helfer to men of influence, and pointed out how desirable an exploration would be of some of the little known parts of India.

Major Hutchinson's introduction secured him a polite reception everywhere, and he met with a hearty welcome from some scientific men—among them James Prinsep; but, generally speaking, he found but little sympathy with his tastes. People in this vast empire were too busy with more important affairs to trouble themselves about natural history.

As the distance from Cassipoor prevented our keeping up much intercourse with the city, we moved into Calcutta, reluctant as we were to leave our hospitable friends. As our stay there, however, was never intended to be more than temporary, we did not wish to set up housekeeping, and went to a well-managed boarding-house in Chowringhee. From the windows of our bed-room, which was high up, we had a fine view over the finer parts of the city, which greatly pleased us, as the plain all round Calcutta affords no point for a general view.

It was interesting to watch the roof and gallery of Government House, which were every evening decorated with living statues. The birds called adjutants, a species of stork, much larger than our storks, with broad bare skulls and long beaks with a pouch, always made it their rendezvous. They took up their station every evening at the same time on the balustrade of the gallery, and stood there motionless, on one leg, till darkness concealed them from view. In the day they walk about the streets as if they formed part of society. No one thinks of interfering with them. They stand for hours on one leg, looking on the ground as if in the deepest meditation, philosophically ignoring the impertinences of the small birds until one of them makes so bold as to come too near one of the storks' heads. He is then caught and disappears down his long throat, the stork standing as before, looking as if nothing had happened.

The birds are very bold in these countries. The rooks, so shy with us, used to pay us visits at breakfast time; at first they only came to the window-sill, then inside the window, and at last to the breakfast-table, where they helped themselves without ceremony. I was at last obliged to close the jalousies to get rid of their thievishness.

We became intimate here with some agreeable families, who showed us much kindness; among them I may mention Sir Charles and Lady d'Oyly, in whose house we were warmly welcomed. Sir Charles was an excellent landscape painter, and although his time was much occupied, as he was a member of the Board of Control, he was so condescending as to give me lessons in drawing, saying that I might visit many interesting places, and should be sorry not to be able to take sketches.

These lessons and the society of Lady d'Oyly were the bright spots in my residence at Calcutta, and they were afterwards the cause of a turning-point in our lives.

Helfer continued to direct attention to various branches of natural history, deserving the attention of Europeans and the Government, not only from a scientific but from a mercantile point of view. He gave a course of lectures in the town-hall on various subjects of this nature —among others, on the silkworm, showing the advantages of its systematic culture, and how well the natives would be adapted for it, as it would afford profitable employment to many who are unfit for severe labour.

His lectures excited some attention. The 'Friend of India' took up the question, and urged the Government to profit by his suggestions. Still they did not produce the desired effect among the influential classes. In spite of the politeness with which he was treated, it seemed as if something inexplicable frustrated his wishes.

Weary of idly waiting, and not disposed to be dependent on the favour or disfavour of other people, and always keeping his eye on Central Asia, he thought it would be best to approach it by a journey to Lahore, of whose ruler, old Runjeet Singh, of his liking for Europeans, and of his desire to turn their knowledge to the advantage of his country, he had heard a great deal.

There was much to be said for and against this scheme; for one thing, he was reluctant to expose me to an unsettled life again. He tried, therefore, to collect as much information about Lahore as possible, to enable us to decide.

Among others, we had made the acquaintance of a wealthy and distinguished Indian, the Nabob Dwakanat Tagore, a man who had thoroughly imbibed European culture, and associated chiefly with educated Europeans. He had built himself a villa in a splendid park, complete and well-appointed in every respect, a great contrast to the palaces of Oriental grandees in general, in which, with all their splendour, disorder and dirt abound.

A gallery of pictures selected by connoisseurs, a collection of engravings, a well-stocked library, and a beautiful music-room, gave evidence of the refined taste of the master of the house.

The most curious sight, however, was himself, as, in rich Indian costume, he sat at the piano, and sang an Italian air. Not that his singing was anything remarkable, but the whole scene was so unusual, and his desire to appear thoroughly European so evident. He wished to adopt everything that came from the land of industry and the arts, and asked Helfer to teach him some German songs that had been admired.

He was so generous and hospitable that his country-seat was quite a rendezvous for European society, and often a resource for newly-married couples who were not able to take a long wedding journey, and yet wished, according to English custom, to spend the honeymoon in retirement.

This remarkable man greatly interested Helfer; they often held long conversations as to the practicability of his ideas about culture of the soil, and the Nabob at length proposed that my husband should carry some of them out at his expense in his extensive territories.

The proposal was gratifying and advantageous to Helfer, but it altogether set aside the end he had proposed to himself, and would have turned the man of scientific research into an agriculturist, for which he did not consider that he had any vocation or talent.

He hesitated between these two plans, sometimes advised to the one, sometimes to the other by our friends. The editor of the 'Friend of India' encouraged him to wait, and continually urged the Government in its pages to avail itself of Helfer's services, and said that it would be a reproach if it allowed a scientific explorer, of whom there were but few in the service of the Company, to escape it, and probably to be outdone by Runjeet Singh in appreciating him.

These well-meant but not always judicious harangues having failed of their object, Helfer inclined to go to Lahore, and took measures to secure a favourable reception there, when an unexpected circumstance again gave a turn to events entirely in accordance with his wishes.

One day when I was with Lady d'Oyly, she received a call from a Frenchman, General Allard, who had long been in the service of Runjeet Singh. He had taken his beautiful wife, a lady from Cashmere, and her children to France, and was now returning according to promise to his master, who placed great confidence in him, and had entrusted him with the command of his military affairs. He availed himself of a short stay at Calcutta on his way to call upon the chief personages in the Government circle, and thus it happened that I became acquainted with him. He did not speak English, and Lady d'Oyly but little French, so it fell to my lot to be interpreter, and thus the general's attention was more attracted to me than it otherwise would have been.

When he heard my name, he repeated it thoughtfully to himself; then as if something he had forgotten had come into his mind, he said : 'I have heard your name before; I believe I even have something for you.' This seemed to me very unlikely, for there could be no relations between us; but he continued : 'Allow me to hasten home; I shall doubtless find it among my papers.' So he left, begging permission to call next day. I shook my head incredulously, but awaited in some suspense the solution of this curious incident which the morrow was to bring.

Soon after breakfast General Allard was announced. He looked much pleased, and held a sheet of paper and a letter in his hand which he handed to me, saying: 'I have great pleasure in delivering this letter from Count Mülinen, from Paris, and at the same time to be reminded by it how warmly he commended you both to me.'

It must be mentioned in explanation that I had, at Paris, made the acquaintance of the family of Count Mülinen, the Wurtemberg ambassador, and had enjoyed their friendship. During our travels I had from time to time informed them of our adventures, and had mentioned our intention of going to Lahore.

General Allard's stay in Paris, of whose influence in Lahore Count Mülinen was aware, gave him the opportunity of recommending us to his protection on his return, and to prevent our being forgotten by a busy man, and knowing how much good connections are thought of in certain circles, he had mentioned in the open letter of introduction that I was a niece of the celebrated Prussian general Count Bülow von Dennewitz.

Without a suspicion of the influence which this paper was to exert, I was gratified by receiving a proof of interest in us from Europe, as well at the prospect it afforded my husband of protection in Lahore. But it was to have other and much more important consequences.

Our friends in Calcutta took advantage of the letter of introduction from Count Mülinen, and cleverly contrived that it should get into the hands of those in authority.

What wonders were worked by these few lines. Although neither the recommendation of cultivated men, nor Helfer's own lectures, had been able to procure for him the recommendation he deserved, it was effected by a few words, which accredited us with being well-connected! So it was, so it is, and so it ever will be, in spite of the advance of equality and fraternity.

The very next day Helfer received an invitation to a scientific soirée at Government House, and was asked to give an address on some scientific subject. It appeared as if this was ostensibly a final test of his qualifications, for the same evening he was confidentially informed by Sir Edward Pehyn, the Lord Chief

Justice, that his Lordship, the Governor-General, was disposed to entrust him with a mission for which he might offer himself.

Although Helfer could not feel much flattered by the moving cause of this proposal, nothing could have been more welcome to him.

But before making up his mind, he consulted General Allard about his prospects in Lahore. He strongly advised Helfer against going there, and described the state of things as neither brilliant nor settled. 'Runjeet Singh,' he said, 'is a clever but capricious and arbitrary man; everything depends on whether he takes a fancy to a man at first sight; and if you were so fortunate as to please him, your future would be very insecure, for from his great age there may soon be a change in the government, the consequences of which, under Asiatic despotisms, are incalculable. I myself,' he added, with some emotion, 'have left my family, having taken them to a place of safety, to return to Lahore according to promise, with little prospect of seeing them again.'

And he was right. Runjeet Singh did not sit much longer on the throne of Lahore. Disturbances ensued after his death, and General Allard died there without seeing his country and family again.

Our thanks were also due to our friend Nabob Dwakanat Tagore for his kind offer, although it was not accepted.

His preference for Europe induced him soon after to leave India, and take up his residence, first in London and then in Paris. I saw him there afterwards, very much altered by the cold climate, and after a few years he succumbed to its effects.

Helfer hastened to present a memorial to the Government, in which he offered his services as naturalist. In reply, he immediately received a commission to undertake an exploring expedition in the provinces in the peninsula of Malacca, not long before conquered from Burmah; he was requested to organise a plan for it himself, to name the requirements and the salary he should demand.

Thus, at last, he saw his fondest hopes realised; all his dreams were to be fulfilled. Although Central Asia and Cashmere were not the countries he was to visit, these were still less known, and their tropical character offered a most interesting field for the naturalist and collector.

On the last day of 1836 he received, as a new year's gift, the official notice of his appointment with instructions specifying what was required of him.

He was not only to collect specimens in every department of natural history, but to investigate the nature of the soil, with a view to discover for what it was best adapted, to send in seeds, plants, and specimens of wood for the botanical gardens, to take meteorological observations, and make mercantile and statistical returns. Further, he was to visit the vast teak forests, which furnish the best timber for ship-building, and the old tin mines; the search for coal-fields also, which was of great importance for the intended steam navigation to China, was a point specially insisted on.

The selection of the various instruments, chemicals,

arms, drugs, and other requirements for the equipment of the expedition, was left entirely to Helfer, and the officials were directed to furnish all he required. When asked what salary he should expect, he replied with German modesty, 'Five hundred rupees per month'—a sum which appeared high to him; he was answered with a smile: 'Not more? You will certainly receive as much as that.' The salaries of the officials on previous expeditions of the kind had been three or four times as much. He did not care for money in the least, and had no head for figures, though it was capable of everything else.

Our pedigree having been certified, and Helfer having received an appointment under the all-powerful Company, we all at once became the fashion; the house of the Governor-General was opened to us. Invitations to dinner, the chief factor in social life there, soirées and balls, were showered upon us, and we were even welcome guests in the boudoir of the Hon. Miss Eden, Lord Auckland's sister, who did the honours of his house, especially Helfer, as this clever lady took great pleasure in music, and sincerely regretted not having profited by his musical talents before.

For many this change would have had great charms; we valued it only as ensuring the accomplishment of our objects.

As a finale to our adventures in Calcutta one more surprise was in store for us.

Helfer one day received a summons to attend in a court of justice without notice for what purpose. In the court two rather degraded looking men were placed before him. 'Do you know these prisoners?' With horror he recognised the pretended princes, our travelling companions, who had succeeded in gaining his entire confidence, and had so shamefully abused it. The elder of the two brothers had the audacity to offer his hand, saying, 'Good morning, Dr. Helfer. How do you find yourself in Calcutta?'

Helfer started back indignantly. He had so sincerely believed in their honour, and was so really attached to them, that he felt all the more deeply wounded and betrayed, and could not bring himself to say a word to them. He was requested by the judge to state the circumstances under which he had been cheated by them, and to name a sum as compensation, but he begged to be excused from giving evidence against them, preferring to renounce all compensation. His only desire was to get out of their presence as quickly as possible.

As the fates would have it, they crossed our path once more. They were afterwards transported for several years, for their many crimes, to a penal settlement in the Tenasserim provinces, from which, as the custom is with Europeans, we wished to take servants and workmen, and these very men were offered to us.

Imagine our taking for sweepers in our house these men who had eaten bread with us, with whom Helfer had studied philosophy, history, and national economy, and who had been the means of so important a turn in our fortunes. We of course declined their services, and they ceased to haunt our steps.

We devoted the last few days to our first and best

friends at Cassipoor, and spent some pleasant hours in Major Hutchinson's family circle, until we received notice that the vessel was ready to sail. On the 21st of January 1837, we embarked on board the schooner *Elizabeth* from the Coolie Bazaar without returning to Calcutta.

CHAPTER III.

MOULMEIN, AND EXPEDITION UP THE RIVER SALUEN.

It was blowing a gale, the waves were tossed hither and thither by the current, the rising tide, and the contrary wind.

The captain paced the deck, looked now at the sky, now at the waves, now at the weather-vane, which veered about in all directions. At length he gave orders to sail, relying, as he said, on the good qualities of his ship. Captains place unbounded confidence in their ships, as mothers do in their children, however little it may seem to be justified to other people.

We began to steer, or rather to be driven down the river, for the strong current made it impossible to keep in the right channel. The storm became a hurricane. After a futile struggle with the elements, the *Elizabeth* returned to her anchoring-ground.

We had to stay on board to be ready to sail at any moment. During the night the wind ceased, and in the morning we set sail.

I now had ocular demonstration of what had always appeared to me incredible—that the short passage from the mouth of the Hoogly to Calcutta is more dangerous than the sea voyage from Europe.

On both sides of the river lay vessels, aground, dismantled, or entirely wrecked. The most astonishing sight was a pretty large sea-going vessel, lying on her side on shore behind a factory. The waves had lifted her up and cast her ashore. Nine vessels, we were informed, had been wrecked.

We were glad to be on the open sea.

I never saw the sea so calm, or under a more cloudless sky; we glided over the water as if sliding upon ice. For the first time I was free from sea-sickness, was able to enjoy the voyage, and to be almost constantly on deck, inhaling the sea breezes, and now and then making interesting observations.

One day when the crew were at leisure, I observed a Lascar pretending to be asleep, but from time to time watching his neighbour out of the corners of his eyes; when convinced that he was asleep, he searched his jacket, very carefully took hold of an insect, which politeness forbids me to name, between his finger and thumb, and deposited it on his neighbour's jacket, thus ridding himself of a torment without loading his conscience with murder.

I noticed that the Lascars, in preparing their food, never made use of the kitchen, but cooked their rice over vessels made of clay filled with Indian earth; in this manner they satisfied their consciences, and evaded the law which forbids them, on pain of losing caste, to cook their food anywhere but on the sacred soil of India.

However cunningly legislators, secular or religious, may devise fetters for mankind, the inventive mind will discover methods of breaking or evading them, when they are opposed to common sense or justifiable rights.

On the 7th of February we arrived in the Gulf of Martaban, and cast anchor at the mouth of the Moulmein river, near the town of Amherst.

The tide having begun to ebb, we had to wait till it flowed, as it rises over eighteen feet, and therefore a considerable expanse of the bed of the river is alternately covered and left bare. But the mud is hidden from view by the mangrove trees. Except where steep cliffs project into the sea, this curious tree protects the whole coast from the inroads of the waves; it grows with peculiar luxuriance in the brackish water at the mouths of the rivers, where the thick, gnarled, twisted roots form a dark web of network, which when laid bare at low water appears to float in the air, and the holes and hollows are the favourite haunts of alligators.

On the 8th of February we reached Moulmein, our temporary destination, the capital of these British possessions, and the residence of the Governor.

The first view of it from the river was not prepossessing. The huts were scattered about in the wildest confusion. But no sooner had we landed, and left them behind, than the scene changed, and an entirely new world opened to us.

Anyone who has ever seen a recent settlement knows the interest of the sight—doubly interesting here, where the struggle between the wild profusion of Nature and the beginnings of cultivation strikes the eye so forcibly. There a wilderness has just been cleared, here are some dwellings just finished, and others in progress; here a garden planted with all sorts of things, there gigantic primeval trees, surrounded with ornamental shrubs for a park about to be laid out. There huge trees are being uprooted, here flowers cultivated. The ground is being levelled for streets, which in spite of all obstacles are to be laid out in a straight line. Life and activity everywhere; wherever you cast your eyes, there is something to interest you. It is the same sort of interest that we feel in a promising child, when we ask ourselves: What will he grow up into? The hope of rapid progress here was founded on the favourable situation of the place, at the junction of three navigable rivers. The Atta-yan, Gyeng, and Saluen unite to form the majestic Martaban or Moulmein river. The scenery of the island of Bilookioun formed by them, with its richly-wooded shores and heights, adorned with picturesque pagodas, is particularly fine. The salubrious climate, and the security afforded by British rule, ensured prosperity.

By the treaty of peace between the British Government and the kingdom of Ava, in 1826, the provinces of Martaban, Yeh, Tavoy, and Mergui, called together the Tenasserim provinces,[1] with the Mergui Archipelago, were ceded to England. They constitute a narrow strip of land between the 11th and 20th degrees of north latitude, 140 geographical miles long, and scarcely 30 broad. They are bounded on the west by the Bay of Bengal, on the east by the mountains which traverse the peninsula lengthways, and form the boundary

---

[1] Now more commonly called British Burmah.—Tr.

between the British territory and Siam. In the north they are separated by the Saluen river from Burmah of which, before the war, they formed a part.

An incredible number of rivers have their rise in the mountain chain, which is a continuation of the Himalayas, and is the watershed between the Bay of Bengal and Siam; they make their way through the ridges, running parallel with the main range, and after a short but rapid course empty themselves into the Bay of Bengal, and during the monsoon they are often swollen into rushing torrents.

This territory had been for centuries the theatre of perpetual, destructive wars between two equally powerful and equally barbarous states, Burmah and Siam. They conquered it by turns, but neither ever retained it long, and it was their custom, which had been reduced to a system, to carry away whole nations into bondage, or to compel them to emigrate by oppression. Thus 40,000 Thalians from Tenasserim emigrated to Siam after the usurper Alompra had wrested these provinces from the Burmese, about 1760, and devastated the country as far as Mergui. At the time when the English took possession, the whole territory of 30,000 square miles had but about 100,000 inhabitants—not much more than three to a square mile. They lived chiefly on the coast, and in the four towns Moulmein, Yeh, Tavoy, and Mergui.

The interior was for the most part destitute of inhabitants, except a few scattered Karens, probably the aboriginal inhabitants, who had taken refuge in the mountains and forests from the persecutions of the conquerors.

The coast only, and its seats of commerce, had from time to time been visited by Europeans, but never for more than short periods; but little, therefore, was known of it, and nothing at all of the interior.

This was about all the knowledge we had of the country which Helfer was thoroughly to explore, to investigate its resources, and to open up to European intercourse. It promised much that was new and interesting to his observant mind.

We were politely received on the shore by Mr. de la Condamine, the Assistant Commissioner, who had been apprised of our coming. He took us to the house of the Governor, Mr. Blondell, who was absent on a tour of inspection.

Hotels, or other accommodation for strangers, there were none. Everybody who lived here had enough to do to provide for his own wants without troubling himself about those of other people. Everyone who landed here had some special vocation, and made his arrangements accordingly, or claimed the hospitality of the settlers.

Mr. de la Condamine was commissioned by Governor Blondell to invite us to take up our quarters in his bungalow, and assigned two spacious rooms to us, in which we soon felt at home; without being luxurious, they contained everything necessary for comfort.

The bungalow was on a height above the town, in a newly laid-out park, in which some nutmeg shrubs in spots near the house, specially selected, were conspicuous. It was the first attempt to acclimatise these products of the Spice Islands; but they did not thrive in their new home, neither climate nor soil suited them.

These bungalows were quite different from any dwellings we had seen before; in appearance they were rather in the Chinese style, and their construction was specially adapted to protect them against heat and damp. In order to give the air free access they are raised from the ground on wooden poles from five to ten feet high, and suspended, so to speak, between earth and heaven.

Mr. Blondell's bungalow was distinguished as the residence of the Governor by being built of varnished teak. The external as well as the partition walls consisted chiefly of jalousies, which occasioned a strong current of air throughout the house. It was only one storey high, square in form, and consisted of three divisions, all of which were provided with bath-rooms, besides spacious drawing and dining-rooms in the centre; a pointed roof, *à la Chinoise*, overhung the walls from six to eight feet, affording a protection against the sun and the monsoon rains, quite indispensable in the absence of window-shutters.

A broad wooden staircase outside led into the drawing-room. The floor of teak boards, covered with fine matting, was a match for our best parquet floors.

Mr. de la Condamine took us into his own bungalow to breakfast, and regaled us with tea, coffee, fish, and curry. Curry made with the mountain rice which grows here is the chief diet both of natives and foreigners. The grain is very large, and when prepared it looks like snowflakes. It takes the place of potatoes and the rather indifferent bread, as an addition to all other viands, and is always on table. Mountain rice is much more nourishing than that grown on the plains, and the Bengalese, accustomed to the latter, find it indigestible.

Our host surprised us with a fruit that was new to us, and whose aroma filled the room. It is called the durian, and is like a rolled-up hedgehog, only larger. The prickles are so sharp that to the uninitiated it is difficult to handle. The inside contains five rows of kernels imbedded in a white pith, about the size of chestnuts, enveloped in a bright yellow cream-like mass. This cream is the edible portion; it is taken out with a spoon, and tastes and smells like a combination of all the spices of the tropics; it is heating, and strangers generally find it too pungent at first, so that Mr. de la Condamine was surprised at our liking it.

This fruit is considered such a delicacy by the natives that when the King of Ava ceded these provinces to England he had a clause inserted in the treaty, granting him an annual shipload of durians, for they do not thrive in the more northern climate of Burmah.

It grows on a tree which reaches a great height; the long, upright trunk ends in a crown, from which the fruit hangs down. The hard wood is said to be used by the Chinese for shipbuilding. Unfortunately, the durians cannot be preserved, and every attempt to bring them to Europe has failed.

We were not long content to stay indoors. We

had seen too much and too little during the short walk to Mr. Blondell's bungalow not to wish to see more. To the astonishment of Mr. de la Condamine, after breakfast, about 11 o'clock, we proposed a walk to the Pagoda Hill, the highest point of a range of hills to the north of the town.

Although the heat here on the 13th degree of latitude is not nearly so much dreaded as at Calcutta on the 23rd, the idea of walking at this hour appeared preposterous to our host. Perhaps Helfer felt all the more desirous to prove our adaptation for the wanderings before us; at all events, he persisted in his plan. But Mr. de la Condamine, in spite of the gallantry indicative of his French descent, declined to accompany us; he, however, compelled us to accept the services of his chattah-bearer.

A chattah, without which neither man nor woman of the higher classes goes out here, is an umbrella made of folded oiled brown paper, about the size of a carriage-wheel, carried by a servant, sometimes by two, over the head of his master.

We perambulated part of the town and the bazaar. The houses are raised so high on bamboo poles that you can stand under them, and are constructed entirely of bamboo without any iron. The walls, made of open lattice-work or scantily covered with broad pieces of bamboo bark, fastened with wooden nails, permit you to look out and to see in. The floors are also made of slender bamboo canes, nailed with wooden pegs to beams underneath, so that they tremble at every step. Such a house is something like a hanging bird's-nest, and not much firmer. In storms they are swayed hither and thither, but withstand them better than more solid constructions.

The space beneath the house affords shade, and the currents of air between the poles coolness.

The porous water-vessels, wound round with damp straw, are hung up here, and the water becomes icy cold.

In the bazaar there was a Chinese coffee-house, decorated with large inscriptions, variegated paper lanterns and bannerets. There was even a street inhabited by Chinese, so early had this industrious people appropriated a share of the space.

The shops, like our market stalls, built of light bamboo poles, three or four feet high, contained mostly articles of daily consumption, fish, rice, fruits, &c., as well as a few articles of luxury, particularly potzos, silk scarfs, over three yards long and two feet wide, of the gayest colours, and mostly with chequered patterns in blue, green, red, and yellow. The potzo is the holiday dress of the men; they wrap it round their loins, and throw one end picturesquely over their shoulders.

The Burmese are of Mongol race, and are a great contrast to the slightly-built Hindoos, with their Caucasian type of countenance. They are short, thickset, and strongly built, with a peculiar formation of the legs and loins, which are carefully tattooed all over with hieroglyphics in blue. This painting, which, under the knee is like a broad blue ribbon, makes their want of clothing far less repulsive, as it looks as if they had short blue trousers on. Many of them are also tattooed on the breast and shoulders, as a sign that they belong to a higher class. The tattooing is a very painful process; it cannot be completed all at once, but is done at different times, between the ninth and fourteenth years.

A broad face with large cheek-bones, a flat nose, projecting lips, small grey eyes slanting upwards, and a pale yellow complexion, something the colour of an unripe lemon, does not sound like a charming picture, and yet there is something attractive in the appearance of the Burmese men which I cannot exactly describe. It is, perhaps, an independent, manly expression in the faces of the older men, and in the younger ones a careless, jovial, daring air which characterises their looks and movements.

The women are of the same type as the men, but more delicate. Their round, childish faces, with their pug noses and roguish expression, make them, although not pretty, more attractive than the renowned Indian beauties.

They wear as their only garment a large square shawl of silk and wool which hangs down close to the body from the waist to the ankles, the upper ends being tied together under the left arm—an anxious sort of costume in windy weather. Since the English dominion, their feeling of propriety has induced them to cover their bosoms and shoulders with a jacket of coarse English net.

It is surprising, on coming from Mussulman countries, to see the women not only unveiled but going about as freely as the men, and taking part in all the business of life. They serve in the shops, buy and sell, and transact all sorts of business which I had before seen regarded as the exclusive privilege of men. Their bearing was self-possessed and dignified, free alike from boldness and servility.

The favourable condition of the women, and the free, independent character of the men under a barbarous and arbitrary government is to be explained in the first place by the cheerful views of life fostered by Buddhism, which is free from caste, fanaticism, and intolerance.

The worship of the Deity in the manifestations of Nature, where she showers her gifts in luxuriant profusion on purpose to be enjoyed, must tend to foster a happy, careless temperament, and this is, in fact, the characteristic of the Burmese nation. The oppression of the despotic rulers was less felt in these outlying provinces than in those in close proximity to them. It was chiefly confined to the collection of taxes by native officials, and occasional systematic house visitation which the people contrived to elude by hiding their valuables, or they were only deprived of their luxuries, not of the necessaries of life; of these, with their scanty wants, they always had abundance.

They could even in some measure escape from the devastating wars, when not actually in the field, by retreating to the mountains and forests. It did not concern them very much if their villages were burnt down and their fields desolated, as they are obliged to pull down their houses and rebuild them about every three years. Thus even under despotic governments they maintained a surprising amount of freedom and independence; and they seem to have granted it also to their women, more perhaps from indifference than sense of justice. However that may be, it has had salutary effects on the female sex.

I learnt that in this land of the far East woman possesses the same rights as man—a step in legislation to which even civilised Europe has not yet attained. She may carry on trade and commerce, possess land, and manage it herself. She is not legally subject to her husband, and can dissolve the marriage bond, which is only entered into for a time; indeed, she can do so before the time, by refunding the sum paid down on entering into the contract. But this is a rare occurrence, not more frequent than divorce with us. Polygamy is allowed by law, which consistently allows a woman to have several husbands; but, to the honour of the sex be it spoken, there was only one instance of it. A rich woman had expended her money on this luxury, but earned for herself universal contempt.

A broad steep path with steps led to the top of the Pagoda Hill. There were high poles on both sides, to the tops of which, bells, Æolian harps, cymbals, and other instruments were fixed, which, as they were stirred by the breeze, gave forth pleasant sounds. The pagoda on the platform on the summit was built of brick with chalk facings, in the form of a bell with a gilt top. All round the walls were niches of various sizes, the projecting roofs of which also terminated in gilded points, so that the whole circumference of the pagoda was adorned with them, and the bells and harps fixed to them were probably intended to salute the large ears of the gods in the niches with perpetual sweet sounds. Near the large pagoda were several smaller ones just like it. They were shaded by a fine group of trees.

My interest was greatly excited by a store room—I can call it by no other name—full of gods. It was a large open shed full of images of Buddha of all sizes. He is always represented as sitting cross-legged. But here there was one image of him lying down, thirty feet long, with well-proportioned hands and feet, arrayed in a gilt garment, like the women's dress, and with a high, black, pointed cap. Of course the faces of these images are of the Mongul type, like the people themselves. They are all representations of one and the same divine incarnation—Buddha, who assumed human form for man's benefit. The making of these images is deemed a meritorious act. I was told that the King of Siam employed himself in this way, and made one a day. Nevertheless, they attach no particular sanctity to them, and freely give them away.

Near the chief pagoda there was a gong hung on a cross-beam between two poles, used like our bells for calling the people to religious observances, or to announce the hour. Gongs are made of the finest bell-metal with a large admixture of silver.

Novel as these sights were to us, the panorama from the height soon proved more attractive. At our feet lay the rising town struggling with the wilderness, and near it the cantonments of the English garrison, looking like a well-kept garden intersected by neat paths and a broad avenue, on both sides of which were the officers' houses built in the bungalow style before described. Beyond was the mirror-like Martaban, having become a majestic stream by the junction of the Saluen, Gyeng, and Atta-yan, looking like a lake with picturesque islets. On the opposite side was the town of Martaban bounded by a range of wooded hills surmounted by pagodas.

Mr. Crawford, one of the earliest and most intelligent travellers in this district, calls this view one of the most striking of tropical landscapes. In the east were the higher ranges covered with dense forests, then, during the dry season, like our woods in autumn, clad in the most varied tints. The loftier mountains melting into blue vapour bounded the horizon.

I have never seen so harmonious a picture, yet it was far from being the grandest scenery which I saw in this country, so rich in natural beauties.

Social ceremony had found its way even here. Mr. de la Condamine thought it his duty to introduce us into society consisting of the families of two English regiments stationed here.

The proximity of Burmah and the, as yet, unhealed wounds inflicted on this empire by the late war made this strong garrison in Moulmein necessary.

Helfer, therefore, accompanied by Mr. de la Condamine, made calls upon the officers, beginning with the Brigadier; these were, as in duty bound, returned, and were followed by invitations to dinner.

Impatient as my husband was to set out on his journey into the interior, he had to wait for the Governor's return, and he did not arrive till the 24th of February. He was delighted to see more respect accorded to the provinces entrusted to him than had hitherto been the case, and the unknown portions of them selected for exploration, and at once took measures to provide liberally for our comfort. It afforded us an opportunity of gaining an insight into the character of the people, and of comparing their condition under the previous despotism with the results of the present British rule.

Mr. Blondell commissioned his officials to obtain suitable men to accompany us as collectors, bearers, and boatmen. Of course no compulsion was employed; they could only be requested to offer themselves for suitable remuneration.

The idea of a government not compelling its subjects to work, but only offering it to them for payment, leaving them free to decline it, was, from their previous experience of life, quite incomprehensible to the natives.

At first, therefore, they could not reconcile the proceedings of the Company, which they supposed to be a woman, with their notions of a government. After the English had taken possession of the country they expected a stern requisition of their treasures, as had always been the case before. They had, therefore, carefully concealed them, for in the absence of other luxuries they set great store by them. On the occasion of grand processions, the women did not, as usual, wear gold chains and bracelets, in order not to attract the cupidity of the barbarians. As the expected visitations did not take place, they said it was nothing but cunning, that they might make more sure of getting possession of them in the end. But when feminine vanity had to some extent triumphed over fear, and the women began again to adorn themselves, and still the dreaded seizures did not take place, they were reported to have said among themselves, compassionately touching their foreheads, that the Lady Company could not be in her right mind.

Here was a nice opportunity for the men to put the forbearance of their rulers to the test. They declared unanimously that they would not go. The Gyown-Yowk (Burgomaster), reported this unheard-of contumacy in despair, fearing that he would have to pay for it, and begged earnestly to be allowed to obtain the men in his own way.

When Mr. Blondell coolly replied that the Burmese were free to go or not, as they pleased, and that he could get other people for less than he had offered them, the burgomaster was astonished beyond measure. He made this reply known, and before long crowds of young men offered themselves.

The first expedition was to be but short, and to be confined to the province of Amherst, as it is impossible to traverse these countries during the monsoon, which begins in April. The excursion was to be made chiefly in river boats, and would never be out of reach of the haunts of men, so that it was but a foretaste of what was before us in the interior; still, in Mr. Blondell's opinion, more preparation was required for it than we had supposed.

Helfer required an interpreter with his Burmese

retinue, their language, a corruption of Chinese, being different from any we had heard; it has such delicately modulated sounds, that our organs of speech and hearing can scarcely distinguish some of the differences, and we were only able to do so after long practice.

A half-caste of Portuguese and Burmese origin, who spoke English and Burmese, was engaged for this office, but he could not make himself understood by the Karens with whom we soon came in contact. An interpreter was therefore required between him and them, and an old elephant hunter was found who was accustomed to bring his booty to market at Moulmein.

Helfer selected ten hardy young Burmese as collectors in the various departments of natural history, whom he meant to instruct in their duties.

A Malay from Sumatra, called Abdarahma, an orthodox Mussulman and a capital body-guard, was selected for our personal attendant, and justified the choice by his rare fidelity and devotedness. A Christian Malabar, black as ebony, took the situation of cook. He had learnt the noble art under French tuition in Pondicherry.

A young Burmese woman, with whom unfortunately I could only communicate by signs, accompanied me as lady's-maid. A Bengal tailor was also engaged, as it was thought indispensable to have one to repair the clothes torn in the jungle. These servants, with the boatmen and bearers, formed a considerable retinue.

Stocked with provisions for some weeks, and with letters of safe conduct to the authorities with whom we should come in contact, ordering them to comply with all Helfer's requisitions, on March 3 we left Moulmein, and proceeded up the river Saluen in three large boats.

In about half-an-hour we landed on the island opposite. It has a mineral spring hidden in a palm grove, which is said to possess valuable medicinal properties, and in course of time it may become a resort for invalids. It then poured forth its healing waters unheeded.

The young Burmese are much at home on the water, and rowed us on with lusty strokes, amidst singing and laughter, amusing themselves with splashing each other, and although we, too, got our share, it was impossible to take it amiss. Before long we reached the village of Palien, which had been destroyed in the late war, but was now rebuilt. The Gyown, who had been informed of our arrival, was waiting for us on the shore, and invited us to his house; that is, he had had it entirely emptied, washed within and without, and placed it entirely at our disposal, instead of the zayat intended for strangers. The evacuation of such an abode is soon accomplished. A few cooking utensils, the sleeping mats, a gun hanging on the wall, and, with the more wealthy, a chest of clothes, silk potzos, and feminine ornaments, are all there is to move; the dah, however, is never wanting, the chief weapon of the Burmese, as well as the implement used in their work.

The dah is a large knife, a foot long, in shape like a razor, the forepart of the blade of which is strong and broad and fixed to a long strong handle. With this knife they fell the largest trees, and defend themselves against tigers, but it is also used for their finest work, for they split reeds with it to a hair's breadth. A sharp dah of good steel is the pride of a Burmese or Karen inhabitant of the jungle, and he always carries it in his potzo.

Our Burmese youths kindled several fires round the dwelling, and then went to forage in the place. Although this was strictly forbidden, the hospitality of the villagers required that they should season their boiled rice for them with Burmese dainties, consisting of dried and powdered fish.

We had an appetite for a curry of chickens, as there were numbers pecking about near the house. Our host said, however, that with all due deference to us, he could scarcely bring his mind to kill one of these creatures, in which the soul of one of his relations might be living; but if we would kill them ourselves, he had no objection. Our attendant therefore killed some, and the cook having prepared a savoury dish, the scrupulous man found his relations very good eating.

The ruddy flames picturesquely illumined the groups of figures in the woods, cooking, smoking, and chatting, and displaying the youthful elasticity of their limbs with every movement.

Interesting as was this spectacle, however, we needed to be cooled before going to rest. The dwelling was divided off into bath and sleeping rooms by hanging up mats. My maid was very expert in administering improvised baths without a tub; they consist of pouring cooled water over you, which runs off between the interstices in the floor, leaving a refreshing coolness. The beds with curtains, which we had brought with us, ensured us a good night's rest, unmolested by the buzzing inhabitants of the forest.

Helfer determined to stay a day or two here, and to begin his work of exploration in the neighbourhood.

Early next morning he assembled the young men selected as collectors, and, as well as he could, with a novice for an interpreter, instructed each in his duties.

To one, stones and minerals were shown, that he might search for them, and bring specimens. Another was to bring blossoms from shrubs and trees; a third was provided with a butterfly-net, and a fourth with a fishing-net. Our body-guard was to shoot every animal within reach of his gun. Helfer went himself with some of the men to teach them to search for almost invisible insects, and was in great danger of his life from a herd of buffaloes belonging to the village. These animals, which wander about in numerous herds round the villages in the plains, where they are used in rice culture, are far more dangerous to Europeans than the wild beasts of the forests. Too much accustomed to men to fly from them, always on their guard against wild beasts, and ready to combat them, they attack every strange object, and such, of course, is a human being in clothes. No sooner did they see Helfer in his white suit than they gave the alarm, formed themselves into a compact circle, with their young ones in the middle, and their thick bushy heads outside, and rushed full tilt at him. Being in the open field he would scarcely have been able to save himself, had not two of the Burmese concealed him with their naked bodies, while a third fearlessly confronted the herd. He spoke kindly to them, they stopped, stood still, as if considering, and then turned peaceably away.

Helfer, as was his custom, ascended the highest point of a hill near to take observations, and employed the rest of the day in seeking information about the country.

The systematic lying of the natives makes it very difficult to acquire correct information. They consider it the first law of prudence never to speak the truth, even when they have no reason for suppressing it. It is a vice which they share with all other Asiatic nations, and was the only one we observed among the merry Burmese. Added to this, our interpreter did not turn out efficient. In order to be able to dispense with him as soon as possible, Helfer addressed himself diligently to the study of the language.

Towards evening our collectors returned from their first excursion, heavily laden with stones, ores, branches of trees, fallen leaves, and decayed wood; they had also caught butterflies and fish. As will readily be imagined, there was a good deal of rubbish, still it was evident that they had apprehended their duties tolerably well, and that useful service might be expected of them by-and-by.

For Helfer and me—his assistant—the work of the day now began, in sorting, examining, writing notes, preserving insects, pressing plants, &c. It occupied us till midnight, and was almost daily repeated.

It is not my purpose to impart the scientific results of my husband's researches. They are printed in his reports to the Government in Calcutta, in Acts of Parliament, and in the journal of the Asiatic Society of Bengal, and were afterwards translated into German, and published in a separate form by the Imperial Geographical Society of Vienna. The task I propose to myself is to relate our adventures, and only selections from these, for interesting as our daily wanderings were to ourselves, and numerous as were the novel sights that attracted our attention, it would be wearisome to recount them in detail. I have therefore refrained from presenting them in the form of a diary. Moreover, my pen fails me to record the impression which this free, unconstrained life, amidst the grandeur and luxuriance of nature, made upon me, or the profound consciousness of the Divine presence I experienced amidst the shades of the silent forests. I could not, even at the time, clothe my feelings in words which did them justice, much less can I now find adequate expression for the charm which, in spite of their hardships and difficulties, the recollection of these wanderings has for me.

As we proceeded on our voyage our Burmese often sprang into the water up to their breasts, and with loud shouts dragged and pushed the boats over sandbanks. Thus we drew near to an isolated and picturesque range of limestone hills, which we had already seen in the distance, rising to a height of 2,000 feet. As we saw them without lights and shadows in the white mist, which fills the horizon at this season, they looked like an unbroken mass.

This haze is so thin and ethereal that it is more like a veil of thin gauze than our more northern mists; it tempers the burning rays of the sun, and lends to the landscape a soft, melting hue, in which the lights on the mountains, richly clothed in wood, blend softly with the lilac of the shadows. I have never seen any other colouring like it, and should a painter attempt to transfer it to his canvas it would certainly incur the charge of being unnatural.

Early in the morning of the 9th, Helfer made an excursion to the highest point of this ridge. He took with him some of the best of the men, and the zockey, or chief man of the place, as a guide, a rule which he always observed, both to inspire the villagers with respect, and to keep order among the bearers, who were changed at every village.

A plain, many miles in extent, opened before him, which, during the monsoon, is under water, and there were many swamps and pools full of fish, affording food to a multitude of herons. He had often to be carried on the back of a sturdy Burmese till he came to a Karen village, where he made a halt, and the men cooked their rice. Thence he took a Karen as a guide, and making their way through an almost impenetrable jungle, they reached the top of Zoog-ka-beeg, at the foot of which was a primeval forest. A large pagoda stands on the top of the mountain, which is a great resort of pilgrims. A path led up to it, with steps here and there cut in the rocks. It was an arduous climb, particularly at that season of the year, when it was very slippery from the fallen bamboo leaves, varnished, as it were, with a coating of melted silicious earth.

On a platform half way up was a halting place, and near it a cave, containing a large gilt figure of Buddha, and a deeply excavated basin, into which fresh spring water is conducted through bamboo pipes. Harps, fiddles, &c., were hung upon the dilapidated pagoda at the top, and their melancholy sounds broke the stillness of the place. The view was very fine. Helfer returned late in the evening, very tired, his followers laden with spoil.

The next day they had a rest, while we sorted and packed the specimens, to be sent back by boat to Moulmein, for it was desirable to lighten our baggage, and to deliver the first-fruits into Mr. Blondell's hands.

On the 16th we reached the island of Kow-loon-kioun, at the junction of the Yeng-baing. It was, for the most part, overgrown with impenetrable jungle; lofty trees with splendid tufts of blossom towered up out of it, only to be obtained for the herbarium by felling the trees. Our people discovered tracks of tortoises, left upon the ground when they come up out of the river at night to lay their eggs, and leave them to be hatched by the glowing hot sand. It is curious to observe how sagaciously they select spots high enough up not to be reached by the water, and yet sufficiently moist, from being under the water when at a higher level, to enable them to dig holes a foot or more in depth, which can be filled with dry sand. In these they lay their eggs, twenty or more at a time, as we were told, and cover them with loose sand. In returning to the river they try carefully to efface the marks of their feet with their tails, that the eggs may not be discovered.

We certainly should not have observed their tracks, but they did not escape the practised eyes of the Burmese, looking as if carefully swept with a rice-broom. Following these from the water, they found several of the holes filled with eggs, to their great satisfaction as well as ours, for they made a welcome addition to our scanty fare. But it is necessary to be careful not to eat too freely of them, for they are not very digestible.

The egg of a river tortoise is about the size of a duck's egg, quite round, and flattened at the poles, and instead of a hard shell it has a tough skin, like that of a soft hen's egg, and a large dark yellow yolk.

After the sun has performed its maternal duties and matured the egg, for which a period of from three to four weeks is required, the young creatures escape from their shell, pierce the roof of their cradle, and hasten to the water, where they take care of themselves, without maternal help or teaching.

We followed the Yeng-baing up stream for some days, between lofty walls of rock, far from the haunts of men. It is like a mountain stream, and during the monsoon must be a rushing torrent. Here, for the first time, we heard the tiger quite near our river encampment; at first a kind of shrill yell, then deeper and stronger. As tigers frequent the shores of rivers, and proved by the chorus of many voices they gave us that there were several near, large fires were kindled round the camp. These frightened them away, as well as a flock of monkeys, of the sort called howlers, who had come near us with impudent curiosity, and mingled their unmelodious voices with the roars of the tigers.

After we had returned to Yeng-baing-kua, on the Saluen, we made an excursion to the teak forest, six miles off, which was a special object of interest to Helfer, on account of the value of the timber for ship-building.

We could not set out till about mid-day. The way led us at first through a district bare of trees, which had at some time been under cultivation, at the foot of some hills, which reflected the sun's rays, and kept off the cool breezes, which generally come from the mountains at noon. But we were protected by the large bamboo hats, pointed at the top, after the Chinese fashion, the very best preservative against the scorching sun. We trudged steadily on, only now and then making a halt to collect specimens and look about us. But we soon found ourselves in the midst of rustling, waving, tiger grass, six to eight feet high, which closed over our heads, and threatened to stifle us.

The spots where this grass grows are the most dangerous. They are the favourite haunts of the tiger, who takes his siesta after dinner among the high reedy stalks, or pounces on his prey from concealment amongst them; for, strong and bloodthirsty as he is, he is a coward, and avoids an open combat when he can.

His cowardice makes it easier to protect yourself against him, for he is easily alarmed by unwonted sounds, and sneaks away, unless too strongly impelled by hunger.

A tremendous noise, with shrill instruments and loud clappers, interspersed with shots, was therefore made by our company. Our elephant hunter headed the troop, holding his antiquated gun, with which he boasted that he had slain many a monster, in readiness. He was followed by the Burmese, dahs in hand, we being in the centre, as they always would have it, and they eagerly watched the waving of the grass, from which they descried the movements of a crouching tiger, imperceptible to us. The reedy grass closed over the footsteps immediately, so that each one had to make his way laboriously through it. Its growth is so strong that it is a real plague.

After a most fatiguing march of several hours, the smell of burning announced that a wood was on fire, a frequent occurrence at this time of year, or that a piece of ground was being cleared for cultivation by burning the underwood. We soon came in sight of some isolated Karen dwellings, standing amidst smoking heaps, under half-charred forest trees.

The Karens, a people but little known, retreat far into the hills and forests, purposely concealing their existence as much as they can, from fear of being carried off into slavery, as has too often been the case. Treated with contempt by the previous conquerors, the

Burmese, they avoid all communication with them as much as possible; one or two of them only coming to the towns, to procure indispensable articles by barter.

They settle in little communities of from ten to fifteen families, near some brook among the mountains, set fire to the underwood, the flames reaching up and consuming the branches of the lofty trees, and in the soil beneath, mixed with ashes, they grow rice, plantains, cucumbers, betel-nuts, and sweet potatoes; these products, birds, and the chase suffice for their wants. The cotton plant furnishes them with clothing; it is woven by the women, and often tastefully ornamented with embroidery, and they are more decently clothed than the Burmese.

They cultivate the ground round their huts in the most primitive style, so long as it yields enough for them, and then move to some other spot, often at a great distance, for the sake of fresh soil. They build new houses, and, as they help one another, one can be finished in a day; but they are still more lightly put together with bamboos than those in the towns. I did not venture in, for fear of my feet slipping between the staves.

It is surprising to see how safely children, not more than a year old, who with us can scarcely crawl, make their way about these floors, and even climb up the ladders, twelve to fifteen feet high, at the entrance, without coming to any harm. The danger from wild beasts at night, especially tigers, which might spring into a low house, if driven by hunger, makes this elevation necessary. The ladder is removed at night, and the inhabitants feel themselves as safe as our knights of old when the bridge over the moat was withdrawn.

The Karens are not so strongly built as the Burmese, and the Mongolian descent is less strongly marked. The cheek bones are less prominent, the eyes do not start so much, and the complexion is brighter, more like that of southern Europeans. The colour in their cheeks is striking, and I was surprised to see the girls blush slightly, which I had not observed among any other Asiatic races.

Under continued oppression, and in default of the physical strength or mental superiority to enable them to maintain the contest with their enemies, patience, cunning, and, as a last resort, flight into the woods, have become the sole weapons of defence of this harmless people.

Their rather rude language had no written characters, and as they were entirely uninstructed, they were destitute of the higher religious ideas. Perceiving inexplicable powers in the forces of nature, they ascribe them to 'nats'—good or bad spirits. They offer sacrifices to them of rice, fruits, or flowers, which they place in concealed spots in the forest, or in the hollow trunks of trees. Having no regular system of worship, nor any leading idea, they follow the instinctive impulse to fear, or reverence, according to their individual temperament, an incomprehensible Being above them, an instinct which none of the children of nature can escape from; it is only the speculative, hyper-cultivated intellect that succeeds in doing so.

If you question them about their ideas of supernatural things, as, for instance, a life after death, an idea which all the children of nature eagerly grasp, they will answer: 'We know nothing about it, neither do we think about it; all we know is that we come into the world, and must go out of it again, and as it is so beautiful in the world, it will most likely be good hereafter.' But they are not without ability, and are quite capable of receiving instruction, as we soon had the opportunity of observing.

The teak forest did not come up to my expectations. The Government farmed it to private persons, and received a rupee for every trunk sent to Moulmein. As no control was exercised, greed had made sad havoc here. The finest timber trees had been felled, and had knocked down others in their fall, which had been left lying about, as less available, in confusion. On some the foliage was still green, others were mouldering away. The forest looked like a great battlefield, where not men, but gigantic trees had been the combatants.

We preferred to encamp outside the village to occupying the hut of the Karen zockey. The Burmese put a hut together for us, of bamboos and mats, near a clear stream, in no time. It is wonderful how quickly they clear a spot from underwood and roots, and prepare it for the, to them, strange wants of Europeans. They themselves encamped round about, cooking their rice at the watchfires, singing, smoking, and chewing betel, a habit they are all addicted to, and which still more disfigures their ugly mouths.

The fruit of the areca palm is broken up into small pieces, folded, with some slaked lime, in the leaf of the betel shoots, and chewed, as the Americans chew tobacco, only instead of blackening the teeth, it stains the mouth red, as if it were filled with blood, and leaves a dark stripe on the edges of the teeth. This luxury, for which they care more than for eating and drinking, has become indispensable to the natives.

It is curious that these antipodal races, representatives of the earliest and latest epochs, should so resemble each other in their customs, or, rather, bad habits.

The villagers had grouped themselves, gravely and silently, as their custom was, at a respectful distance, and watched the joviality of the Burmese with perfect equanimity, now and then looking attentively at us.

Having had our repast, and sorted the specimens, wearied with the labours of the day, we retired to rest, but it was not of long duration. About midnight we were awakened by human voices, proceeding from men and women alternately, now in a major now in a minor key; the sounds were melodious, but not like European singing. They increased and died away in regular cadences: too wild and irregular for singing, too melodious and expressive for wailing.

We learnt that a child of the zockey had died, and had been buried that morning. But one of their elders and wise men (they have no priests) had declared that the day was unlucky, and the body had been exhumed to be buried again next morning. The ceremony of the dance of death, which would last till the burial, was just beginning. We resolved to attend, and sent a message to that effect to the zockey, with a request that he would not disturb himself on our account.

We found a numerous company of men, sitting round the wall in double rows. In the middle of the long side of the wall there was a large fire, round which were vessels of rice, meat, and other viands. The sorrowing father sat near, presiding quietly and with dignity over the ceremonies, as he afterwards did at the feast; the mother, with an infant at her breast, was crouching in a dark corner. In the middle of the space, the possessions of the dead child, clothing, ornaments, beads, metal rings, &c., hung like trophies on bamboo canes. It is considered honourable to exhibit these treasures to the company at a funeral, and many things are never worn, but kept for such occasions. Among the trophies we observed a flat parcel done up in a mat; this, we were told, contained the body. It is the custom to crush it flat immediately after death, to tie it firmly up, and to hang it up in the room.

The death dance round the body was now begun by young girls, two and two, at a slow pace, followed by young men in the same style; it was accompanied by a dirge, which, even close by, was not unpleasant, and compared with the wild noise of drums, cymbals, and pipes, which passes for music among other Asiatic nations, it was remarkably harmonious, and in good time.

The alternate lights and shadows, occasioned by the fire, on the figures of the old men and women and the young men and maidens, as they danced, lent a wild, romantic aspect to the scene. Dance and song lasted till dawn, then followed the funeral feast, after which the body was laid in the earth in a pleasant spot in the wood.

A year after burial, the body is again exhumed, and exposed to the elements on the top of a mountain—a strange custom, of which we failed to get any satisfactory explanation; it appears as if some vague idea of renewed life and rejuvenescence must be at the bottom of it.

That this people, without any religious system of their own, have lived for centuries under Burmese rule without voluntarily adopting Buddhism, or having been compelled to adopt it, shows, on the one hand, the isolation in which they have lived, and on the other, the absence of bigoted zeal for conversion among the Burmese Buddhists.

At funeral feasts the Karens have a custom of drinking the blood of a freshly killed pig, which, repulsive as it is, must not be taken to evince a bloodthirsty character: they are, on the contrary, a quiet, gentle people, who show less disposition to bloodshed than any European nation, for no instance of wilful murder has been known among them. When we were preparing to start next morning, we observed that the villagers also were packing up their scanty possessions, driving their poultry and pigs together, in short, making all preparations for emigration. When asked the reason, they said: 'We are ignorant people, have no one to help us; we know of no medicine for our sick; if one of us dies, we cannot live any longer in the place, we seek another air, that is our medicine.'

Ready at any time to leave their homes, they live a life of perpetual wandering. Their home is the green forest, among whose cool shades they pass a lonely existence, with but few pleasures, but in contentment. They were like a blank sheet of paper awaiting the pencil, which shall trace on it the characters of civilisation. That this pencil was not far off we had pleasing evidence before long.

We returned by another route, less difficult, though longer round. All at once we remarked a change in the vegetation, betokening a warmer climate, and made a halt, to examine the spot. We found a lovely oasis, adorned in the freshest May green, while all the surrounding landscape was of the russet hue, produced by five months without rain.

Cocoa-nut palms, which we had never before seen in the forests, but only in the neighbourhood of cultivated spots, surrounded the underwood, with their lofty crowns; among them were fan and other palms, overgrown with a network of creepers and parasitic plants. Then there were the shrubs and aquatic plants, peculiar to a hot climate, with broad leaves and flowers. In the midst we observed steam rising as if from a valve.

It was not easy to make our way through this exuberant vegetation. Our Burmese, to whom, just as to children, any novelty was a delight, cut the beautiful shrubs and flowers with their dahs, right and left, to make a path. But the ground became not only more slippery, but hotter at every step, till it was like hot pap, and we could only get along by leaping from hillock to hillock. I had to give it up, but Helfer, carried by two sturdy fellows, reached a hot spring of 40° Reaumur (122° Fahr.), which had produced all this luxuriance.

The remains of mouldering masonry, encrusted with a deposit of sulphur, showed that the spring had not always poured forth its health-giving waters unheeded as now. The proximity to the rising settlement of Moulmein will assuredly before long restore its importance. It was impossible to remain near it long, not so much on account of the hot steam, as from a vast number of huge leeches.

They were called elephant leeches by our attendants, and they soon swarmed round their naked feet; their bite is much more painful than that of an ordinary leech, and leaves a venom behind, which makes the wound malignant and even dangerous. Our people, who would have courageously fought a tiger with their dahs, and had interposed their own bodies between Helfer and the furious buffaloes, now retreated in alarm. Lifting first one leg and then the other, they tried to beat off the hideous creatures with sticks, but in vain; numbers of them soon clung to their legs, attracted by the rare taste of human blood. We were in danger of being bitten ourselves, for they tried to gain entrance through every opening in our clothes.

We were obliged to turn back, but, in spite of all difficulties, Helfer and his assistants had collected many valuable specimens in the short time. There was a profusion of flowering shrubs, many of which are not generally found in blossom in the dry season.

When we returned to our camp and the hut that had been erected for us, we found our meal ready, but the hut and the air were full of huge mosquitoes, which fell upon us with bloodthirsty fury, and the thin texture of our clothing was no protection against their long stings; neither tobacco nor the smoke of the fire drove them away, there was nothing for it but to get under our bed-nets, which were put up in haste, and arranged for sitting up; so at last we were able to enjoy our supper in peace, and to sort and note down the specimens.

Even our attendants, less susceptible than we were, and better protected by rubbing the skin with cocoa-nut oil, complained so much that we determined to leave the neighbourhood of the hot spring immediately.

We had not as yet experienced any of the dangers described in books of travel, and looked forward to with curiosity and dread; we had seen no tiger lurking in ambush for us, no trail of venomous serpents, ready to dart at us, in the grass, on which we had so often reposed; we had never met with a panther climbing the trees ready for a spring, nor a rhinosceros, which will attack every living creature indiscriminately; but now we had to run away from such miserable little creatures as leeches and mosquitoes, not unknown to us at home. Just so in life; it is the petty ills and contrarieties of every-day existence that rob us of our equanimity and peace of mind.

Having returned to the Saluen, we had a voyage of considerable variety. Sometimes we were overshadowed by the giant branches of the trees of the primeval forest, beneath whose leafy arches the river pursues its course undisturbed; next we steered between laughing rice fields and banana plantations, with their ripe red and yellow fruit, among which human habitations lay scattered; then followed an impenetrable jungle. We landed at Melaych-hua.

Helfer undertook some arduous excursions here, to explore the sites of ores that had been brought him, as well as to search for coalfields, the chief object of his explorations.

He saw the first traces of elephants, and at night heard their trumpet-like cries; also tracks of the rhinosceros, which are far more rare. He did not catch sight of them, however. His labours this time were rewarded by the discovery of copper, and indications of former mines.

He brought me back a plaything, 'for lonely days,' not that I found my solitude wearisome, for, besides other occupations, catching butterflies for my private collection took up a good deal of time. But I was pleased with his gift, a pretty little monkey, which he had exchanged with a Karen girl for a string of beads.

He was of the long-tailed species, had a smooth greenish-grey skin, and an intelligent face, with eyes far more wise and expressive than many a human face can boast. He was very shy and timid at first, and hid himself as much as he could. Lest he should make his escape during the night, I fastened him with a little chain to the foot of my bed; but the poor little fellow, having never worn fetters, cried so bitterly that I was touched. So, to avoid disturbing my weary husband and being kept awake myself, I took him into my bed. No sooner did he find himself under the clothes, and by my side, than he was pacified, and clung fast to me with his arms round my neck. Unwelcome as such close quarters and the caresses of the little creature were, I could not get rid of him, and we peacefully fell asleep.

When he awoke he looked earnestly at me, as if aware that I was not his accustomed bedfellow; but as I looked kindly at him and stroked him, he threw his arms round my neck again with great vehemence, as if impelled by some special impulse. From this moment our warm friendship, if I may be allowed the expression, was sealed; he was constantly at my side, though I no longer gave him a place in my bed but at my feet. He soon found out what liberties were allowable and what were not, and altogether showed an intelligence and attachment far beyond what are generally attributed to monkeys. Full of good humour, he did not carry his jokes too far, but learned to see from my looks when I had had enough of them, and lay down, as obediently as a child, in my lap. But he could not resist the temptation to carry combs, brushes, and mirrors, &c. to the tops of the highest trees, in order to make his toilet. I often looked for him, called him by his name, and thought he was lost, while he was combing and brushing himself at the top of some tree. He would wait for a favourable moment to come down, put the things in their places unobserved, and appear with a look of affected innocence, which betrayed an evil conscience. If I showed displeasure, and wanted to punish him, he would lie down quite crushed at my feet, and submit to the chastisement, without complaining or defending himself. But, nevertheless, he could not withstand the temptation again. So I had to lock up all things of the sort, which made him quite out of spirits for a long time.

When he stayed away for hours on his excursions, swinging himself from bough to bough and tree to tree, I was always afraid that he would find himself happier among his comrades, who often trooped into the neighbourhood; but he regularly returned with special haste after a long absence, sprang into my arms, and overwhelmed me with caresses, as if to beg my pardon.

He accompanied us on our marches, generally, however, taking his own way over the tops of the trees. Among underwood, or in places bare of vegetation, he would go a few paces before me in the narrow path, closely following our pioneers, as we called the men whose duty it was to cut a way for us with their dahs, but he often stood still and waited for me. A regular walk on his four legs, however, was not to his taste, he soon wearied of it, gave me an imploring look, and, if I gave an assenting nod, he would spring on my arm, and then on my shoulder, whence he could overlook the procession before and behind. His triumphant and self-complaisant air was then quite comic, and seemed to say: 'Look at me sitting up here and being carried, while you, poor fellows, are obliged to walk!' It seemed to us that words only failed him to express human thoughts and feelings.

Once when we were crossing a pretty wide river on a bamboo raft, my pet was not on it, and was nowhere to be seen; he was sought for everywhere, but in vain. We could not delay longer, and landed on the other side without him. Looking back in concern, hoping to spy him, I saw him leap into the water from a lofty tree and disappear. I thought he was drowned, not knowing that monkeys can remain a long time under water, or that they are fond of fish. Great, therefore, was my delight when he reappeared on our side of the water, shook himself, and then came to me with a wistful look, as if wishing to know how I had enjoyed the joke.

In a village where we had encamped near the river, the shores of which were undulating sand hills, the children collected together to look at my monkey's sports. With timid curiosity they stretched out their necks to watch him. He did not at all approve of this, and looked at them with great contempt. When they ventured nearer, he seized a stick, very long in proportion to his size, and drove them away. Having pursued them a little way, he deliberately returned with an air of triumph, and hid himself behind a sand hill, and when they ventured near again to look for him, he sprang from his hiding-place and again put them to flight. This mimic war lasted for some time, he always finding a fresh ambush, until he was tired of it, and laid himself down in my lap. None of these artifices had been taught him, but came out of his own little head, which appeared to harbour many thoughts, which he sought in vain to communicate.

No one who knows these droll creatures only from seeing them in menageries, and their spitefulness when in exile, can have any conception of what they are when at liberty in their native climates.

My little fellow accompanied me, capering about at his own free will, until we returned to Moulmein. But in Mr. Blondell's house, out of regard for his mahogany and damask, and the rest of the elegant furniture, I was obliged, notwithstanding his intelligence, to tie the lively little animal up, which made him so miserable, and even sometimes so spiteful, that I was moved to compassion. I resolved, with a heavy heart, to set him at liberty, and sent him back, with many presents, to the Karen girl, with instructions to take good care of him till I should claim him again. Will anyone accuse me of weakness, when I confess that I shed tears on parting with him, for he looked so disconsolately at me, as if he understood all about it.

We were told of a hill, said to be a long way off, which no one ventured to ascend, because the gnomes took possession of anyone who made so bold as to attempt it. Helfer was desirous to visit the place, and to investigate what could be the origin of this superstition, for there is generally some explanation of legends of this kind.

It was with great reluctance that an old Karen could be persuaded to be our guide, and not until his female relatives had been propitiated with presents.

Our way led through a tract of country which had once been cultivated and then abandoned. The spongy soil was overgrown with weeds of amazing strength, which had overpowered the products of cultivation, and turned the land into a dense and thorny jungle. It is much more difficult to clear such spots again than to prepare a piece of the primeval forest for cultivation, just as it is more difficult to civilise a degenerate race than the children of nature.

There were, however, fortunately for us, some well trodden paths left, wider roads succeeded, and we conjectured that we were again nearing the habitations of men. But it was not so. Elephants, attracted by the bananas, their favourite food, had laid out these highways in accordance with the rules of art. We afterwards also had frequent occasion to admire the sagacity with which these giants lay out their roads, over mountains and through defiles, like intelligent engineers.

At this time of year they are mostly in the mountain regions, where, as they are less affected by drought, they still find succulent food; but their occasional trumpet-like calls, during the night, announced that they had not entirely forsaken the neighbourhood.

We contrived to make our way through the thickets without giving our tailor too much to do in the way of repairs, and at length entered a bamboo forest, a sight which was a great surprise to me; for notwithstanding the many forms under which I had seen this valuable product of the tropics, and much as a few isolated specimens had excited our admiration, we now beheld for the first time a whole forest of bamboos.

The stems grow up, like reeds, from the roots, in regular rows at equal distances, like artificial avenues or plantations, to a height of from sixty to eighty feet, and are about a foot in diameter. These slender stems are bare about half way up, and shine as if washed with a bright yellow varnish. From the middle they branch off, with feathery green foliage, in all directions, and intertwine their boughs with wonderful regularity, as if artistically arranged for vaulted roofing. The bamboo tolerates no underwood, but covers the firm ground with its own glossy fallen leaves, so that you see unhindered through the rows of stems, as through a pillared hall, and the feet glide over the ground as over a parquet floor.

Perfect silence reigned; wild beasts do not find safe covert in these forests, nor food in the hard and, in some species, prickly foliage; it does not even attract insects, and is indigestible to the voracious caterpillar, so that they are free from vermin of all sorts. Neither do the feathery boughs afford food or a safe retreat for birds. Only some flocks of toucans rose screeching out of the wood. This silent temple of nature induced a peculiarly solemn feeling, and we were quieter than usual beneath its dome, until we heard the babbling of a brook, and hastened on in anticipation of the refreshment it would afford us. We made a lonely spot beside it our halting place, under a group of remarkably fine bamboos.

Our young people, having cast off their burdens, and

levelled the ground as if for a dance, made a mat hut for us with even more than their usual dexterity. Our personal attendant and my maid, both of whom had acquired considerable skill in their duties, unpacked our things, and prepared the baths, while the cook made ready a meal, frugal enough, but seasoned with good appetites.

Who, in a spot like this, and under such circumstances, could fail to experience the contentment so well expressed in Schiller's robber song: 'A life of liberty lead we, a life of rare delight?'—though not as robbers, but as harmless wanderers, who amply requited the poor Karens for the rations extorted by their saucy attendants, did we yield ourselves to the enjoyment of this free, unconstrained life, impervious to its thorns.

Our cook had lost or forgotten his tinder box, searched everywhere for it, and was quite nonplussed at not finding it. A young Burmese looked on, evidently enjoying his perplexity. As he could only communicate with him by signs, he significantly tapped his forehead, took two pieces of bamboo, removed the outer rind, and rubbed the bark quickly together; in a few minutes there was a little smoke and sparks of fire.

And the bamboo served not only for striking fire, but as vessels for cooking rice. The canes contain a fluid which is as good tasted as the purest drinking water. One side of the canes is opened, they are filled with rice, closed, and thrown into the fire. Before the cane is burnt through the rice is done, and is as delicate as the nicest boiled rice.

As all proccedings revealed fresh properties of the bamboo, we began to feel a sort of veneration for this wonderful product, capable of satisfying most of the few wants of man in a state of nature. The young shoots, which sprout out of the ground at certain seasons, are an excellent vegetable, something like our asparagus.

We were specially struck here, and had often had occasion to admire before, the nice sense of propriety which the reverence for nature, fostered by Buddhism, had instilled into the minds of these men, uncivilised as we call them. It had inspired them with a refinement and delicacy which police regulations fail to impress upon civilised Europeans in many a splendid capital.

After a zigzag course—from which it was plain that our guide did not know the way—we reached a hill destitute of vegetation. Our followers halted, and could not be persuaded to go further; up there, according to them, you would be bewitched, and unable to get away. Fear and astonishment were depicted on their countenances when Helfer and I at once began to ascend the hill; some of the young people, who had become attached to us, tried to dissuade us from the perilous enterprise, and followed us with anxious looks.

On the top, Helfer at once observed large bare masses of pure loadstone, the magnetic effects of which may have given rise to the curious superstition. The natives may possibly have been sensible of the attraction in the daggers in their girdles, and have attributed it to the supernatural powers which untutored human nature is so prone to believe in. But we were surprised that, as they make so much use of iron, this property of the magnet was unknown to them.

They thought at first that Helfer had broken the spell, by the aid of a more powerful magician, for after seeing how chemical preparations changed colour and form under his manipulations, they took him for a magician. They did not believe him till he brought down a piece of loadstone and showed them experiments with it. Their astonishment was very great, and they wanted to see and understand more, but who could explain to them the properties of the magnet? They all rushed up the hill, stamped about the ground, as if avenging themselves for the fear with which it had inspired them, just as children will beat and pull a bugbear to pieces when they have discovered the secret of the mechanism which has frightened them. They knocked and hammered, loaded themselves with the heavy metal, and would fain have carried away the whole hill, for they all wanted to show their people a bit of the supposed wizard; but Helfer could not allow them to add to the baggage, already much increased, and almost more than the bearers could manage.

An unfortunate occurrence was near depriving us of our Malay attendant and guard.

Our stock of provisions was exhausted, and we had nothing but rice for all our meals, which, after great exertion, is not sufficient for Europeans, accustomed to meat. Helfer, therefore, told the guard to shoot some game fit for food, not an easy task, seeing how all creatures shunned us. However, the man was fortunate enough to track a large elk. He fired at him, but fearing he was not fatally wounded, he loaded his gun again, this time too much; it went off, and wounded the poor man dangerously in the head.

Alarmed by the two shots, we hastened to the spot, and found the elk lying on the ground, and our guard leaning up against a tree, bleeding, and in great pain, covering his singed face and dazzled eyes with both hands. By dint of a bandage put on at once, and the application of effectual remedies, with which Helfer was well provided, we were comforted to find, after a few days, that the patient had recovered, and that his sight was preserved. The accident left no other effects than numerous blue spots on his brown face.

We now took a different direction, in order to regain the boat, which had meanwhile gone further up the river. In so doing we had to traverse part of the road, so called, by which large transports of cattle are driven every year from the Tenasserim provinces to Yunnan, a province of Siam. While yet some way off, we heard a crackling and snapping like small shot, which Helfer could not make out, but our people seemed to be acquainted with it; they nodded to one another, as much as to say, 'There it is!' and when questioned, they said, 'The road is on fire!' Smoke and smell soon confirmed their statement, and, on approaching, we saw a part of the road we had to pass in flames.

In order to produce better feed for the cattle driven this way, the long dry grass and underwood are set fire to at the end of the dry season. This produces a more luxurious growth of pasture during the monsoon, the soil having been thus lightened and manured with ashes. A broad strip, the end of which we could not see, was on fire, tongues of flame darting up and running along the ground.

We looked right and left, and sent scouts in all directions, to discover how we could best get round it, but they all brought back the unwelcome news that it would take a day's journey to get to the end of it. Helfer was at his wits' end. To turn back and overtake the boat by an arduous march was out of the question, both for us and our people, but they did not seem much disconcerted by the fire. They tied sandals made of bamboo canes on their naked feet, made large switches of green boughs tied together, dipped them in the drinking water we had with us, and beat down the flames with them. They went courageously on, always taking care to make a passage for us; we helped by also damping the flames with wet boughs, and thus, by dint of jumping from one clear spot to another, we passed unharmed through the perilous element, though we were nearly stifled with the heat and steam. It took us nearly half-an-hour to cross this sea of fire, and we were dismayed to find that our drinking water was all used up.

There was neither spring nor brook to moisten our parched lips. Some of the Burmese were spying carefully about, while we, exhausted by the exertion, lay down to rest in the shade. Then an exulting shout was heard: 'Water, water! Come here and drink!' And one of the youths brought us a refreshing draught in a red jar. 'Where did you get it?' asked Helfer. 'Oh,' he replied, 'the women put it here for travellers.' 'What do you mean?' asked Helfer. 'Come and see.' With these words he led us to a shady spot beside the burning road. There was a kind of stage under a roof, and at a moderate height were placed many of these vessels of red clay, filled with good drinking water. On further inquiry we learnt that it is a sacred injunction to the women to set these jars up by the wayside, and to keep them filled with fresh water for thirsty wayfarers, though they have often to carry them for miles.

Who would not be surprised at this good Samaritanism among people whom we call barbarians? Here are women sacrificing their time and ease, and exposing themselves to great dangers, in order to provide a reviving draught, or it might be to save the lives of strangers whom they have never seen, without reward, and unobserved.

Our road led us to the place where these women lived, and we were glad, with the aid of the zockey, to find some of them out, and to present them with such things as they value, mirrors, handkerchiefs, &c. They were petrified with astonishment, and could not imagine what they had done to deserve them. Carrying the water seemed to them as much a matter of course as quenching their own thirst. I almost repented having awakened them out of their innocence and acquainted them with the value of their good deeds.

Near this village there was a cave, the coolness of which we at first found very pleasant, but then began to shiver, and it certainly would have produced injurious effects if we had stayed in it long. Vast numbers of particularly ugly bats were hovering about it, and in the water, which was very cold, there were some curious fish, with heads like frogs, whose fins were said to be poisonous. There are also poisonous fish in the Saluen. A few days before, a Karen had been stung by one of them, and died shortly afterwards. After hearing this we gave up bathing in the river.

On the 29th, which was a Sunday, in the evening we were approaching a Karen village, Melaych-hua. When some little way off we heard singing, not unlike the singing in our Protestant churches, but in the simple, pensive tunes of the Karens. There was nothing to disturb the illusion but the unwonted sound of the gong at intervals, which reminded us that we were in Burmah and not near one of our own churches. On reaching the village we found the whole population assembled in one of their larger houses, and singing a hymn with much solemnity. Our entrance did not seem to disturb them; with pure and softly modulated voices they finished their simple but touching hymn, whereupon an aged man uttered a short prayer, unintelligible to us, to which all devoutly listened. Then a young man, the zockey of the place, came forward, addressed us with dignity, and asked us what we desired. The younger women and girls were evidently pleased to see us, and offered their hands to welcome us, colouring slightly as they did so, which is very becoming to them.

We learnt, though, unfortunately, only from an

ignorant interpreter, that a white lady was going about from village to village, and telling the poor, despised Karens about Jesus, who had died for them, would teach them, and make them good and happy; she taught them beautiful hymns to their old tunes, and many other good things. She had washed them all clean in the river, and made 'Isocriten'[1] of them. They followed her advice in everything, and revered her as a good 'nat.'

This white lady was an American Baptist, belonging to the Missionary Society in Moulmein. She had devoted herself to the instruction of the Karens, recognising in their gentle, patient characters, a favourable soil for Christianity. Preaching, singing, and teaching, she penetrated to the most remote spots, lived exclusively for her mission, amidst deprivation and danger, without any reward or acknowledgment, save the approval of her own conscience.

We often came upon the beneficial results of her labours, but we never met with her.

There was not a sufficient number of these devoted missionaries; they could only visit their converts a few times in a year, and were unable to introduce any regular and continuous instruction.

Helfer, having succeeded in finding a bed of loadstone, an accidental piece of information was now to lead to the discovery of silver in the Pakah mountains, surrounded by the Saluen and Thou-Khan rivers.

This group consists of a number of jagged peaks,

---

[1] The native name for the Karen converts to Christianity.—TR.

intersected by gorges and narrow valleys, the highest range reaching a height of 2,500 feet. It is a wild region, densely clothed with wood. Although about thirty miles long, and from eight to ten broad, it was quite uninhabited. The nearest dwelling places, three Karen villages, lay, about eight miles apart, along the winding course of the Yengbaing river.

A Karen, departing from the usual reserve and taciturnity of his race, manifested some interest in Helfer's investigations, and seeing him examining all the stones about, he told him that he knew of a gold mine in another place, and offered to take him to it. This was the only instance we met with of a native giving correct information about the existence of ore; they usually maintained strict silence on the subject, or still oftener tried to mislead by some false statement. They had a great dread of being compelled to work in the mines, as they formerly were.

Having laboriously followed the beds of the mountain streams, and the ridges above the ravines, after a march of a day and a half we came to a spot where the rugged outlines of the limestone cliffs were more plainly seen. We had surmounted the main range, and were on the northern declivity. Perpendicular walls appeared in all directions; the rocks were split by deep clefts, large caverns at their feet alternated with these fissures, and huge, loose blocks lay scattered about on the summits or below the walls of rock.

Along one of these walls of rock there was an abandoned shaft of a mine of the rudest description. The vein of quartz had been hammered out without removing the stone round it. The passage sloped downwards; so far as could be seen it had been hewn out, and the lower part filled with deads.

Helfer had the filling up removed as far as he could, when it appeared that the shaft had not been continued further down. He succeeded in breaking off some of the ore from the quartz; it was not gold, but a mixture of silver, copper, and antimony.

On further examination it appeared that the ore had been smelted on the spot, for he found, under the deads, two pieces of half smelted metal. He had not the means of tracing the veins further, but the existence of the ore was ascertained.

This mine must have been abandoned for a long time, as the whole region was uninhabited, and the wild Karens, as they were called, the only people who were acquainted with it, knew nothing of its existence. The man who was our guide had heard of it from his father, who was a native of the Shan country, where there was a tradition about the wealth concealed in this hill, which they called Baindrawn; he had been there before only once himself. The wild Karens have maintained themselves without any ruler in their inaccessible wilds, and have therefore maintained a more independent character than the rest of their race, though, like them, they are peaceful and harmless.

It is probable that in early times the Siamese possessed this strip of country, and that the existence of silver was unknown to the Burmese, who came after them, or that they had not the means of working it.

Our destination now was the range of the Elephant-tail Mountains, whose summits we had seen at times through openings in the forests. It is the course of rivers and brooks that affords these occasional vistas; if it were not for them you might wander about, as it were, in the dark, without being able to see what you are coming to.

Our Burmese were very unwilling to accompany us; they do not like forests and mountains, the water is their element; they feel at home on it, and are very efficient. Many of them were sick and exhausted; their usual diet is not sufficient for the great exertion of long marches and bearing heavy burdens. It was all the more gratifying that their attachment to Helfer, which was based on his authority as well as upon his mental superiority, induced them to accompany us notwithstanding.

Having crossed a series of spurs of the mountains of moderate elevation, we were surprised to see a fruitful plain, covered with fresh and luxuriant vegetation, but it was extremely hot, and threatened us with fever. Some of our suite dragged themselves wearily on, and were bent on turning back; but the time was not yet come for this, we had to push on at all hazards. To encourage them, however, they were told that when we reached the Saluen again they should be sent home.

We were both much exhausted ourselves, but had, as yet, been free from jungle fever. Our huts had prevented us from being so immediately exposed to the malarious exhalations during the night, and had been the means of preserving us from it.

On April 9, the Karen zockey, who had voluntarily accompanied us from Yengbaing-kua, was despatched with ten Karens to find out the most practicable way to the foot of the mountain. They started very early, and did not return till late in the evening with the news that they had surmounted the spurs, but had not reached the foot of the main part of the mountain, for where they could not follow the elephant tracks, they had had to cut their way with their dahs.

Helfer now resolved to make the ascent himself the next day. The invalids were allowed a day of rest, and we set out, accompanied by scarcely anyone but Karens. The scarcity of bloom on the vegetation in this district was striking; the fresh green was exchanged for a russet hue; it was thirsting for the rainy season, when it would again adorn itself in its former luxuriance.

At the foot of the chain of mountains forming the boundary of Siam, we arrived at a remarkable lake, estimated by Helfer to be about 110 miles from Moulmein, and called Lambret by the Karens; it had the appearance of an immense crater, though there was no trace of volcanic origin to be seen. On the western side quartz rocks were scattered about, all more or less rounded, no doubt brought there at some time by the action of water. These blocks were full of particles of tin ore, not measuring more than a quarter of an inch, which Helfer did not find anywhere else in the province of Amherst.

This region swarmed with wild beasts; we even saw the wild cow, one of the rarest and shyest of animals. They almost all withdrew into the thickets on our approach, and at the unusual noise that we made, but during the night we had a concert, not of the most agreeable kind, from the most various throats, in which the trumpet notes of the elephant prevailed over the rest. Several tigers were seen, but the huge fires round our encampment protected us from making too close an acquaintance with them. The Karens were not afraid to go out alone. Shy and timid as they are in intercourse with men, they are so accustomed to the perils of the wilderness, that they know how to protect themselves against them. Armed with his dah, a Karen will fight a tiger.

The next day we continued our march to the mountain itself. Sometimes following broad elephant-tracks free from underwood, and sometimes making our pathless way on the edges of precipices and gorges, we came to a steep wall of rock. But here our followers absolutely refused to go further. The Burmese said that they could not carry the loads further, and the Karens were terrified at the idea of getting to the Siamese frontier at the top. They had too great a dread of the slavery into which their forefathers had been carried. They said that their enemies were always on the watch for them, and attacked all who ventured to ascend the mountain.

In vain Helfer represented to them that, with our numbers, and under the leadership of an Englishman, they had nothing to fear; in vain he promised extra pay. Having no means of compelling them, he began to ascend the mountain alone, armed with a gun, and cutting his way with a dah. They had never permitted this before, a few of the most courageous had always followed him wherever he went. To put them to shame he ascended to the highest point alone. But the distant view he hoped to gain was shut out by the vast forest that extended to the top. He could not possibly cut any vista through it alone, and returned very much exhausted and out of humour, but, to my inexpressible delight, safe and sound. He sternly repelled the Burmese, who went joyfully to meet him, not vouchsafing them even a friendly look, which they took much more to heart than many serious admonitions before.

The Karens, meanwhile, had shot an elk and some flying squirrels; the elk was cut up and his flesh distributed; it was high time to replenish our stock of provisions.

But we had not made the arduous march to this spot quite in vain, it was soon rewarded by the discovery of lead mines.

The temperature, at this distance from the coast, where the sea breezes do not penetrate, and the western sun strikes with full force against the mountains, was intolerable; the air vibrated with heat.

We returned to the lake to which the sick and exhausted had been brought, and found them somewhat revived. We encamped in a romantic spot, and were delighted with the picturesque view of the mountains across the broad lake.

We wished now to get to the Dagyaing, a tributary of the Saluen, but had a difficult march before us. We came at first to a brook, and alongside of its clear waters there was a winding path for a considerable distance, and perpendicular cliffs on the other side threw a grateful shade. But they soon began to close in the path, and before long a lofty rock, projecting into the water, obstructed it entirely. Further progress seemed impossible, but it was equally improbable that a well-trodden path should suddenly come to an end, and we soon discovered that it went straight across the brook to the other side, and then along its banks again.

A stream is not much of an obstacle to men whose only clothing is a tattooed skin, and who are as fond of the water as amphibious animals. Without any ado they tied ratan rods together to make a seat, and invited me to sit upon it; this was a novelty, they lifted me up with shouts of delight and carried me through the rapid stream. But the bottom was not firm, the loose stones rolled under the feet of one bearer, and the foot of the other slipped, so that I was in danger of falling into the water, and was nearly as wet with the splashing as if I had gone over on my own legs. We continued our way along the edge of the cliff, which unfortunately afforded us no shade on this side, but reflected back the sun's rays in full force. Bathed in perspiration, we reached a point where the path was cut off by a rock on this side, and crossed the stream again. The water was shallower here, but instead of pebbles there were great masses of rock in it, round which it whirled and foamed and formed cascades. Having come so far, going back was out of the question, neither was it possible for me to trust myself to be carried over.

After the fearful heat, however, the cold mountain stream appeared most inviting, and trusting myself to the guidance of two powerful men, I stepped in without delay, and safely reached the opposite shore, dripping wet and shuddering with cold. But in a few minutes our clothes were dry, and we were again in a bath of perspiration. Five times more I made the experiment of a natural vapour bath, which one could certainly only do without peril in such an atmosphere. Helfer preferred to remain in the water, and performed the distance swimming and wading. The sun was sinking, and we had not reached the Dagyaing. We could not go any further, and had to pass the night near the stream, already swollen to a respectable little river.

Our brave Karen zockey, whom Helfer thoroughly liked and trusted, offered to go to a village near and get some boats, as the river had become navigable, to save us further fatigue. Before we had emerged from our curtains next morning, we heard the shouts of the Karens announcing their return, and had scarcely breakfasted when all was ready packed in the boats. After a short row we reached the Dagyaing.

This river, which we now descended, is a mountain stream, twenty feet broad, very deep in places, and in others so shallow that the boats had to be dragged along. On the shores considerable patches of wood had not long before been set fire to by the inhabitants to protect themselves from the tigers, who had robbed them of many of their pigs.

After an hour's voyage we lay to near Konoh, a

large village sixty paces from the river. We preferred encamping on a nice shady spot on the bank. With the help of the Karens a large pent-house was contrived for our hut, which made us a shady drawing-room.

Helfer now sent the sick and exhausted men, after they had been revived by a good meal, in several boats to Moulmein, to get there as quickly as they could.

We received news here of the arrival of the boats which had been sent up the Saluen from Moulmein, but they had not been able to get so far as this from want of water. The messenger also brought us the much-needed stores of tea, coffee, spirituous liquors, &c., letters from Mr. Blondell, who was anxious about us, and a packet of letters from home by the last mail from Europe. We had long been anxiously looking forward to them. Here, on the utmost boundary of the habitations of men, in the Anglo-Indian Empire, the loving words of our beloved friends were more welcome than ever to our hearts; we felt how strong were the ties which bound us to our native land, for the thousands of miles between us, and the total contrast of our surroundings to everything at home, made it doubly dear to us.

The Karens, who had come so far with us and patiently borne the heavy loads, were now dismissed. We were glad to be able to regale them before they left with a glass of gin, of which they are very fond, and had had to do without for several days.

Our brave zockey was rewarded in princely style, and took leave with all the demonstrations of affection at his command. Helfer held out hopes of a speedy return, for he was so attracted by the beauty of the Elephant-tail Mountains, and so firmly believed in the practicability of some of the schemes he had projected, that he thought it probable he might settle for some time in these parts.

The Burmese, who wanted to make a feast, also received gifts from the stores, which put them in high good humour. It was a day of general rejoicing, and in the evening we had the novel spectacle of a monsoon storm.

The sultry atmosphere had announced the approach of the rainy season. But we had not paid much attention to the gathering clouds in the otherwise clear sky, so that we were startled by distant thunder, succeeded immediately by tremendous peals much nearer. The flashes of lightning and the reverberations of the thunder among the mountains were fearfully grand. A shower of rain, the first for six months, poured down. It was a great blessing to us, and still more so to the parched ground. All vegetation, and the various species of spice trees and shrubs exhaled their sweet perfumes, till the scent was almost overpowering.

Refreshing as it was, it was none the less a warning to reach the boats, as quickly as possible, which were to take us back to Moulmein, to place ourselves and our collections, particularly botanical specimens pressed in blotting-paper, in safety, before the monsoon set in in full force.

All arrangements were made, everything packed in

five little boats, which the zockey of the village procured for us, and on a Sunday, April 16, we began to descend the Dagyaing. Not far from the village we had to pass a dangerous whirlpool, formed by two huge blocks of rock, and the boats often had to be dragged over shallow places; but we steered safely down the picturesque stream and arrived at about 3 P.M. at the village of Paina-kiounyua.

The inhabitants came in a friendly spirit to see us, but seemed surprised that we should travel on that day. This was explained in the evening, when, at the sound of the gong, we heard the hymns we had heard before, and learned that the inhabitants were 'Isocriten,' who, as newly-converted Baptists, strictly observed the Sabbath. They were not to be persuaded to render us any help on that day.

Safe in the roomy boats, on the rapid Saluen, we happily reached Moulmein, after an absence of six weeks, and were received with the greatest kindness by Mr. Blondell, who again invited us to be his guests.

CHAPTER IV.

EXPEDITION TO THE THREE PAGODAS.

HELFER returned to Moulmein well content. We had happily surmounted all the difficulties, dangers, and privations of an arduous journey, and borne the climate well; no accident had befallen any of our attendants, though they had frequently been alone when collecting specimens, and exposed to great dangers. He had good reason to hope that the results of his explorations would be satisfactory to the Government in Calcutta, and at once set to work to arrange his ample collections.

He also began to study the Burmese language grammatically, in order to be able to dispense with an interpreter, and to publish some of the results of his observations in the *Moulmein Gazette* in Burmese; daily practice had already enabled him to speak it with tolerable fluency. He succeeded in such an incredibly short time that he often wrote his articles in the presence of others, that he might be able to prove his authorship. He pursued a peculiar method in learning this unusually difficult language. He used to put a sheet of paper, on which he had written down the words and idioms learnt during the day, under his pillow. Whether it was that his dreams were full of them, or that his memory did not slumber during the night, anyhow they were fully impressed on his mind next morning, and by the time he undertook his next expedition into the interior, in November, he was perfectly well able to communicate with the Burmese without assistance.

It was pleasant to me to find myself again in civilised society; there was a peculiar charm in the sudden change of scene, from the thickets of the jungle to a ladies' drawing-room. Moulmein society seemed much less wearisome to me than it had done on first acquaintance. Mr. Blondell, who was unmarried, and regretted that he could not, on that account, invite ladies to his house, took the opportunity of my being there to do so, and asked me to do the honours. This opened a new and hospitable rendezvous to English society in Moulmein, to its great satisfaction.

The storms of the monsoon, which reaches its height at this latitude, increased to hurricanes, the lightning flashed like fire from heaven, the earth trembled beneath the terrific peals of thunder, the rain literally poured down in torrents, and once flooded the earth with twenty-three inches in twenty-four hours. During this period, which was generally a weary time for society in Moulmein, we tried to break the daily monotony by little fêtes, music, games, and theatrical representations, such as we have in Germany, but they were quite a novelty to the circle here.

Mr. Blondell also invited some of the Burmese magistracy, under his rule, to these parties. Seated on mats along the wall, they watched the sprightly doings with evident interest, but when they beheld their stern master in the ranks of the dancers, they at once turned their faces to the wall, and covered their eyes with their hands. Respect forbade them to look at their ruler frisking about in that way.

I, however, felt more attraction to the leader of the American missions, Mr. Judson, and his estimable wife, than to the so-called fashionable world. Mr. Judson had preached Christianity in these lands as a missionary before the English had taken possession of them, and had penetrated as far as Ava. But there, in the immediate neighbourhood of the golden throne, offence was taken at his proceedings; he was forbidden to teach and preach, and as he did not obey, the despotic ruler threw him into prison, where, laden with heavy chains, he languished, without hope of release. He would certainly have died of starvation, if his courageous wife had not dared, and found out the way, to provide him with the necessaries of life; but, in order to watch her opportunity, she often had to spend whole days and nights outside his prison. When he had regained his liberty, in consequence of the victory won by the English over the Burmese, he transferred the seat of the missions to Moulmein. The scars left by the fetters on his hands and feet were as indelible as the traces of grief and anxiety on the noble countenance of his wife. Both, however, devoted themselves with unflagging zeal to the spread of Christianity.

Mrs. Judson had undertaken the task of inventing characters for the Thali language, a dialect spoken in Pegu, on the Lower Irawaddy, to translate the whole

Bible into Thali, and to make extracts for the use of the people—an undertaking that one would have supposed too gigantic for a woman's powers. Mr. Judson had established a Burmese school, in which he provided not only religious but secular instruction. Unfortunately his success was not proportionate to his efforts and his great powers of mind.

The Burmese have no inclination to change their religion. The religious views of Buddhism, which they have retained in its purity, entirely satisfy their spiritual wants. They compare the incarnation of Buddha to the incarnation of God in the person of Christ; the purifying process of the transmigration of souls, until they are absorbed in the Infinite All, seems to them analogous to the repentance, remission of sins, and return of man to God the Father through the Son, of the Christian religion, and, in fine, they consider that the moral precepts of their religion are in no way behind Christian morality. Then they are by nature a careless, joyous, happy race, who, as yet unacquainted with luxury and the pursuit of pleasure, can easily satisfy all their modest wants. Such a people do not furnish the soil adapted for the teaching which says: 'Come unto me all ye that labour and are heavy laden.'

Neither have the threats of eternal damnation and hell, with which fanatical missionaries have sought to frighten them into Christianity, made more impression on them. The Burmese generally asked them: 'Where do you suppose our forefathers are?' And on receiving the reply: 'In hell, because they died unbaptized,' they said: 'Then we will go there, too.'

They were mostly only degraded subjects who had been persuaded to be baptized, for the sake of worldly advantage, as they received pecuniary support. If this ceased to be given, they generally collected their bibles and tracts together and burnt them in some public place, saying: 'We won't be Christians for nothing.'[1]

In the external forms of Buddhist worship there is a surprising similarity to those of the Roman Catholics. The altars with many tapers, processions, pilgrimages to holy places, the rosaries, the tonsure and celibacy of the priests (pomgys), the grades into which they are divided, up to the episcopal dignity, present the most curious analogies. The Burmese also have convents (khiowngo), but they do not possess any property, the priests live solely on gifts, and as they devote themselves to teaching boys, the convents are more like schools.

The regulation is that every boy shall spend a certain time in a convent, where he wears the yellow dress of the priests, and is instructed in writing, reading, ciphering, and geography. He is usually there from the age of ten to thirteen, and then decides whether he will remain a priest or return to secular life. Limited as this instruction is—for example, according to Chinese ideas, China includes nearly all the world, other countries being only a little appendage thereto—and although their books, which consist of leaves of the fan palm stitched together, contain nothing but the precepts of their religion or chronicles of the court, still

[1] It must be remembered that this refers to a time between thirty and forty years ago.—Tr.

a certain amount of school instruction is universal, down to the lowest labourer; but it is not often that a Burmese makes any further progress.

The doctrine of the transmigration of souls, according to which the dead appear on earth in all possible forms for their purification, mostly, however, in the shape of domestic animals, causes the latter to be treated with great kindness and consideration; an ill-treated or overladen beast is scarcely ever to be seen, and still more rarely will a Burmese kill a domestic animal. They live on vegetables, fish, and wild animals.

Reverencing nature as divine, and living so much in the open air in their genial climate, they consider it an honour and a privilege due to their priests, that their bodies should not be permitted to decay, but should be returned to nature and the air. This idea is the origin of the Burmese custom of blowing their deceased pomgys into the air. These ceremonies are general popular festivals, and are performed with great pomp and circumstance, so that the funereal rites of several priests usually take place at the same time, the bodies of those who have died some time before having been preserved from corruption. The bodies, beautifully decked out, are laid, with great solemnity, on a lofty wooden stage, under which a quantity of powder is laid; the powder is fired, and the explosion blows the dead, and the stage, reduced to atoms, to the four winds of heaven.

The people, who assemble in solemn procession at the place, make a great point of securing a morsel of the body, a shred of the garments, or even a chip of the stage. There is a general scramble for these relics, which are kept as charms.

Perfectly tolerant, or rather indifferent towards other religions, the Burmese are inaccessible to conversion. Their priests carry on long disputations with the missionaries, but maintain that their own religious writings are as old and incontestably true as those of the Christians, and demand mathematical proof to the contrary. They regard the zeal of the various Christian missionaries with stoical imperturbability, and these, unfortunately, carry on their hateful sectarian controversies even here, and their mutual abuse is disastrous to Christianity.

On the other hand, the Burmese priests permit Buddhism to be openly abused by the Christian sectaries in the streets without inciting the people to demonstrations against it, though, from the consideration in which they are held, they could very easily do so.

The Burmese have no castes, and are free from prejudice of race, readily acknowledge the superiority of Europeans, and are eager to learn from them. They consider their connection with them to be an honour, and readily give them their daughters in marriage, provided only that the marriage contract is concluded in accordance with their laws, by which the husband must pay down a sum of money according to his position. The woman then considers herself the legitimate wife of her husband, and demands not only to be treated as such by him, but lays claim to the honours appropriate to his rank, consisting chiefly in a suitable abode, and the number and dimensions of the chattahs (umbrellas) carried after her when she goes out.

Many of the English officers were married to Burmese women. In the cantonment there was a smaller bungalow, close to their own, in which the wife lived. She attended to the domestic affairs, took her meals at her husband's table, and not seldom acquired great influence over him, or gained his devoted affection. Many instances have occurred in which, on the removal of a regiment, some of the officers have not been able to make up their minds to part with their wives, but have preferred to leave the service, and remain in the country.

There were no girls of bad character, or immoral houses, at Moulmein, such as usually abound in garrison towns. The girls were too proud and independent to enter into any other than a marriage relation. The children of these unions, though not distinguished for beauty, were generally intelligent; the mental characteristics of the European father, combined with the happy temperament of the Burmese mother, were evident at an early age. The people were universally fond of these children. I have now and then even seen a Burmese caressing a child of his wife's whose blue eyes and light hair unmistakably betrayed a foreign origin. A new, gifted, and it is to be hoped, happy race will arise under British rule.

We were to get a sight of a royal Bengal tiger in the middle of the town, which we had not done when these animals were close to us in the jungle. One evening, when the sky had cleared after torrents of rain, the moon and stars were peculiarly bright, and we were taking tea out of doors for the first time after a long interval, and reading by moonlight the European papers which had just come in, an officer came up and called out to Mr. Blondell, in a voice trembling with excitement, 'My dog—my favourite dog has been carried off by a tiger.'

'How so? Have you been hunting?'

'Oh no; then it would have been likely enough; but here, in the middle of the town, it is incredible.'

He then related what had happened.

He had been sitting, in the twilight, comfortably smoking a cigar, in the verandah of his bungalow, which was in rather a retired situation, surrounded by underwood, and raised about five feet from the ground, his dog, as usual, lying at his feet. Perfect stillness reigned around, not a sound betrayed the presence of a living creature, when a tiger made a sudden spring from under the verandah, seized the dog, and made off. This was enough to disturb the equanimity of the bravest, but the officer quickly recovered his presence of mind, seized his gun, and followed the tiger, but no cries of the dog showed the direction he had taken. To pursue him in this uncertainty would have been madness, as he would have dropped his prey and turned upon his pursuer.

The dog could not be rescued, but he had to be avenged, and the town to be ridden of the audacious intruder. Measures were therefore at once taken for pursuit of the tiger, it being assumed that he would not at once leave the neighbourhood after his meal.

Before daybreak, a spirited troop, headed by the officer, sallied forth to hunt the marauder, and were lucky enough to find and kill him. He was a splendid animal, six feet long, with immense claws and jaws, and his fangs looked terrible, even in death, while the soft, finely marked skin was inviting to the touch.

Four men, adorned with green boughs, carried the monster tied by his four legs to a pole. The procession was everywhere greeted with triumph. The slayer, already handsomely rewarded by the owner of the dog, received twelve rupees, besides the premium paid by the Government for every tiger killed.

An amusing incident made us acquainted with some of the curious relations between men and animals which prevail in the beliefs and manners of these countries.

The King of Ava wished to give her Britannic Majesty a pledge of reconciliation, and selected a white elephant—according to the ideas of the country the most honourable present, for white elephants are very rare, divine honours are paid them, and they may only be the property of a king.

On the way from Ava to Calcutta he came to Moulmein, where he met with a suitable reception in a bungalow erected for the purpose in Mr. Blondell's yard. He was a young animal, and affably received the honours paid him, looked down graciously upon those who approached him to pay their devoirs, and devoured their offerings of sugar cane, plaintains, and rice with great satisfaction.

I was delighted with this miniature copy of the sagacious denizens of the forests, who looked as if he was made of sugar. But my fancy for him was near getting me into trouble. One day, when I was about to stroke him, I observed angry looks among the bystanders. Happily, Mr. de la Condamine, who was close by, seized me by the arm, and prevented my touching the animal. It would, he said, have put the people in a rage, from which even Mr. Blondell's authority would scarcely have protected me.

The presence of this sacred animal was the occasion for great festivities at Moulmein; arrayed in their best, and with all their valuables hung about them, the women made ceremonious pilgrimages to him in solemn procession, followed by games and festivities.

Among the games there was one which displayed much grace and agility. Young men, with many-coloured potzos round their loins, the ends flying fantastically about their heads and shoulders, their black hair encircled in white muslin shawls, formed themselves into long processions four to six abreast, and, as they slowly passed, good-sized balls, made of ratan withes, were tossed from one to the other. The ball is thrown, not with the hands, but with the soles of the feet, and must be caught and thrown back in the same way. This, of course, demands great elasticity and suppleness of limb, for it implies very rapid changes of position. These columns of ball-players paraded all the streets of the town, animated by the applause and laughter of the lookers on, who took the liveliest interest in the spectacle; it may, to some extent, be compared to our ballet dancing, but propriety was never outraged in the least.

Amidst amusements of this sort, graver occupations and studies, the time of the monsoon, usually so dull, passed very pleasantly away.

In October, the rains became less violent and frequent; the sun began to have more power, and to dry up the soaked ground. But it was some weeks before the country was accessible, and it was not till the middle of November that Helfer could think of undertaking his second mission into the interior. It was to occupy six months, the whole period of the dry season, to include the provinces of Yeh, Tavoy, and Mergui, and to extend to the south-east frontier of the British possessions.

We had had ample experience, on our former journey, that the equipment provided, splendid as it appeared to us at the time, was by no means adequate for the preservation of health and strength during a six months' tarriance in uninhabited jungles. The climate, the scanty fare, often ill suited to Europeans, and the unremitting exertion, were all factors any one of which was enough to undermine the strongest health.

Mr. Blondell was perfectly aware of this; he provided, in a far-seeing and most liberal style, not only for our wants, but for those of our suite, and for all the scientific requirements. There was to be a large double tent to protect us from the night exhalations and the burning sun when at work during the day; a table and two chairs were provided for our convenience in arranging collections, a four-post bedstead, and two little tin drawers in a wooden frame were to make it easier to keep clothes and toilet apparatus in order, so that the interior of the tent might look more comfortable.

Large stores of tea, coffee, sugar, and spices for curry were taken for our suite as well as for ourselves. Preserved meats and other viands prepared in Europe, sherry wine, spirits for our people, and the pale ale, so much used in India, were packed in large quantities. One would not have thought ale adapted to the climate, but it is particularly useful, as Europeans, accustomed to good diet, when their digestive organs are weakened by the heat, cannot, without it, assimilate sufficient nourishment.

For the conveyance of all these household effects, and other apparatus, two elephants and fifty bearers were provided, and there were to be two riding horses for our own use. To the former collectors, artists as we playfully called them, an animal stuffer was added, provided with arsenic, sublimate, and other materials for preserving animals. A laundry man was added to our personal attendants, and my Burmese ayah was exchanged for a young black girl from the Malabar coast, who, like most of her people, could speak English.

It will appear that we were exchanging our modest German ways for Indian magnificence. But it would be unfair to attribute all this care to effeminacy. The result showed that we Northern foreigners preserved our health and strength, while the natives, sleeping in the open air, and living on their scanty vegetable diet, fell sick, and several times we had to have reinforcements.

The descriptions of some travellers, who, with a gun on their shoulders, have provided themselves with food, whom the vault of heaven has served for a tent, and the cool but damp grass for a couch, may sound very delightful; and to some it may appear superfluous to drag all these goods and chattels through forests, over mountains and rivers, simply for the convenience of two persons; but it must be borne in mind that it is one thing to rove about at your own free will, without any particular aim, and quite another to have various special objects in view, which demand all your powers, both mental and physical. Our attendants had no time to provide us with food by the chase; it was their business rather to be on the look-out for the rarest animals for museums. Besides, the game is so shy that it would always be difficult for a troop of people, following a particular direction, to kill a sufficient supply. Expert hunters know well how much time, patience, and perseverance are required for the chase in the wilderness. And as for sleeping in the open air, it may sound very pleasant to those who have never tried it, but he who has once experienced the waking up with stiffened limbs, and wet through with dew, and knows anything about the night exhalations in tropical forests, is well aware that it almost invariably leads to jungle fever.

But well adapted for the purpose as these complicated preparations were, they had their shady side. They demanded forces not readily procurable. There were new and strange elements added to our previous suite, Thalians, Shans, and Chinese; and we soon found that they were not so tractable as our young Burmese, and it made strict discipline necessary. In order to enforce it, the Gyown Yowk of the district, whose jurisdiction extended to the town of Yeh, was to accompany us so far. But, unfortunately, he had but little authority over his foreign subjects.

Helfer's impatience to set out increased with every fine day, and would not allow him to wait till the end of the monsoon.

On November 14, we set out in six boats, and rowed up the Atta-yan to a point where our riding horses and the elephants, which had been employed in dragging wood from the teak forests, were to await us.

Borne along by the tide, which flows a good way up, we reached a Karen village, where heavy rain warned us that we had set out full soon. The boats, and the bales of paper for pressing plants, were sheltered from the downpour in a spacious cave. Nothing special occurred till the 18th, when we reached the site of the former town of Atta-yan, which had been entirely depopulated by the voluntary emigration of the inhabitants to Siam, and there were but two huts left standing.

Near here there is another warm spring, with a temperature of 122° Fahrenheit. Having with great difficulty cut a way through the thicket, we came to the ruins of a temple overgrown with plants not common to the district. The water, which is something like broth, swarmed with the redoubtable leeches, like the hot spring on the Saluen, and they immediately fastened in clusters on the naked bodies of our attendants. No sooner had they got rid of one than another got hold. They were most repulsive to me, for though I can handle almost any creature without disgust, I have a great aversion to those which have an incalculable power of contraction and expansion; it was, however, but a foretaste of what was before us.

As mosquitoes of the most malignant sort also made the spot intolerable, we did not stay long, having taken our repast under shelter of the bed curtains.

Our little flotilla then went on, the shores of the Atta-yan becoming more and more romantic, and the forests more dense.

We came to a place which the natives consider to be bewitched, and sacred to the 'nats.' Forty years before a gigantic tree had been felled, to be hollowed out for a war boat, but it fell, unluckily, and killed over a hundred men. Ever since the spot had been in ill odour as under the immediate influence of the spirits. A little wooden house had been erected on the stump of the tree, in which every passer by placed an offering to the gods, of rice, betel nuts, or something of the sort, in the firm conviction that it would protect him from jungle fever.

On the evening of the 23rd we came to the influx of a tributary of the Atta-yan, considerably swollen by the rains, and taken advantage of for floating teak wood from the forests above. Ten Karens awaited us here, as a reinforcement of the bearers, and as pioneers in the wanderings now soon to begin.

The boats were carried up one day's voyage further by the tide. There, to our surprise, we found the horses and elephants which were to have joined us higher up. The driver, a Thalian, as almost all the elephant drivers are, pretended that he could not find the way any further; and he had not executed the commission to exchange a useless female elephant for a powerful one in the teak forests. He tried to justify his contumacy by all sorts of pretences, and showed himself to be altogether a refractory subject; to our surprise, the Gyown Yowk held his peace and did not interfere.

This was the first instance of disobedience among our followers, and it showed Helfer plainly enough that he no longer had people like the tractable Burmese to manage, that the new elements were striving for mastery, and that there would be an end of all discipline if they once got the upper hand. He perceived that, for the sake of our personal safety, as well as the success of the expedition, he must at once put down this first rebellion against his authority. As remonstrances were vain, and the elephant driver persisted in refusing to exchange the useless beast, Helfer coolly ordered the baggage to be packed into the boats again to return to Moulmein, where the governor would inquire into it and punish the delinquents. This took effect, and the scene changed in no time. The Gyown Yowk, who had remained passive, and perhaps was secretly speculating on assuming the leadership himself, all at once changed his tone, and offered, when the driver was discharged, to go himself to the teak forest, and bring back a good elephant. He went, and sent back a messenger the same evening to say that he would come himself next day with a number of elephants.

Meanwhile, without any particular reason, except to teach his new subjects how to submit unconditionally to the despotic will of their master, Helfer ordered the camp to be pitched on the other side of the river, and the animals to be sent over too. The next day the Gyown Yowk arrived, with nine splendid elephants to choose from, and they also had to be brought over. It was interesting to see how circumspectly the huge creatures slid down the steep, slippery shore. Sitting on their hind legs like dogs, they felt about with their fat but sensitive fore-paws for a firm spot whence they could slide down slowly into the water. This proceeding, as well as the swimming, was evidently very unpleasant to some of the novices. They uttered cries of distress, and could only be made to move by severe castigation. One elephant disappeared in the water beneath his rider, who only saved himself by swimming. His feet had become entangled in the roots in the river; in vain he tried to extricate himself, he sank deeper and deeper, till even his trunk disappeared. Strong poles were pushed under his body, but what could men do in unsteady boats with such a weight? It was impossible to help him, but at length he made his own way up. Slowly, and evidently exhausted, he swam to shore, and had to rest for some time before he could climb up the bank. It is always an agitating sight to see a creature in danger of perishing helplessly before your eyes, even if only an animal.

Before taking leave of the river, and beginning the

land journey, the collections already made were packed up, letters for Moulmein, Calcutta, and Europe closed, and all sent back by the boats. This done, the bridge between us and Moulmein, and the rest of the world, was broken down behind us. So long as we were near the river, we felt that we had a clue to guide us back to our kind; but now, take what direction we might, we had to make our way through pathless woods, and being the only two white people among a crowd of motley attendants, we felt rather lonely and desolate.

I suppose, in reflecting on our situation, I must have lost my usual hopeful expression, and have looked rather downhearted, for Helfer playfully called out to me, in the purest Lusatian dialect : 'Now, don't be afraid !' (*Nur keene Furcht niche* [1]), which made me laugh, and thus restored my good spirits. How often a very few words suffice to change our mood, to inspire us with courage, and make us feel equal to anything, or else to send us down into the depths of despair.

Our Karen pioneers were sent forward to our destination, the Three Pagodas, an elevated spot, forming the boundary of Siam, and the watershed of the eastern mountain chain. It was said to be five or six days' march, and they were to discover the most practicable route, and when necessary to make it passable for the horses.

On the 26th, our column was ready for the march. The loads were carefully distributed, so that no one should be overloaded. The lion's share, the heavy tent

[1] Comparable to some English provincial dialect—Somersetshire, for instance, ' Don't 'ey be afeard now.'—TR.

and chests, of course fell to the elephants. On one of them our cook was enthroned, with an apparatus of burnt clay, which enabled him to begin his operations on the march, when we were late in reaching our encampment. Slowly and laboriously the procession made its way through the tangled growths of the long, thorny rods of the ratan palm, by which large tracts were overgrown. Then we came to vast forests, and often had to alight from our horses to escape the fate of Absalom.

My attention was almost exclusively devoted to observing the sagacity with which the elephants bore their burdens unscathed through all obstacles. This remarkable animal always sets down his columnar feet in measured tread, trampling down the lower underwood as he goes. He calculates precisely how far apart the trees must be, and how high the boughs, not to interfere with his load. If the trees in his way are not too large, he seizes them with his trunk, bends them down, and treads them to the ground. In the same way he breaks off the boughs with his trunk that hang too low for his burden, generally putting one into his mouth. Thus, he stalks phlegmatically along amidst the crackling of the broken trees and branches, making way for himself right and left, up and down, and munching as he goes. It seems really marvellous that he can so well estimate, not only his own bulk, but that of his load. If the baggage on an elephant's back is well distributed and secured, it is very seldom that any accident happens to it.

We always considered ourselves fortunate when we

found the tracks of wild elephants in the direction we were taking, for their roads are laid out through difficult ground, and along precipices, with a sagacity that would do honour to an experienced engineer. It seemed to us almost incredible that they were made by animals and not by men.

After a long march we came to the teak forest, with its splendid trees, in which the timber was being diligently felled. Here, too, the elephants employed excited our admiration. We saw them fastening strong ropes, with cleverly tied knots, without the help of man, to the fallen trees, and drawing them to the edge of the river, where they undid the knots, and began the process again. Twelve elephants were thus at work, under the supervision of one man.

Conscious of his strength, the elephant will bear ill treatment, to a certain extent, patiently and without retaliation. But if carried too far, and once his wrath is roused, he will not spare even his driver, to whom he is otherwise faithfully attached. The drivers often treat them very roughly, urging them on with sharp-pointed goads while riding them, although they know that if once their forbearance is exhausted their own lives are in great danger. Among our company there was one which, a few days before, had thrown his rider, and trampled him under foot.

Just as in life, things high and low, noble and vulgar, are found in close juxtaposition, so here, beside the animal next to man in intelligence and sagacity, we found a miserable worm covering water, ground, and bushes, in distressing multitudes.

The Indian leeches contract still more than the European ones into a thin black thread. When the ground is soaked after the rains they leave their usual haunts, the pools, and crawl about the ground, the wet twigs, and leaves, and fasten themselves to every living thing having veins, within their reach. No precautions were of any use. While we defended ourselves from the disgusting creatures with hands and feet, our large hats swarmed with them from our being under the trees, and they dexterously contrived to get from them to the head, and other parts of the body, and sucked away with a prick scarcely felt. I used to find them, on undressing, in my hair, or hanging swollen under my clothes, to my unspeakable disgust.

Of all the repulsive things I had to put up with on my travels these were the worst. Fortunately they only infest the country like this for a short time, only so long as the earth is saturated with moisture, and the trees and shrubs are still wet with the rains. As soon as the sun has regained its power they retire into their holes and corners.

Nevertheless, in spite of my disgust, I found some interest in observing their instinct, and could not help making experiments to discover how far off they would smell warm blood. If I stretched out my foot they quickly crawled towards it, and if I turned it in another direction they turned too. We were plagued with them for about three days.

Following the banks of the Natshanna, a tributary of the Atta-yan, up the stream, we made for our destination, the Three Pagodas, in an easterly direction.

But the river soon began to wind in all directions; still, for a time, we followed its course; one does not willingly part from a bad guide when there is no better to be had. But as the bends became greater and greater, and took us west instead of east, Helfer saw that he could not follow it any longer. None of our people knew the way, or could give us any information; all were getting weary, and could only be urged on with difficulty. Helfer then had recourse to the compass, and gave orders to proceed directly eastward. The people stared, and said it was impossible, they would all be lost, and perish in the wilderness, if they left the banks of the river, where they might hope to come upon the habitations of men.

One of the bearers, who was fond of leading the opposition, threw himself at Helfer's feet, and handed him his dah, saying that he would rather he should cleave his head in two than compel him to go in that direction.

Helfer, who could not see any such great danger in leaving the river, but recognised plainly enough another attempt to dispute his authority, felt that he must not give way on any consideration. He did not feel sure that this very man, while maintaining that it was impossible to go on, did not know of ways that he wished to keep secret. The great difficulty in dealing with these people, so entirely without any sense of truth, is to find out the right moment for defying them and carrying out your own will, or for being guided by them.

Helfer quietly took the dah, called his young 'artists' together, who formed a sort of body-guard, and asked: 'Who will follow me?' They were unanimous for going on, so without concerning ourselves about the others, we left the river, and journeyed eastward by the compass. As we expected, the rest soon followed. What else could they do? To stay there was impossible, and they did not dare to go back. We made our way laboriously, for some hours, through a tangled mass of interlacing trees, creepers, and mouldering trunks, until we came to a valley more wild and romantic than any we had seen, a gorge in which the sun had not dried the dew on the foliage at mid-day. The branches of the trees on the steep mountain sides overhung it, forming a beautiful leafy roof, sometimes united by creeping plants in splendid bloom. The entrance was choked by thickets of the ratan palm, and grass as high as a man's head; it would have been impossible to get through it had not the elephants formed a broad and firm highway by their passage. All the beasts of the forest seemed to have chosen this spot for their rendezvous. Though our approach had scared them, we saw by their excrement and marks of paws and claws of every shape and size, what a variety of animal life this temple of nature must harbour. Herds of elephants must have passed through not long before. Prints of the feet of the rhinosceros, the most unmannerly and malignant of all the herbivorous animals, showed that he was not wanting in this great zoological garden, though he generally only leads his wild life in impenetrable thickets and mire. We also noticed here and there traces of the deer tribe, from the large elk to the elegant fawn; neither were marks of the huge claws of the tiger and his species wanting on the moist ground, and there would be no lack of prey for them. In short, Noah seemed to have opened the doors of his ark here. Nevertheless, deathlike stillness reigned; all the creatures had fled at the approach of the lords of creation. Only the monkeys, his caricatures, who reflect all his lower qualities, had the audacity not to get out of his way. They sat in groups on the trees, from the largest to the smallest species, looked down at us in surprise, as if aware of the relationship, flung leaves, twigs, and nuts at us, gnashed their white teeth, let themselves down so low by their tails that we could have caught them, turned somersaults, and leaped from bough to bough, went on, in short, as we see them do in menageries, only their gestures are not at all to be compared to those they exhibit in a wild state; the loss of freedom and a colder clime is exceedingly depressing to all the monkey tribe.

Inviting as it was to linger in this charming spot, and weary as we were, we yielded to the wishes of our followers to push on. They did not wish to be overtaken by the shades of evening here, and were probably quite right, for, in spite of fires, we might have made closer acquaintance with some of the inhabitants than we desired.

Having emerged from the gorge, we found, near a running stream, the indispensable requisite for a camping ground, a spot under lofty bamboos free from underwood, which is best adapted for a resting-place, as no living thing can approach unobserved.

Both men and beasts were exhausted, and we readily

gave them and ourselves a day's rest, which we employed in arranging the collections.

We started early next morning, following the brook at first, which we had to cross several times, but when it no longer followed the direction we were taking, we again struck off into the jungle, hoping soon to find an elephant track. We could not venture to place our own elephants, which had been excellent pioneers, in the van, lest they should attract the notice of their wild brethren. They evince a furious hatred towards the tame animals, attack and kill them wherever they fall in with them. This is contrary to their usual peaceful nature, for, except at certain seasons, they seldom act on the offensive.

It is their custom to forage for food in large numbers, and they post a circle of guards to watch; if anything suspicious approaches, they give a trumpet-like alarm, on which the troop is scattered, and takes flight in various directions, so that it is not difficult to escape an encounter. Their alarm was always a signal for us to collect, to place our elephants in the middle, and to keep them thus surrounded, until our scouts had discovered what direction the herd had taken. It was easy to do this, for their tramping through the jungle was always accompanied by a crackling, like the firing of small firearms, but it was not so easy to overcome the mutual aversion of our elephants and horses. The elephants trumpeted on seeing the horses, which had to be prevented, in order not to attract the attention of their wild comrades, and the horses pranced, and got beyond control at the sight of the colossal creatures, so that we had to divide our train into detachments.

The plain which we had been traversing now began to rise, and after mounting for a time the sound of waters met our ears; the thicket opened, and a perpendicular wall of rock, more than 2,000 feet high, met our astonished eyes, over which a waterfall tumbled, glittering in the sun.

We made a halt to enjoy the magnificent spectacle. The wall of rock, lying north and south, closed our way, and prevented further progress eastward. To climb it was impossible, and Helfer felt that the right moment was come for testing the views and experience of our followers, who generally knew more than they pretended to. He therefore consulted the confidential man, the Gyown Yowk, who was willing to reconnoitre, and did not appear to be so ignorant of the district as he had affected to be. He discovered a path which could not have been trodden by elephants only, as there were marks on the trees which were obviously the work of men. The Gyown went with some others of the attendants to try and find them out. In less than half an hour one of the scouts returned, with the joyful news that a village had been discovered, and that assistance and rice would soon be sent. Almost immediately afterwards we heard voices in an unknown tongue, which we might have taken for the chattering of monkeys, if about twenty men had not soon appeared, whose physiognomy and dress differed from those of any of the natives whom we had previously seen.

Their faces were of the Caucasian type, and reminded us of those of the Asiatic Jews. Their clothing consisted of a long white shirt, the edges, short sleeves, and girdles of which were embroidered in coloured cotton. Their coarse black hair was shorn, except a tuft in the middle, and their heads were wrapped, turban fashion, in black and yellow handkerchiefs. They had strings of beads round their necks, and bunches of red and white flowers in their ears. They were armed with spears and muskets. Their manners were free, open, and fearless; their leader especially, in whose smiling mien there was a spice of cunning, behaved with great dignity and self-possession.

They stated that they belonged to the Red Karens, and had left Siam a few weeks before to trade with Yediko, which place, however, we could not find on the map. They denied that they lived in the neighbouring village, and tried to dissuade us from visiting it. Nevertheless, they had brought various provisions and an elephant from it; another, they said, had broken his foot and become disabled.

We had long been aware that the existence of many a village in the interior was concealed by the inhabitants, with, or without the knowledge of the overseer of the district, in order to escape taxation, and resolved to visit the place.

Leaving our suite at the encampment, we went to the village with only a few attendants. It consisted of about ten dwellings, and we found, besides the disabled elephant, a great many others there. It appeared that these Red Karens, so called, had migrated here about a year and a half before; they carried on a lucrative trade in ivory and elephants, which they were very adroit in capturing, and were, so to speak, well off, which accounted for their so assiduously concealing themselves.

Among the women we discovered several beauties, of a type belonging rather to Western than Eastern Asia.

Whether their appearance only, or any other reasons, had given rise to the idea that this tribe, differing so much from all the neighbouring races, was part of the lost tribes of Israel, I cannot say. It was a favourite theme with the missionaries, with whom we afterwards discussed the subject, and they advocated it with much erudition.

Helfer had become convinced that our suite was uselessly numerous, for many of them could not carry much more than they wanted themselves, he therefore dismissed some of the bearers, and hired another elephant instead, to go as far as the Three Pagodas, three days' journey off, to which a newly engaged Karen, who professed to know the way, was to be our guide. By the 'way,' however, nothing more must be understood than the direction to be taken, for these people seldom know anything about a particular place any distance off.

We could not obtain anything but a little supply of rice from the villagers. They had no poultry or other edible domestic animals; they have a contempt for rearing them, and for meat confine themselves to the produce of the chase. European industries and luxuries were entirely unknown to them. The erection of our tent astonished them greatly. Airily and quickly as their own dwellings were built, they had never seen one put up in a few minutes. The tailor's nimble handiwork, and our wearing gloves, amused them very much, but their curiosity was never obtrusive. One of them astonished us by his marvellous dexterity in climbing. Helfer wanted a bunch of blossoms from a tree, whose stem rose up like a polished pillar a hundred feet high, without branches, and at this height the splendid crown of flowers unfolded itself. Our Burmese climbers had essayed the task in vain; when they reached the middle they slid down again. One of the Karens had looked on with amusement, and then began to climb the tree like a cat. How he supported himself on the trunk, which was too large to grasp, we could not imagine. He brought down the rare blossoms in triumph, and thus saved the tree from the axe, beneath which large forest trees often fell to enrich European herbariums. He was rewarded with a pistol, the most valuable present to a dweller in the forests, and was delighted with his new possession.

Helfer made some interesting discoveries here, and we remained till November 29, having made ourselves very comfortable in our encampment.

The evening before we were to start, and while the loads were being packed for the next morning, our faithful companion, a pure bred American bloodhound, was lying near us in the long grass. Suddenly he uttered a cry, and we saw a little green snake crawling away through the grass. On examining the dog, Helfer found a small, almost imperceptible wound. He gave him the best antidotes for serpent poison, but they unfortunately took no effect, for before long his body swelled to a great size, there was a rattling in his throat, and he fell into convulsions. It was terrible to me to see the poor creature suffering like this, so as he could not save him, Helfer sent a ball through his head. Death, apparently, followed instantaneously, and our body-guard laid his favourite on a bed of moss in a thicket close by.

Our start was always accompanied by a great deal of bustle, much more than was necessary, for our young Burmese performed all their labours with noisy joviality, and we were only too glad to allow them this little compensation for all their privations.

Putting together the poles of the tent, which was always left standing as long as it could be, was the signal for departure. We were just mounting our horses, when a rustling was heard among the bushes where the dead dog, as we thought, had been laid, and he crept out, whining, on his belly.

The sensation and joy occasioned by his appearance were indescribable. He looked imploringly at us, as much as to say, 'Don't leave me lying here.' The well-known sound must have announced our start to the poor fellow, and the fear of being left behind have given him strength to crawl out. On examination it appeared that the ball had gone into his neck behind the ear, between the throat and the loose outer skin, and passed out on the other side of the neck.

Helfer looked at him with amazement. Whether the effects of the poison had been neutralised by the great loss of blood, or by the shock to the nerves, his knowledge did not suffice to determine. The patient was cleansed from blood, carefully laid in a basket, and placed beside the cook on the elephant, that he might perform the journey as easily as possible. I shall never forget how gratefully he looked down upon us.

The Karens were certainly more successful than the Burmese in finding their way among these pathless forests, hills, and dales, as well as among the network of rivers and brooks which carried the mountain streams to the Atta-yan, and which we had to cross sometimes on foot, sometimes on horseback, and now and then mounted on elephants. Even the Karens, however, were sometimes at a loss, doubled back, climbed lofty trees to reconnoitre, and missed the marks which they had made on the trees on previous journeys. We did not reach the Zamie-Khioung, a main tributary of the Atta-yan, till December 6.

We had often questioned the Karens about their method of catching elephants, but they maintained strict reserve on the subject. One day, however, the grateful owner of the pistol came up to us on the march, and beckoned us aside to a place where at first we saw nothing but heard groans, as if from a subterranean vault, until he pointed out the trunk of an elephant, peeping from amongst boughs, with which the earth was covered. On going nearer, we saw the animal in a pit, the high perpendicular sides making escape impossible. He had, already, been there six days. Hunger and thirst, vain attempts to extricate himself, rage, pain, and despair, had exhausted him to the uttermost. He greedily took the food offered him by our guide, and allowed him to stroke his trunk. 'In a few days more he will be ripe,' said the man, meaning that he would be tamed and ready for use.

For catching the elephants, deep pits are dug along their paths, and covered with green boughs, so that even these sagacious creatures suspect nothing. Then, to the shame of the sex be it spoken, feminine arts are employed in enticing them to destruction. Two female elephants, well trained for the purpose, are associated with one of the wild herd, and lead him, probably amidst all sorts of blandishments, to one of these pitfalls, into which he is innocently entrapped.

At first the prisoner is stunned; by degrees he realises his situation, and tries to climb out. Rage doubles his strength, but it is of no use in the confined space. Finding every attempt fruitless he falls into despair, foams at the mouth, trembles, and is covered with sweat, utters piercing cries, and at length sinks down exhausted. His captor then, generally at the end of two or three days, thinks it time to approach the pit, and give the thirsty beast a drink. The struggle between his eagerness to quench his thirst, and hatred of his tormentor, is said to be very curious to witness, but the former gains the day, and he even shows his gratitude by looks. After two or three weeks, one side of the pit is dug away, the tamed animal obediently follows the man who has fed him, and is ready for work.

The capture of wild elephants is the more remunerative, as they do not breed in confinement.

I was very fond of feeding the splendid creatures

with a basket of paddy (rice in its natural state), which we gave them occasionally. But in that part of the country working elephants were not generally fed, as in Bengal, but have to find themselves, at night or during the hours of rest.

In the camp I could approach them without fear, but in the evening, when they were set free to forage over a wider range, it was dangerous to meet them, as they were then very suspicious, and showed hostility to anything that came in their way. They often get loose, and sometimes we had to wait for hours till the drivers brought them back. But they never made their escape altogether; they felt themselves cast out by their free brethren.

On a height near the rapid stream of the Zamie-Khioung, we found quite a paradisiacal camping ground, under the shade of teak, iron-wood, and olive trees, and could see out freely between the lofty slender trunks, as there was no underwood.

The ground within and without the camp having been swept as clean as the floor of a room, and the furniture being arranged, our personal attendants served the repast. Afterwards I watched the setting sun, while Helfer comfortably smoked his cigar, and contemplated the various groups of his subjects.

On our right were our 'artists,' occupied in pressing plants in blotting paper, skinning and preparing bladders, looking for and preserving insects in spirits, pinning out butterflies, and sorting stones and ores.

In front of us, lying upon mats round a huge fire, the Burmese cooked their rice, the younger ones playing their favourite game of ball, or making harangues in honour of Buddha, in which they are equally expert. On our left, our swarthy cook, conscious of the dignity and responsibility of his office, stood before an improvised fireplace, from which issued tongues of flame, and near him my little black ayah, chatting volubly in their mother tongue. Not far off sat the dirji (tailor), anxious to heal before nightfall the wounds made in our clothing by thorns and briars, and further off the shoté, busy drying the washing. Apart from the rest sat the Karens, so different from all the others in physiognomy and dress, solemnly singing their melodies.

On the other side the bearers were encamped round a fire of their own. They were mostly Thalians and Shans, and the Burmese would have nothing to do with them. We did not know then that they were secret opium smokers. Our horses lay on the grass close to the tent. One of them was a very nice creature; he had once played the part of buffoon among the horses in a Chinese circus, and still liked to play his little tricks. Wherever we encamped he used to lie down by my side, and would take the ginger biscuits out of my pocket as cleverly as a pickpocket. He would not tolerate anybody on his back but me or my husband.

Behind the tent, in the neighbouring bamboo forest, the crunching and snapping of boughs and twigs gave evidence how acceptable our elephants found them.

In a larger circle the watch fires were burning, well kept up by the watchmen; any neglect in this department was sternly reprimanded.

The temperature in this elevated region had sunk to about 60° Fahrenheit, and obliged us to seek shelter from the cool air, for the first time since our landing. It reminded us of a spring evening at home, and turned our thoughts and conversation homewards. How I wished that I could transport my poor Lusatian country people from their barren sands into this paradise, that they might partake of the rich gifts showered by nature even upon him who does not work in the sweat of his brow, and repose in peace after their day's labour, which, at that time, only brought them in four groschen (five pence) a day.

Large tracts of country, adapted for crops of any kind, and yielding a hundredfold, were unoccupied. The climate is mild and healthful, there is easy natural water communication, security under British rule, and no danger from the scanty and peaceful native population. What a country for colonisation. We resolved to set it on foot, and, God willing, to spare no pains to carry it out.

It was well that we were permitted to enjoy these cheerful hours, for evil days were in store for us.

Next morning there was a busy stir in our camp. Twelve bearers who had not proved efficient were to be despatched, under conduct of a Burmese, by the most direct course to Yeh, to the westward of us, for on our return from the Three Pagodas, our most easterly point, we meant to make our way thither. They were to take part of the collections, some of the baggage we could spare, some luxuries, sugar, &c., of which we had a superfluity, a case of highly-rectified spirits of wine, and even a box containing 600 rupees in silver, for in the jungle, where there was no call for cash, it was only a useless burden.

The chief of the district of Yeh was ordered to send fresh bearers to us here, with stores of rice, our stock having sensibly diminished. We expected to meet them on our return from our excursion eastward, or to wait for their arrival, which might be expected in about ten days. We gave them our old elephant hunter as guide, who was a native of Yeh, and said that he knew the way well. The rest of the men, mostly Thalians, declared themselves willing to go under his guidance.

Part of our remaining stock of rice was equally distributed among the men who were going off, the rest was hung up on trees, and some other things, which we could do without for a few days, were buried.

By noon all these arrangements were completed, and we set out for the Three Pagodas. We had to cross two arms of the Zamie-Khioung, and then came to a ridge of hills of calcareous formation, their lofty sides on our left rising abruptly out of the earth.

We had to give up the hope of reaching the Three Pagodas the same evening. The Karen zockey said that, further on, among the hills, there was no water, and we could not encamp where there was no supply of this element, so indispensable for man and beast. Helfer, therefore, had to give way, and had the camp pitched at Mikeli-Khioung, said to be the source of the Atta-yan. It rushes through the narrow pass of the

Three Pagodas, as we soon discovered. Helfer's endeavour was to find the golden mean between insisting too strongly on obedience to his orders and yielding too much to the local knowledge of the guides, in order not to incur the responsibility of all contingencies. But the mendacity of the people, and the contradictions in which they involved themselves, made it very difficult sometimes to come to the right decision.

If a native is called to account for a lie he laughs, or is amazed that anything else should have been expected of him, and throws the consequences on him who has believed him. Of this we had another instance the next day. The zockey, when asked about the distance to our destination, said that it would take four hours, but we had scarcely proceeded half an hour when we beheld the Three Pagodas, so called, before us, on the slope of the calcareous hills, surrounded by a few trees—in reality, nothing but three heaps of stones, nine feet high, piled upon the crumbled brick walls of the Pagodas that once stood here.

Fragments of bamboo, palm roofs fallen in, broken jars, &c., gave evidence of frequent visits to the spot.

All that is known about the origin of the Three Pagodas on these remote hills is that they were built long ago, as a token of peace between the Shans and Burmese. The middle one, as the mark of the boundary line, is said to have been built jointly, the northern one by the Shans, and the southern by the Burmese. The spot is marked even on otherwise incorrect maps, ancient and modern.

Our followers, with the exception of the Karens,

made reverent obeisance to the ruins. They then climbed up to them, cleared them from grass and briars, covered them with large umbrellas, hastily made of bamboo, and planted flags on them, for which they used some of their best cotton handkerchiefs, and they were quite delighted when I honoured them with a piece of stuff, some yards long, for a larger flag, in the English colours, red, blue, and white; it was planted with great ceremony on the southern pagoda. Helfer explored the whole neighbourhood, and with the *élite* of his men ascended several mountains, one, 4,000 feet high, from which he obtained a view towards the east and south, and of the network of tributaries of the Atta-yan that we had crossed. He also had an extensive prospect over Siam, a fruitful plain as far as the eye could reach.

Our Karen zockey had, meanwhile, gone on a hunting expedition on his own account, from which he returned in triumph to the camp, having shot a large elephant. Three men carried part of the meat, the trunk, the tusks, and feet, and a heavy load it was. He offered us a suitable tribute of part of the feet and trunk, the dainty bits, as he assured us.

This was a joyful event for our people; they had had no meat for a long time, and required it much more under their great exertions than at home. The next day was given up to cooking and feasting.

My disinclination to partake of this species of game, though I also sensibly felt the want of meat diet, was overcome by the cook's assurance that he would dress it in French fashion! But he would have done better to adopt the Karen recipe, for his cutlets were so hard that we could not eat them, while a curry of part of the trunk was very good. The flesh of the elephant is like something between beef and pork, and is nourishing but indigestible. Our people dried what they could not eat either in the sun, or over the fire, and took it with them.

On the morning of December 10 we set out on our return, although I was very unwell, and could hardly keep my seat on my horse. Trusting to my good constitution, I concealed my state as well as I could, as it was impracticable to make a delay, owing to the want of rice. I was not disappointed, for a few hours' hard riding set me up. We soon reached our last camping ground, and, leaving it on one side, passed the night again near the Zamie-Khioung, on one of the islands formed by the three arms of the river, and at a considerable elevation above it. Some of the elephant meat was eaten again, but I did not partake of it, and preferred a lean wild pigeon.

On the 12th we reached the spot whence we had despatched a detachment of our people to Yeh, and where we had hidden our rice—a scanty store in proportion to the number to be fed; but the certainty, as we thought, of getting a fresh supply in a few days kept up our spirits.

At this spot the way to Yeh diverged from that by which we had come, and which the Siamese Karens took to their village. Besides the pay agreed upon, Helfer gave them presents of such articles as they set great store by. It was the interest of the Government to gain over these capable people, and to favour a large immigration of them, and as they are exempt from taxation for ten years in British territory, while in Siam they have to pay a tax of ten rupees per house per annum, it was likely to take place. They left us with the assurance that many of their people would soon follow them, and thus we had been able to forward a not unimportant object.

We were not spared the consequences of eating elephant flesh. Helfer, who had eaten very little of it, was nevertheless seized with severe colic, as well as several of our men, and four were attacked with jungle fever. After much consultation with the Gyown Yowk, it was decided to follow the men sent to Yeh without delay, that we might the sooner meet the bearers with fresh and more wholesome food.

Having made a fresh distribution of the provisions and baggage, which always occasioned great loss of time, and placed the sick under the care of one of the older and more intelligent Burmese, provided with rice, medicines, and coffee, which we had found specially beneficial to them, we left them, under the conviction that we should be able to send them succour all the sooner, and set out for Yeh on December 15. The course taken by our envoys was, as had been agreed upon, distinctly marked out. On both sides, the bark of the trees at regular intervals was cut with the dah, and elephant tracts which crossed our path were closed up, so that we could not miss our way. It led us through a fertile plain at the foot of the mountains, broken by ridges of hills, and intersected by streams.

Lightly loaded, and in good heart, we went on at a quick pace. They were the last happy hours on this route, for they were succeeded by anxious days.

As we wound round a hill, to our no small surprise, we saw six of the twelve men whom Helfer had sent on to Yeh twelve days before, sitting dejectedly on the grass. It was very difficult to discover from their accounts, evidently interwoven with lies, how they came to be there.

They said that they had followed the right direction to Yeh for three days, then, having come to a great mountain, their guide had missed the marks which indicated the way, and as there was no water there, and some of them, including the Burmese, were very ill, they had returned to a place, which the rest of the men, who promised to go on, would have to pass on their return. They had waited three days for them, until all their rice was consumed, and as the sick could no longer live on roots and leaves, they had resolved to set out to meet us by the way they could not fail to find.

Among the men was the one to whom the chest of money had been specially entrusted, and after a rigid examination we learnt that among those who had gone on were several men who were in bad repute as opium smokers, and it appeared to us probable that, intending a theft, they had persuaded their comrades to return.

During this forced and arduous march we had to cross a rushing stream ten times, in which our horses, up to the girth in water, could hardly keep their feet on the loose stones. On the evening of the second day we reached the halting place of the other detachment of men. Instead of going on to Yeh they had stopped there, and were in a wretched plight. They had broken open the case of spirits of wine, and drank it till they lay unconscious on the ground. All their provisions were consumed, the money, however, was untouched. The momentary enjoyment of the drink had had more charm for them than the possession of a considerable sum of money, which they could so easily have stolen.

All that they knew of the guide was, that he had lost his way, had left them several times to seek it, and at last had returned no more.

Helfer was in the most painful perplexity. For the first time he had to deal with criminal conduct among his subordinates, which could not be overlooked; and worse than all was the utter incompetence of these people to find a way out of these difficulties. None of them had ever been at the place, nor could give any advice, except to follow the elephant tracks, though they intersected each other in all directions.

Utterly ignorant of the country, and fully aware of the extreme difficulty of finding the way, Helfer keenly felt the great responsibility resting upon him. He, therefore, thought it best to consult the Gyown Yowk, and some of the older men, and to follow their lead, as the natives are, at any rate, acquainted with the elephant tracks, and are accustomed to take the stars as a guide as to direction.

Leaving behind all the heavy chests, even without concealing them, early on December 16 we began our march, following the stream we had so often crossed the day before, well knowing that human habitations would only be found near the water. We soon found ourselves in a narrow valley, where it was so cold that we shivered, even in our cloaks, and we felt it the more from having to cross the stream numberless times. To our great delight, before long we found the marks made by our old hunter and guide on the trees, and in one place he had written upon a stone: 'Don't cross the water any more, but ascend the hill.'

So we ascended it, but the further we went the steeper it became. Before long we left other ridges behind us, and had occasional peeps to the east and north-east, and the country soon lay like a map before us, the fantastic summits of the mountains we had passed a fortnight before being prominent objects, and when we reached the top we found ourselves on a chain, running through the whole peninsula, from south-west to south-east, and could see the sea to the west.

Up to this time the way-marks had been recognisable, and continued for about 500 paces down the other side, when they suddenly ceased. Not a sign indicated the direction the hunter had taken, and we searched about in vain for any trace of him for some time. We were in great perplexity, and some decision had to be made at once, for a longer tarriance on the top without water was dangerous for man and beast. The Gyown hesitatingly engaged to guide us down, and as he hoped, into the right path. There was nothing to be done but to follow him, and after a short halt we set out again, making our way through dense thickets. But the man had quite lost his head, for he was leading us towards the east instead of the west.

Helfer again ordered a halt. He called all the people together, and asked if any one of them could undertake to guide us. The silence of these usually voluble people showed plainly enough that none of them could do so. He then asked them whether they were willing to follow his lead, and all having agreed, he took out his compass, and indicated the sea-coast in the west as the only direction which must be taken in the long run.

But it was of little avail to know the right direction when there was no prospect of finding any path. Perpendicular precipices, 1,000 feet high, sank down into the dark depths below; towards the south, other points of the chain lifted their snow-clad summits to the sky, and towards the north, dense forests obstructed all distant views which might have aided us.

The day was already far advanced. We heard water rushing in the depths below, but all attempts to reach it failed, though we were tormented by burning thirst. Helfer at last undertook, in the urgent necessity, to climb down, accompanied by three lusty young fellows, in the direction towards the north-east, which he thought the most practicable.

It was with a heavy heart that I saw him go. How easily he, too, might lose his way, and how, in that case, should we find each other again! But after an hour of anxious waiting we heard the concerted signal, and one of his companions appeared, to guide us down by a most difficult, but still practicable way. The whole caravan followed, and as night closed in we reached a gorge, where there was water, but hardly level ground enough to pitch our tent.

The greatest foresight and frugality were needed in the use of our diminished provisions, lest we should be exposed to extreme want. The men had used their rations unequally. Some still had rice, some very little, others none, and yet no one could be left without food. Helfer ordered an equal distribution. He made each one turn out what he had left on a cloth that was spread out, and they were much surprised when we added all that remained of our own stock to it; they had probably never seen a chief put himself thus on an equality with his men.

When the rations came to be distributed there was even less for each than we had feared; each of the fifty-one hungry people received a cup and a half of rice. This was to last until we reached inhabited regions, which, according to our calculations, could not, at the best, be in less than three days.

All were looking downcast, and as I sat under a tree I was looking anxiously at my share. I heard the Burmese whispering together, then one after another came to me, and poured his rice into my lap. 'There, take our rice,' they said, 'you white woman can't live on roots and berries in the woods as we can.' My surprise and emotion at this proof of noble unselfishness, in men whom we are accustomed to consider far beneath us in morality, may be better imagined than described.

I took the rice to keep it for the time of greatest need. Not only the tremendous exertion, on insufficient food, but anxiety about the five helpless men left behind, had sadly upset me in body and mind. I thought of them, prevented from coming on by sickness, perhaps perishing from hunger, or a prey to wild beasts, and dreaded further misfortunes yet in store for ourselves, and which only too surely happened within the next few days. When we set out next morning, two of our people were left behind with fever, without Helfer's knowledge. Much of our baggage was left behind here, too, in order that we might get on faster, but again we wandered blindly about the whole day.

Following the river, we arrived at an old elephant track overgrown with bamboos, through which every inch of our way had to be cut with the dah, and after three hours we descended from the hateful mountains into a valley, and from this into a lower one, traversed by a rushing mountain stream. Although it ran north and south, Helfer followed its course, taking it for a branch of the Yeh. We frequently had to cross it.

More baggage having been left behind, we came to a plain where we could take a direction towards the west. To our inexpressible delight we recognised, by cuts in the trees, a path from north to south that must have been traversed by men. Uncertain which direction to take, Helfer chose that of the course of the stream, but it soon turned to the east; he, therefore, called a halt, and went on to explore with the Gyown and some of the strongest men. He found that the marks became more and more rare, and at length disappeared among the mountains to the east.

He came back to us much depressed by these disappointed hopes. It was by that time too late to resume our march westward, and the day closed without any solution of our difficulties. Our people had killed some monkeys, some large birds, and a snake, not venomous, and prepared a meal from them. I was glad to be able to give them a handful of corianda seeds, three onions, and ten peppercorns, which I had found, to season it with.

It was but a scanty meal for some forty people, yet no murmurs were heard; the men bore all their privations with admirable patience. The cook prepared a large lizard for us, the flavour of which they told us was very good, and I doubt, in fact, whether we ever ate the most dainty dish with more relish. Its flesh was very tender, and much like that of a chicken. We regaled the sick with coffee, which was efficacious in dysentery, now becoming malignant. Some of the stronger men were sent off to bring the two sick ones to the spot to which we had to return.

After a night spent mostly in anxious consideration how to extricate ourselves from our hopeless state, Helfer got up at four o'clock, taking the bright moonlight, on waking, for daylight. He found the people also awake, and ready to start. That we might not miss the way-marks, large bundles of dry foliage were set fire to, to serve as torches on our melancholy retreat. The morning was very cold, the dew falling in large drops. The roar of the tiger and other beasts, disturbed by the torch light, fell on our ears not far off. But our thoughts were entirely engrossed with the consideration how to escape from our perplexities.

Nine of our people were reported sick. During the night, driven by hunger, they had taken an ox-skin from underneath the howdah (saddle) of the elephant, boiled, and eaten it. Two of them were placed on our horses, three others carried on biers. Our caravan thus assumed the aspect of a funeral, and as slowly and silently we marched along. In the course of an hour we reached the spot where the path divided; there we found the two invalids, who, supported by others, now dragged themselves after us.

On December 18, we took the path in the opposite direction. Trodden by elephants and marked by men, it led us to a plain towards the west, and was calculated to raise our hopes; but we had been so often disappointed that we did not venture to indulge them.

The plain became narrower, the ground began to rise, and once more we found ourselves in a gorge, in which both path and marks came to an end. We were in a labyrinth of the mountain chain running parallel to the other, and as no outlet appeared we feared we had lost another day.

Our progress westward was, of course, very small; we had sought for the right track on all sides. Still our people did not complain. I was pleased with their exemplary behaviour, and their confidence in Helfer's guidance, and yet I would almost rather have heard them grumble, this death-like silence was so depressing. No one, however, would or could carry loads any longer. At every difficult spot one and another laid down his burden, and did not take it up again. The bearer of the money-box stumbled, it fell to the ground and burst open; in default of anything better, it was bound up with ratan withes, and left lying in the forest, like the rest of the baggage. Money was of so little value in this wilderness, that we would willingly have given it all for a good meal.

Helfer retraced his steps, still hoping to discover some path that we might have overlooked, but found nothing but yawning clefts and the impenetrable thickets of the ratan palm, into the region of which we had now entered. No one who has not seen its thorny, densely tangled growth can conceive the difficulty of getting through it.

Meanwhile, an old Karen, always one of the foremost in our train, had been carefully spying about, and with better success than Helfer. He had discovered a narrow path, entirely overgrown, which had escaped even the sharp eyes of the Burmese, had followed it for a little way, and found that it led down to a western slope of the mountains. With a loud halloo, a great contrast to his usual taciturnity, he announced his discovery. With hope renewed we went down the steep descent for two hours, by the track made by the elephant, who passed over the most dangerous spots with admirable skill. Thus, the dinner hour arrived, and we were all sadly tormented by hunger; it even drew bitter tears from my eyes, which I never could before have believed possible. As we were approaching a swamp surrounded by high underwood, the Karen gave the signal to halt, and crept alone to the bush, in which we perceived a large animal without distinctly seeing his form. After a few minutes a shot was heard, and immediately afterwards our hunter cried out: 'A rhinosceros, save himself who can!' He had wounded but not killed the beast. All tried to escape from the furious monster.

Helfer and I, with some others, climbed a tree that was leaning towards the ground, but it broke beneath the weight. Just at this moment another shot was heard, and the loud death rattle announced that this time the ball had taken effect.

The people now all rushed to the spot where this ungainly and most dangerous denizen of the forests lay in his death struggle. Abdarahma, our Mussulman body-guard, strove to get to the front, and cut the beast's throat while it was still alive, that he might not be debarred from partaking of it by the precepts of his religion. Up to this time he had steadily refused to eat meat that had not been slaughtered according to its rules, but this cut satisfied his conscience, and enabled him to appease his hunger.

The rhinosceros was one of the rare species with two horns. The horns are highly prized by the people as a universal medicine, and they give a good price for them.

The famishing men pounced greedily on the carcase. Many of them ate great pieces raw, others prepared to cook it and to dry what was left. In a few minutes the skeleton looked as if it had been gnawed clean.

For my part, I had too vivid a recollection of the effects of eating elephant's flesh to partake of the delicacy, and contented myself with a bit of lizard, which anyhow was more digestible.

The rhinosceros feast, however, spared the life of my dear steed, for that evening, although he was used as a transport for the sick, he was to have been killed and eaten by the men. The meal ended, Helfer hastened the start. The thought of the invalids left behind would not let us rest; we were anxious to send them succour as soon as possible. A short march led us into a plain, thickly overgrown with underwood. The path, still traceable, maintained its westward course. There were also evidences of human labour. Boats must have been built here, for there were rollers such as are used to convey them to the water; then followed olibanum trees that had been tapped, places where there had been fires, and others cleared by human hands. But there was nothing to indicate how long ago anyone might have been there, or whether their habitations were near, as the natives go long distances into the forests in pursuit of their occupations.

Meanwhile, it was growing late. Happy to see the hunger of the men appeased, and hoping for speedy release from our difficulties, we had the tent put up, and enjoyed some refreshing sleep.

On the 19th, with renewed courage, we made an early start. We thought our difficulties were over, but were once more doomed to disappointment. When we had been scarcely an hour on the way, the path, to our horror, turned first south, then east, and was lost in a forsaken Karen settlement, which, like all spots which have once been cultivated and then deserted, was overgrown with the wildest thorns and briars.

No living creature was to be seen far or near, save a melancholy crow, sitting on a bough of a charred tree, and no sound was heard but the monotonous cooing of a turtle dove, who loves to build her nest near the habitations of men. That men had dwelt here was plain enough, but when? and whither had they gone? These nomadic Karens often settle a long way from their old homes. There were choked-up paths branching off in all directions—which was the right? We halted and sent scouts out, and on their return chose the track where the marks on the trees were most frequent. After following it for an hour, we came to an extensive opening in the woods, which had plainly been the resort of buffaloes, but had not been trodden for a long time. In this prairie every trace of a path was lost, so that we were obliged to turn back. Once more, relying solely on the compass, we tried to make our pathless way westward; but the more the ground descended, the more luxuriant became the ratan palm and other thorny growths on the humid soil. We reached a deep stream, which seemed to flow westward, and a consultation was held how best to turn it to account. To go along its banks seemed impracticable, on account of the mass of thorns and briars. A young Burmese proposed that we should go down it on rafts. The idea took with the rest, for with their amphibious natures they are at home on the water. They set to work as if electrified; our old Karen, however, said nothing—he did not approve the plan, but had nothing better to propose.

Within the short space of one hour, four rafts were constructed of dry bamboo trunks, fastened together with ratan withes, and, although the water came through and wetted our feet, they were strong enough to bear the load. But the pleasure of this improvised voyage did not last long. We were stopped by gigantic trees lying right across the river, which could not be got out of the way, and we had to land on the other side. We then sought and found another path, but, like the others, it only led to deserted settlements. Once more Helfer had recourse to his compass, and almost resolved to trust solely to its guidance in future.

In spite of thorns and the increasing slipperiness of the ground, we trudged along until another path trodden by men was discernible. It led directly westward, and before long to an open space, where, scarcely believing our own eyes, after so many disappointments, we saw a herd of buffaloes.

How delighted we were to see these ugly spiteful creatures, for where they were there must be men too. The Gyown Yowk had become so dispirited that he would not see that they were buffaloes, but took them for a herd of wild swine. They were grazing on the other side of a wide and, as it turned out, almost bottomless swamp.

Summoning the remains of our exhausted powers, we hastened our steps. Soon the plaintive tones of Karen singing met our ears, and at the same moment we saw smoke rising from an inhabited hut.

In an instant the order of the procession was broken, and discipline was no longer to be thought of. The men rushed in wild confusion into the bog, each having thrown off the remainder of his load, crying, 'Lu, Lu!' (a man, a man!) We also had to wade through it on foot, leading our horses, and sinking almost up to our knees.

The voice came from the solitary herdsman. He

told us that we could not sleep near the swamp, or we should be inevitably attacked by fever. He himself slept in a lofty tree, and only maintained tolerable health by this practice and long use. He was a 'debtor slave,' that is, a man who, to pay his debts, or for some reason or other, sells himself for a time, and had been compelled to take the post of herdsman in this unhealthy spot. Under the English Government these people are called 'debtor servants,' as the English ear cannot endure the word slave, even if the thing is the same.

As he could neither offer us food in sufficient quantity, nor a night's lodgings, we had to march on for three-quarters of an hour to the next village.

With this last and most arduous day's work, however, the difficulties and privations of our nine days' wanderings through a pathless tropical wilderness came to an end.

Our arrival disturbed the night's rest of the villagers, for our famished band made their way at once into every house, clamouring for rice, eggs, fowls, butter, and other eatables. Thus unceremoniously roused from sleep, the inhabitants thought they were attacked by hostile Siamese, and prepared for flight. But as soon as Helfer showed them the Government credentials, they were pacified, and their fear was changed to astonishment and the utmost friendliness.

Large fires were soon kindled, round which boiling and roasting, questioning and narrating, feasting and laughter, went on; all troubles were forgotten. Helfer's first care, however, was for the men left behind, and even before the night was over he sent off experienced villagers with torches and food to seek them and bring them to the camp.

After all our anxiety and distress, we were refreshed by sweet sleep till late in the morning. It was with thankful hearts that we found ourselves out of the wilderness, and once more among the habitations of men; never have I felt so keen a sense of the brotherhood of all men as at that time among these so-called savages. There was nothing but anxiety about the invalids to damp our joy. But we were soon relieved of this also. One after another of them came in, half-led, half-carried by the villagers, till all were rescued, weak and exhausted indeed, but still alive. This was more than we had ventured to hope. Urged on by fear they had slowly followed our track; when their last rice was gone, they had lived on berries and roots, killed a few birds, and spent the nights in trees for safety from wild beasts.

Even the baggage left scattered about in the woods was found bit by bit, and brought to us. It may sound incredible to European ears that even the silver, though it glittered through the chinks of the broken box, which had been but imperfectly fastened together, reached our hands untouched. Anyone who had chosen to enrich himself could have done so unpunished.

Helfer was satisfied with the result of his explorations, and considered that a promising field had been opened up for scientific observations; he was happy also, after the many hardships which his suite had undergone, and the dangers to which his collectors especially had been exposed, not to have lost a single man; for even the old guide, whom we had given up for lost, re-appeared afterwards at Yeh.

Our experience proves that the dangers of tropical countries are greatly exaggerated, when it is said that they lurk behind every bush and under every tree. It is rather that wild beasts fly from man than that he has to fly from them. It is only the lower reptiles who do not shun the lord of creation, and follow closely on his heels.

Our experience had also been very favourable as to the effects of the climate on health. Although some of our people fell ill, it was owing to sleeping in the open air when weakened by strenuous exertions and privations. But we Northerners had traversed a tropical wilderness under most difficult circumstances without contracting any serious illness, though we were exhausted to the utmost.

By prudence, by keeping to your accustomed diet, and, above all, by protection from the night exhalations, ill effects may in most cases be avoided. My black maid was a striking instance of this. When she came to me she was weakly and immature, almost a child. I always had her to sleep near me in the tent, and she visibly developed and became stronger, although she shared all the exertions of the men, and performed the most arduous marches on foot, for I never could persuade her to mount my horse or an elephant.

Splendid tracts of country, as fertile as they were lovely, and adapted for valuable produce, abundantly watered by rivers and streams, affording easy means of communication, had met our admiring gaze. Human beings only were wanted to enjoy these bounties.

Our sick and exhausted men were sent in boats by a circuitous route to Yeh, our long-sought destination, while we reached it by land in one day's march. Yeh is not a town according to European ideas, though it was so considered by the natives, because there were tradespeople there—among them some speculating Chinese and artisans. A Burmese assistant-commissioner administered justice and law, but his office did not give him much to do. He had a salary of seventy rupees a month, and therefore passed for a great and wealthy lord.

He was apprised of our approach, and considered it appropriate to his dignity and ours to give us a ceremonious reception, and came mounted on a small pony to meet us on the frontiers of his domain. A large moustache gave him an odd appearance, as the Burmese are generally quite beardless.

We were lodged in a zayat erected not long before by the well-to-do inhabitants for the reception of Europeans of position—their honoured governor, for instance—and the commissioner was loud in the praises of its beauty and elegance. It was a nice bungalow with two rooms, bath rooms, and a spacious balcony, from which there was a splendid prospect towards the west, over the blue waters of the Bay of Bengal, and towards the east of the triple mountain chain which we had crossed under such difficult circumstances. The

River Yeh, which rises and falls fifty feet with the tide, and rushes rapidly to the sea, winds through the plain.

The internal appointments of the bungalow consisted of a table and two chairs, a great advance on the universal custom of squatting cross-legged on the floor.

The town lies beneath the shade of lofty cocoa-nut and areca palms, and is surrounded by luxuriant rice fields; the houses are quite concealed among the foliage of giant plantains. It would scarcely be a healthy place if it were not that it is kept cool, and all miasma blown away by the breezes alternating between the mountains and the sea.

Helfer resolved to make some stay here both in order to explore the neighbourhood and to recruit our health; for although our strength had held out hitherto, now that the excitement was over we felt greatly exhausted and overdone. I especially required much rest, but my husband soon began to make excursions again.

The 24th of December, the eve when we celebrate our beloved Christmas festival, was approaching, and we wished to observe it as usual. But of what use was it to adorn and light up a tree when Nature is clad in all her verdure and beauty, when the sun would obscure the tapers, and even the moonlight rival their brightness. Amidst such surroundings, a Christmas tree must look rather like a caricature than a symbol of festivity. To make it appropriate the earth should be wrapped in frost and snow, and the windows frosted with floral designs; our thoughts as well as our eyes are then directed to the world within rather than to the world without, and conduce to the festive mood, but circumstanced as we were we could not get it up.

Helfer was urgently entreated by a deputation of natives, the under-assistant at their head, to ascend the Zae-town mountain (Medicine Mountain) with them; they said that many valuable herbs grew there, and that precious ores were concealed in its bowels, but that it was bewitched, and could only be trodden with safety by pomgys—priests, protected by a magical wand. As soon as the people heard of Helfer's expected arrival, they hoped that the great magician who could work changes in Nature (an idea that his chemical experiments had given rise to) would break the spell and make the mountain accessible.

He was convinced that some cunning trick had been played on the ignorant people by the priests, and willingly embraced the opportunity of putting an end to their superstitious fancies.

Provided with all necessaries for an absence of several days, the procession proceeded to the bewitched place by paths not less difficult than those by which we had come. Deep in the forest they saw a torn rhinoceros lying dead, and a tiger still bleeding near it. They had had a fierce struggle, ending in the death of both.

The ascent of the mountain, which was 2,000 feet high, was steep and arduous, though recent marks on the trees pointed out the way. During the ascent Helfer found a staff of some foreign wood, with a peculiar aromatic scent, probably lost by a pomgy. He made his party inhale the smell of the wood, which was new to them. On the top of the mountain he made fires of various colours by means of chemical preparations, burnt the staff, and declared the mountain disenchanted.

The grasses and plants on the top were of course different from those in the plains; whether they really possessed any medicinal properties it would have required more time to discover, and perhaps merely their rarity may have given rise to the idea of their miraculous virtues, the use of which the priests wished to keep in their own hands.

The expedition returned rejoicing over the success of the disenchantment, bringing the ashes of the magician's wand as a trophy.

Helfer earnestly desired that I should no longer share the hardships of jungle travelling, but return to Moulmein without him. But with thanks for his consideration, I decidedly declined the proposal, for I was too much interested in these travels to wish to do so, and was firmly resolved not to be separated from my husband. The hardships were soon forgotten.

Before we left Yeh, a great festival was given in our honour. Two girls of ten years of age performed a Burmese national dance, on mats as smooth as a mirror, accompanied by music, in which time was totally disregarded; indeed, more properly speaking, it was a mere noise of cymbals, trumpets, and a sort of glass harmonicon. While the art of our European Taglionis consists in hovering as much as possible in the air, these dancers never left the ground for a moment. They glided in a circle with their feet closely pressed together without lifting them, and moved only their arms and the upper part of their bodies in curious, almost convulsive jerks. The more rapid and vehement they were the greater the applause, until they stepped on one side quite exhausted. The girls passed for adopted daughters of the under-assistant, but they were in reality slaves, whom he had purchased, and they could have bought their freedom for sixty rupees.

The dance was followed by a dramatic representation. The piece seemed to be well composed, and the actors had their parts well by heart. As far as I could understand, a court intrigue was the subject of the play, through which a minister was dismissed, but reinstated in favour. The part of the premier, the chief person of the piece, was, strange to say, acted by a boy of nine years old, with animated declamatory action, and a very droll figure he cut among his fellow-actors of from forty to fifty years of age. The first scene represented a conference of the dignitaries of state. The king then appeared with his suite, after which the harlequin executed a sword dance.

Between the scenes there was choral singing, also solo recitations and improvisations, some of which evinced unusual facility of expression.

We did not remain to the end, for it lasted until long after midnight, and as we were to start early next morning we wished to retire to rest.

The collections were forwarded by water to Moulmein with the men who were returning thither, and another portion of the luggage, also by water, to Tavoy, which was to be our next halting-place.

Helfer had received letters from Moulmein and Calcutta, among them one from Lord Auckland's secretary, in which he spoke in the most flattering terms of his performances, and of his first report, which had just been printed. He himself did not estimate the results very highly, and only felt the more incited to deserve, by redoubled efforts, the commendation he had earned.

He planned to take the direct route to Tavoy, but to halt at certain points, and make excursions with the *élite* of his troop, while the main part of it remained within range of human habitations.

Proceeding in the direction from north to south we kept the mountain chain to the east in view with the sea at no great distance on our right.

The country we passed through was mostly well cultivated; the inhabitants, chiefly Thalians, are more eager for gain than the Burmese, and are diligent labourers. The temperature rose to 80°—90° Fahrenheit, but it was tempered by the sea, and the climate was very favourable to vegetation.

Our progress was often hindered by the numerous tidal rivers which rise in the mountains, for getting men, beasts, and baggage across always occasioned considerable delay. They are mostly navigable for about thirty-five miles up.

Great caution in crossing them was rendered necessary by the number of alligators which find a safe retreat among the roots of the mangroves on the banks. They look so much like floating stumps of trees that one is in danger of treading on them; it is only on closer inspection that you perceive their watchful greenish eyes and their yawning jaws ever ready for their prey. But though it may sound almost incredible, even an alligator is capable of gratitude, and affection for a human benefactor.

The rising tide often brought large quantities of fish into the broad and deep Karagoun river, and the inhabitants of the neighbouring villages employ themselves largely in fishing. But parts of the fish only are generally used, the heads and entrails being thrown again into the water. In a slimy little bay in this river, a Burmese, standing up to his middle in the water, carried on the trade of killing and cleaning the fish, and by his side lay a gigantic alligator, into whose jaws the refuse fell and disappeared like flies. The monster lay comfortably extended in the slime, now and then raising his stumpy tail out of the water as a token of satisfaction, and eagerly following the man's movements with his glittering eyes. When the provision was for the moment at an end, the man stroked his furrowed back as if to exhort him to patience till he had new matter for his insatiable jaws. Thus the half-tame alligator and the amphibious man lived together on the best of terms, neither harming the other in the least.

On January 16, without accident or anything worthy of record, as there was no scope for Helfer's scientific explorations, we reached the Hinzai river. The elephants, horses, and baggage were left behind here, as we were going down to the mouth of the river. We must have been carried for a thousand paces through the mud to the boats in readiness for us.

Thanks to the tide, in a few hours we were in a fresh-water basin, six miles wide, and from ten to sixteen long. It is formed by eighteen rivers, larger or smaller, all navigable to some extent, which carry their waters through it to the sea. From this point you see the ranges of mountains, rising one above another, to the north and east; towards the south an isolated mountain, overtopping all the rest, and towards the west, shutting in the basin towards the sea, there is a range of hills, from 150 to 400 feet high, with an opening two miles long, through which the Hinzai flows to the sea.

If this passage were navigable for ships drawing much water, the whole English fleet could find anchoring ground in the basin. It was no part of Helfer's mission to investigate this, but he explored a portion of the shore, the peculiar products of which afforded him so much booty that it was almost more than he could manage to carry away.

We encamped on a projecting hill under a Casuarina tree, the first specimen of this Australian species which we had seen in the open air. We called the place Casuarina in honour of it.

The sharp eyes of the Burmese detected some huts, which were only just visible at the water's edge, being excavated in the moist but firm soil. Fishermen from Tavoy were making ngapé, fish ground to powder, which goes through a process of fermentation like cheese, and is then considered a delicacy, but only a refined Asiatic palate is capable of appreciating it. Tortoise eggs are also collected here in amazing numbers, as a lucrative article of commerce. Our people discovered two pits, in which several thousand eggs were stored up in the moist sand. We bought 300 of them for twelve aurah (one florin), which provided us and our suite with several excellent meals. In a hole, which one of the fishermen showed us next morning, one tortoise had, during the night, laid no less than 119 eggs!

After many zig-zags, as Helfer constantly diverged from the direct route to ascend the pathless heights of the Zadie mountains, we reached the town of Tavoy on January 18.

It is situated in a fertile plain, which extends eastward to the foot of the mountain chain, and is bounded by three ranges, rising one above another, in the misty distance. The whole district, enlivened by numerous villages, interspersed with well-cultivated rice-fields, every hill and spur being adorned with pagodas, afforded a pleasing picture of advanced civilisation, unequalled by any other we had seen in the country. The town is built on the broad, navigable river of the same name, amidst the shade of thick foliage, and had at that time about 14,000 inhabitants, mostly Thalians, with a small military garrison. The office of governor, in the name of Her Britannic Majesty, was held by a Scotchman, as assistant-commissioner, but neither the government of his province nor the administration of justice gave him much to do. The cases were very rare in which he had to lay down the law, and equally so in which he had to trouble himself about the maintenance of peace and order. He had so little acquaintance with the doings of his subjects, their weal and woe, that, in order to obtain the statistics he wanted, Helfer had to apply to the natives themselves.

Happy land, where there was so little occasion for legislation or punishment, and where the people could be permitted to enjoy themselves in their own way! Is it still in the enjoyment of this blissful innocence after being longer subject to European rule?

Mr. Blondell possessed a bungalow at Tavoy for occasional residence, which he placed at our disposal. We were supplied with all kinds of vegetables from the well-tended garden of the assistant-commissioner. We had also a cargo of provisions from Moulmein, so that we were able to make ourselves not only comfortable at Tavoy but to enjoy some luxuries and to lay in a fresh stock of strength.

CHAPTER V.

ON THE RIVER TENASSERIM.

Gratifying to Helfer as the results of his expeditions had hitherto been, in other respects he had not yet found what he was most eagerly seeking—coal—a product of inestimable importance, in consequence of the insufficient quantity and poor quality of the East Indian Burdwan coal.

A coal-field in Tenasserim would not only be able to supply steam-vessels to China and the Eastern seas but also the stations on the west coast of Bengal, Madras, Bombay, Ceylon, and those still higher up. Helfer, therefore, directed his unremitting attention to the discovery of this mean looking black stone, as it was called by the natives. But although he was always showing them specimens of it, and inciting them to further search, he could learn nothing; they either did not know or would not say where it was to be found. They brought him many stones and minerals, particularly such as had a shining or glittering look, and once an enormous block of grauwacke, but never any coal. Helfer was, nevertheless, convinced that it did exist in the country. He had neither time nor the necessary materials for mining operations, but, trusting to some propitious star, he cherished the hope that accident, which has been the chief factor in so many discoveries, might lead to the discovery of a coal-field.

Having thoroughly explored the neighbourhood of Tavoy, he fixed upon the course of the river Tenasserim, the most considerable of the rivers in the southern part of the province, as the object of his next journey into the interior. Although it ran parallel with the coast, in the greater part of its course it was but little known, and had never been navigated by Europeans.

The Tenasserim is formed by the junction of two rivers, the Bain-Khiaung and the Kamoung-Thueg-Khiaung. It is said that the capital of an independent state once stood on the latter. The source of the former is in 13° north latitude, among a lofty mountain chain which traverses the country from N.N.W. to S.S.E. It receives sixteen mountain streams all running from S. to N.N.W., until it unites with the Kamoung-Thueg-Khiaung, flowing almost direct from the north, near Metamio, and they form together the upper Tenasserim.

This river became of the greatest importance to Helfer, and not to him only; it will be so for all time, when the lands which it traverses shall be further opened up to European civilisation.

We left Tavoy on January 30. In passing through the extensive rice-fields to the east, with the greatly increased temperature, we suffered much from the heat until the hills and green woods again lent us their grateful shade. The affection of the herdsman for the woods, of the nomadic tribes for their wanderings, the longing of mountaineers for their hills and dales, is very intelligible to me.

Towards evening we entered upon a fruitful vale, in which there were a few scattered dwellings near a rapid stream. We encamped near them, and friendly intercourse soon began between us and the Burmese inhabitants, for we still had a good stock of desirable articles, such as mirrors, knives, scissors, and handkerchiefs, wherewith to incline the hearts of the natives towards us, especially of the women.

The next day we sent the horses and elephants forward by a broader road, and went ourselves on foot by romantic paths up a richly-wooded ravine, through which a wild mountain torrent descended.

There was a troop of children ahead of us accompanied by several dogs, going through the jungle with hearts as light as if it had been a paradise instead of a land full of perils. They were going to school at a convent at a considerable distance. We were told that the dogs were to some extent a protection from tigers, as they always attack dogs rather than men.

The danger from tigers varies in different places. In many districts, about Tavoy and Mergui for instance, no one remembered a case of a man having been killed by a tiger; while at Singapore, on the southern extremity of the peninsula, the tigers have so little fear of man that the labourers in the plantations have to be protected by a cordon of soldiers, and even then are not safe from their attacks.

I had long wished to visit a Buddhist convent, and to see wherein it differed from a Catholic Christian one.

We, therefore, followed the children, who, like school-boys everywhere, beguiled the way with fun and merriment. Instead of primers they carried bundles of fan palm leaves sewn together, on which the uniform-looking characters were engraved with a style. They look like rows of noughts close together, with little hats, sometimes at the top sometimes at the bottom.

The convent buildings consisted of several bungalows forming a square; they surrounded a spacious court which served as a playground. Under a roof in front of the house was a long table, upon which, just as we arrived, Burmese women were placing vessels of a red colour filled with rice and curry; they then retired as silently as they had come. The last of them announced that the meal was ready by sounding a gong, and when they were all out of sight the pomgys, with shorn heads, their rosaries on their arms, and yellow tunics thrown over their shoulders, came out accompanied by their pupils and took their places at table.

There was something so antiquated and formal about the scene that you might have fancied you had an ancient philosophical school with its pupils before you. The important business of eating was transacted with great solemnity, and they then retired into the bungalows. The women then appeared upon the scene again to clear the table and sweep up.

In the Buddhist convent, then, the separation of the sexes was strictly observed; for though the women provided for the physical wants of the men, it was, as it were, with invisible hands. The convent was poor, the monks lived on charitable gifts, and occupied themselves exclusively in teaching the boys entrusted to their care. Among the monks we noticed some of very venerable aspect, but we had no opportunity of making further acquaintance with them, as foreigners are not allowed to enter.

In the afternoon we reached the pass, on the summit of which our people were waiting for us with the animals, and fell in there with a troop of wandering Karens who were going to Palouk. They were carrying all their possessions with them, and, little as the two races have in common, it reminded us of the nomadic Arabs of Syria.

We encamped for the night on a plain overgrown with long grass, as there was clear running water in the neighbourhood.

Our guide assured us that we should reach the shores of the Tenasserim early next day. But after the many proofs we had had of the untrustworthiness of the guides, we did not rely upon his information, and started before daybreak, that we might at any rate be able to encamp at night near the river.

The morning was very foggy, the mountains being thickly veiled in mist. The way, at first very fatiguing, led mostly through deserted settlements, relapsed into wildernesses, or between decayed bamboo stems, whose rotten, hollow canes blocked the way and crackled under the horses' feet. It then turned into a narrow pass, following the rocky bed of a little torrent. The coolness and dampness of the fog were very perceptible, for the sun had not pierced it at nine o'clock.

But at the end of the ravine an elevated undulating

plain opened out, and a pleasant path with fine thick grass on both sides, and shaded by lofty trees, led us to a point whence we could see the rapid waters of the river. There were nice gardens on its banks, and houses of a better sort than the usual Karen dwellings. Just before reaching the place we met a troop of young Karens, whose neat and careful dress surprised us. They started on seeing us, and, after looking attentively at us, exclaimed; 'Another white mother, another white mother!' They at once surrounded my horse, and led us in triumph to their abodes.

In the verandah of one of the larger bungalows a lady was standing, and, as we were about to pass on, she politely accosted us, and invited us to enter.

A reception like this on the frontiers of Siam, and after just passing through a desert solitude, seemed like enchantment, but the enigma was soon solved.

We were at Metamio, the capital and royal residence of a once independent kingdom, of which nothing but obscure legends remain. There are no architectural monuments to bear witness to the existence of the former flourishing town; prolific Nature had long ago smothered the mouldering ruins with verdure.

In this remote but lovely and fertile spot, Mr. and Mrs. Wade, of the American Mission, had taken up a permanent abode, animated by a desire to teach Christianity to the Karens, so susceptible of culture, and yet sunk in ignorance, poverty, and oppression; to impart to them useful knowledge, to improve their circumstances by better cultivation of the land, and to form them into civilised communities. They already saw their efforts crowned by the happiest results, nor had their pupils forfeited their natural simplicity of character.

They had enabled the scattered Karen families to settle in larger numbers together; they had built a chapel and a spacious school-room, in which, to our surprise, we saw not only children, but men and women, old and young, diligently learning to read and write the characters devised for their language. They had unbounded confidence in their teachers, assiduously followed their precepts and counsels, served them in every possible way, loved them as father and mother, and revered them as prophets, lawgivers, and judges.

What an attractive mission for a philanthropist, to be instructor of a people whose intelligence and amiable and tractable character render them capable of any degree of civilisation! But it would be a no less attractive field for a fanatic to set up the throne of infallibility and to forge the fetters of mental bondage.

Happily, Mr. and Mrs. Wade did not belong to the latter class of missionaries, but held moderate views, and were true friends of the people. Mrs. Wade was especially beloved and revered; wherever she appeared she was surrounded by a multitude who listened to her words as to an oracle. The feminine character seems to have a special facility for influencing and gaining the favour of this gentle race, which accounted for my being so warmly welcomed and accosted as another white mother.

Mrs. Wade was then devoting her attention to

training six young men who were to go as apostles to their distant brethren, to take the blessed doctrines to them, and to form them into a united people. Perhaps a flourishing tree may have grown out of this tender shoot.

Mr. Wade had the school-room made ready for us, though we protested against it, as our tent was convenient enough. But he considered it an indispensable act of hospitality, and we readily gave way, gratified by this unhappily rare instance of liberality towards professors of a different creed.

With great alacrity tables and forms were got out of the way, the room was thoroughly cleaned, partitions put up for bath and sleeping-rooms, and we were made as comfortable as if in our own house. The people brought us offerings of rice, fish, game, and fruit, and the girls elegant baskets of flowers, which they presented with unaffected dignity, for even in their outward deportment a surprising change had taken place.

We thankfully accepted the gifts, and were about to give presents in return, when Mrs. Wade interposed: 'There must not be any barter,' she said; 'the people must offer their gifts from unselfish motives. If you wish to leave a remembrance on leaving, I shall not object to your doing so.'

After they had all bidden us welcome in turn, and sufficiently inspected the two white strangers, whom they took, as a matter of course, for spiritual emissaries, on a given signal they retreated, and left us to refresh ourselves free from intrusive curiosity.

Towards evening Mrs. Wade came to take us a walk through the place, and to call on a few of the more respectable families; we were followed by many of the inhabitants, who were proud to show the 'town,' the first built by Karens, to their foreign guests.

There were about fifty houses in the style of small bungalows, built symmetrically on the shore, surrounded by well-kept gardens, and, compared with the wretched hovels of the dwellers in the forest, the place really had the look of a town. The houses were also more orderly inside, and showed the awakened appreciation of domestic comfort. It was Saturday, and they were being scoured and rinsed inside and out, a custom answering to the American white-washing, and, considering the small sense of cleanliness among the Karens, it was well to introduce it here.

I thought their simple dress very suitable for the men as well as the women, except that the long sleeves, which, from an exaggerated notion of propriety, Mrs. Wade had made them wear, were not becoming to the young women.

At sunset the people were summoned to evening worship in the chapel by the sound of the gong. Accompanied by the solemn tones of the organ, played by Mr. Wade himself, the congregation sang in pure, soft tones a touching psalm of thanksgiving and praise. It was evident that the people had received the new teaching into their inmost souls, and that their hearts were raised in gratitude to the beneficent Creator proclaimed to them. I have never attended a more touching service.

The following Sunday was rigidly observed. So great was the effect on us of the genuine piety that we witnessed here, that Helfer abstained from any secular occupation, even from arranging specimens, in order not to jar upon the people's solemn frame of mind. He edified the congregation before and after service with preludes on the organ and singing hymns; these people are very fond of music, and listened most attentively to these to them novel tunes and modulations.

We stayed a full week at Metamio. Helfer explored the neighbourhood, and made several days' voyage up the river, while I enjoyed the interesting society of Mrs. Wade, and for many years, long after I left India, I kept up a correspondence with this judicious, energetic, and amiable lady.

Obstacles of various kinds, which may be overcome by regular navigation, occasioned Helfer to give up the project of going down the Tenasserim from this place. The difficulties were not so great lower down, but in order to reach this point we had to return to Tavoy.

After a few days' stay there we went to Palouk, a pretty considerable place on a navigable river of the same name, where an active trade with the interior was being developed. Here also we spent a few days, endeavouring to acquire information as to the best way of reaching the lower Tenasserim. But neither the Burmese inhabitants, nor the Karens, nor the Shans in the neighbourhood, could give us any certain information about its course or the distance, and so Helfer was once more thrown upon his compass as sole guide.

Following the course indicated, we came to a place

where the path, though it had been evidently much frequented, was closed by an almost impenetrable barrier of interlaced climbing plants. On seeing this obstruction raised by the hand of man, our people started back, and demanded that we should turn round at once, and take some other way.

The barrier denoted that the small-pox had broken out at the place to which it led. In this country small-pox is a scarcely less desolating scourge than the plague on the Asiatic coasts of the Mediterranean. When it appears the inhabitants take flight, scared out of their usual apathy about illness, leaving those who have been attacked to their fate. As a warning, and protection against the further spread of the disease, the fugitives close the way behind them, and years often elapse before a native will enter a village again.

Knowing himself to be protected against infection, my husband went alone to the infected village by going round the barrier, intending, if possible, to give medical assistance to the sick. But none but the dead were to be found in the houses, and as the bodies were in an advanced state of decomposition, and the air very pestilential, there was no room for further investigations.

All the experiments which Helfer made with vaccination in India failed. Neither the lymph taken direct from the cow, nor from European children, produced pustules in the natives; the pricks of the lancet were quickly healed without causing the least irritation of the skin. I am not aware whether medical science has discovered the reason of this singular fact, or has found the means of arresting small-pox in these countries by vaccination.

We did not reach the shores of the lower Tenasserim until March 10; at this point they were quite uninhabited. Helfer was convinced that his intention of exploring the river, and of mapping it for the first time by following its course on land, was impracticable, and decided to go down its inviting waters on rafts. There was ample material, and our practised followers had soon constructed sufficient rafts for the transport of men and baggage. The one intended for us had two comfortable seats, and was manned by a steersman and six rowers. The little flotilla glided gently down the stream, and Helfer began making a survey of the river. He used the compass for determining the directions of its course; and the number of oar strokes, in which equal time was always kept, served as a standard for distances. With the compass before him, and counting the strokes of the oar, he mapped his observations on a strip of paper several ells long, spread out on his knees —no very easy method of making a survey.

The first day passed pleasantly enough; Helfer's attention was so kept on the stretch that he was not sensible of fatigue; but on the second day the shores became more and more steep and bare of trees, until they ended in perpendicular cliffs, between which the sun struck down in full force upon the river, and he was so overcome by exhaustion from the insufferable heat that he was compelled to rest, and to turn over his laborious occupation to me. No doubt my sketches were still less perfect than his; but, so far as I know, this plan, which I still possess, served as the basis for the first map of the course of the Tenasserim.

As it was then near the end of the dry season, the water was very low, so that the banks were exposed to view. Helfer carefully examined their formation, and became more and more confirmed in the opinion that there must be coal-fields in the country.

After we had continued our voyage for ten days, the rafts, so hastily put together, threatened to get out of joint, for they had often come into collision with hidden trunks of trees, or been driven against rocky promontories, and had always been a little the worse for it. The water began ominously to overflow the upper layer of wood, and our feet were thus in a cold bath up to the ankles, while our heads were burning in the sun.

On the eleventh day we saw the first habitations of man; there was a hospitable little village on the shore. We did not find much fresh food there, but there were some useful boats to be had, by which we could continue our voyage more safely and quickly. Two days later we reached a larger village, where we determined to make a longer stay.

The head man received us with all the respect due to our credentials, and lent us all the assistance we required. On unloading our collections from the boats to be sent back, which were here exchanged for larger ones, the eyes of one of the villagers fell on a bit of coal, which had been left in one of them. He kicked it contemptuously away, saying: 'We've got that useless stone here—you need not bring us that.'

The words fell on Helfer's ear as a long-wished-for revelation. With incautious haste, he asked, 'Have you? Where is it?' His eagerness betrayed the importance the white man attached to the stone, which was quite enough to make the other obstinately deny all knowledge of it. 'I know nothing about it,' he protested, in direct contradiction to what he had just said. Incensed at this audacious denial, Helfer threatened him with severe chastisement if he did not tell the truth, whereupon, after long demur, he remembered having once seen stone of that kind in a ship at Mergui—that was all he knew about it. The head man, also, when seriously questioned, concealed the existence of coal in the district, and, taking the man under his protection, confirmed his last statement.

Helfer became greatly excited, and resolved to leave no stone unturned to get at the truth. At a hint from him, his Burmese body-guard seized the delinquent and bound him to a tree. The inhabitants watched these proceedings in gloomy silence. The ratan switch was raised to scourge his naked body, but Helfer could not bring himself to give the word of command for the cruel punishment, and quick as lightning another idea occurred to him. He had the man untied from the tree, bound hand and foot, and then put into one of the empty boats, which was to carry him off immediately.

This at once took effect. The women threw themselves, howling, at Helfer's feet, and entreated him not to take the man away. Their weeping and wailing finally conquered the defiance of the obstinate liar, and he confessed that the black stones were to be found not far off on a tributary of the Tenasserim.

He had to guide Helfer thither without delay, and

there, sure enough, on the shores of the shallow river, was a great layer of coal under a stratum of sandstone.

How shall I describe my husband's intense satisfaction, as, with beaming eyes, he brought back a piece of black shining coal, of the best quality? His efforts were crowned with success, the main object of his explorations accomplished, and his conviction that some happy accident would bring to light what he had so diligently sought had been amply justified.

The further voyage was now given up, and we took the shorter land journey to Mergui, in order to communicate the important discovery to the British authorities without loss of time.

CHAPTER VI.

THE PLANTATION AT MERGUI.

THE town of Mergui is built in the form of an amphitheatre, on the slope of a ridge of hills, 200 feet high, rising gently from the shore. The population was at that time about 8,000. There were broad streets, formed by rows of bamboo houses on piles. Elegant bungalows, inhabited by Chinese merchants and American missionaries, stood beneath the shade of lofty cocoanut palms, which here, so near their native clime, the Nicobar islands, attain a luxuriant growth, and are to be seen in all their beauty. The verandahs are concealed from the passer-by by banana leaves, of a mastic green colour, over twenty feet long, and the entrances to the houses are hidden by the graceful festoons of the Betel creeper, which the natives carefully cultivate. High over this labyrinth of green, with the roots peeping between, the great pagoda, with its numerous adjoining buildings, towers up in the middle of the city, and close to it is the Government bungalow, over which waves the British flag.

The view from this point is delightful. At your feet is the boundless expanse of sea, into which the broad and navigable Tenasserim empties itself on the south side of the town. It is dotted with groups of islands, encircling the safe and spacious harbour. The highest is King's Island, in the west; it is richly wooded to the summit, which reaches the height of 3,000 feet, and protects the haven, ten miles in width, from the dangerous storms of the south-west monsoon.

The broad expanse is enlivened with a multitude of craft, from the slender English clipper to the Malay coaster and the bulky Chinese junk, each carrying its national flag. Little boats ply hither and thither like swallows, and keep up a lively intercourse between the shipping and the bazaar, which extends from the upper town to the strand. There representatives of all the trading nations of the East are to be met with, varying in build, colour, and garb, some transacting their business with noise and clamour, others in reserved and dignified silence.

The well-protected harbour, easily accessible to a whole fleet, as well as its favourable situation, half-way on the frequented route between Calcutta, Singapore, and China, made it appear probable that Mergui would become one of the most important seats of commerce in the East.

The climate, also, is unusually good. With a moderate temperature of 84° Fahrenheit, there is always a pleasant freshness in the air from the mountain and sea breezes, which enables you to dispense with artificial apparatus, such as the punkah, &c. Mergui is considered one of the healthiest places on the coast. An English regiment, which, while stationed on the Malabar coast, was almost destroyed by sickness, had lost no more men after being removed to Mergui. Balsamic odours, exhaled from the fragrant blossoms and fruits of the spice trees and shrubs, fill the air, and to inhale it, combined with the refreshing coolness, is a delight which no words can describe. You seem to imbibe a pleasurable sensation at every pore. It may be that this superfluity of physical enjoyment is enervating, but nothing more delightful can be imagined.

Attracted by so much beauty and so many advantages, we resolved to settle here, and, should circumstances permit, to increase the natural products of the country by improved culture.

We at once took possession of the unoccupied Government buildings placed at our disposal. Helfer then went again in company with an officer of engineers to the coal-field to explore it further, and to make arrangements for working it. On his return, he arranged his notes of the last expedition, and wrote a report of it, to be delivered personally in Calcutta, as had been requested. He also wished to discuss further undertakings.

Although, when possible, I was glad to avoid a sea voyage, I resolved to accompany my husband to Calcutta. The natural desire of a housewife to exercise her own taste in selecting the furniture for a new home overcame my aversion.

But before leaving Mergui, we selected a site for our house, the neighbourhood of which was to be the field of our future labours. We decided on a hill, covered with luxurious verdure, not far from the town, near the sea, and close to unappropriated woods. The prospect was not less fine than that from the Pagoda Hill. When at sunset the ball of fire dipped into the sea, his last rays gilding the crests of the waves, and bathing the landscape in rosy light, the splendour of the scene was quite overpowering.

A Chinese carpenter undertook to build our bungalow. It did not require any architectural skill, nor any great outlay of time or money, for it was soon finished, and cost 300 rupees. It stood upon piles, eight feet from the ground, and the space underneath formed a hall, always cool and shady. The interior included a large room in the centre, two smaller ones at the sides, with bath and dressing-rooms, and a small, half-open drawing-room at the back. A broad verandah ran all along the front of the house, and the thick roof of palm leaves, projecting six feet beyond the walls, afforded protection from rain and sun. The walls consisted of mats, as did also the doors and windows, which could in case of need be closed, but they could not prevent anyone from coming in. Of what use, however, would it be to shut doors and windows when the walls offered no obstacle to ingress? It was in these modest, but, in our eyes, charming apartments, that we intended to set up a permanent home.

After a quick and prosperous voyage, on August 13 we landed once more at Calcutta. With what different feelings did we tread the shores of the Ganges, now that our wanderings and endeavours had found a definite termination, and all that we had scarcely ventured to hope for a year before had been realised.

Short-sighted man, what a blessing it is for him

that an impenetrable veil hides the future, and permits him to play with the roses of the present, even on the brink of the grave! Just at the moment of our greatest happiness, Helfer's voyages among the Mergui Archipelago were determined on, which were to bring his active and hopeful career to an untimely end.

The authorities received my husband with the utmost favour, and acknowledged his services not only in flattering words but by more substantial reward. From the low figure of his expenses they concluded that he must have defrayed his personal travelling expenses from his own resources, and although he disclaimed it, a sum of 12,000 rupees was granted him for expenditure incurred in the service of the Company, as well as a considerable increase of salary. Measured by a German standard, such remuneration may seem high, but it was a mere bagatelle compared with the sums which similar undertakings have cost in India.

Heartily welcomed by friends and acquaintances, among whom, however, I was sorry to miss my dear Mrs. Hutchinson, who had followed her children to England, we once more spent some pleasant social hours in these circles. But nothing could detain us long; we wanted to get back to Mergui to the new and promising field of labour upon which we intended to enter.

We took all that was necessary with us for a comfortable home—we even allowed ourselves the luxury of a fine piano to cheer our leisure hours—and reached Mergui again on September 10. The interior of our bungalow had meanwhile been finished, and it gave me no little pleasure to arrange the furniture, and to turn it into a habitable abode.

We now once more eagerly discussed the plan of forming an extensive plantation. We considered the advantages which would accrue to the country from higher cultivation, and the introduction of valuable foreign products, such as the coffee plant, nutmeg, and other spice plants, and calculated also the profits that we might, in course of time, derive from it ourselves. I also became more and more enthusiastic for the idea which was ever present to my mind—of founding a colony of my German fellow-countrymen.

We proceeded to carry out our scheme, and laid the first stone of the building, that is, we set up in the wood, which we took possession of without scruple, the landmarks of our first plantation.

The appropriation of portions of land without authorisation, and by which you do not encroach upon anybody's rights, gives you a feeling of liberty which can no longer exist in populous Europe, and that it could be done close to the town proves how little the natives cultivated the land. The authorities do not interfere, but permit the cultivator free possession of the land for three years, after which a tax of a rupee per annum per acre is exacted, the punctual payment of which secures future possession.

It was only for a few weeks, however, that we enjoyed these joint labours, and the pleasure which we had so long foregone, of living together in a home of our own. As soon as the monsoon storms abated, Helfer prepared for the expedition to the islands, with the exploration of which the Government had entrusted him. I at length yielded to his remonstrances against exposing myself to wind and weather in open boats, and, averse as I was to it, had to allow him to go without me.

On November 28, 1838, he left the roads of Mergui with a number of his previous suite, in two roughly-built coasting boats. Two small canoes were also taken to enable them to reach the cliffs and rocky islands in shallow water. Before they were out of sight of the harbour, they had to take shelter from sudden squalls behind the Madramacan Islands, and could not continue their voyage until the next day.

A glance at the map of Malacca shows a group of over 4,000 islands between the 9th and 14th degrees of latitude, which constitute the Mergui Archipelago. Many of them are mere rocks, but most of them are clothed with a luxurious growth of wood. The whole forms a labyrinth of straits, passages, caves, and clefts, through which even an expert Ulysses would find it difficult to make his way, and a lifetime would scarcely suffice to explore them.

While Helfer searched the heights and depths of these islands, to discover what treasures they might contain, I superintended the laying out of our plantation.

The Burmese dahs, at my bidding, did great execution among the fine old trees in the forest, until numbers of them came with a crash to the ground, and exposed their tangled roots to view. It was a scene of sad destruction, but a necessary sacrifice for the pursuance of our project. The Burmese are very expert in calculating the fall of trees so that they should lie crosswise over one another, and when they do not succeed in that, the large boughs are cut off and piled lightly up, so that the sun and air may have free access, and by the end of the dry season the wood is sufficiently dry. The aromatic odours which were diffused from this mass of felled timber penetrated into our house till they were quite overpowering.

At the same time Chinese labourers were employed in digging up a piece of ground, clearing it of roots, and preparing it for a nursery. Thanks to their untiring diligence, within a short time the waste ground was turned into a well-kept garden, laid out in every part with the utmost precision according to Chinese taste, and thousands of cocoa and areca nuts were planted in it. A mother cannot watch the cradle of her newborn babe more carefully than a Chinese his garden. He surrounds it with a close-set hedge of pineapples, which, like thistles with us, are carefully excluded from the interior, for, like them, they smother everything if not kept within bounds. Although the pineapple attains a size and flavour of which those grown in European hothouses give no idea, they are so little esteemed here, and are so superabundant, that a boatload of them only costs fivepence, and we fed our horses, which are very fond of them, with them. In my desire to turn everything to account, I fancied that a nice beverage might be distilled from the aromatic juice, but the result was only a sharp extract as sour as vinegar, which was not of any use, even in cooking.

In March, towards the end of the dry season, the

felled trees, then dry, were set fire to. The conflagration and heat produced by a fire extending over a hundred acres may be imagined. The air was so heated, over a wide circuit, that I was obliged to leave our house. When the soil was cooled by the rains, the young trees were planted in the ashes, which were a foot deep. To the annoyance of the Chinese, straight lines could not be kept to, as trees charred but not burnt and roots often came in the way. In order to promote the growth of the young trees, the holes were manured with the refuse of fish, which was to be had in great abundance. My zeal was shared by my hundreds of labourers. I visited them early in the morning on horseback at their work, and mostly spent the whole day, whether in rain or sunshine, among them. Not seldom, when storms followed quickly one after another, I was wet to the skin several times in a day, but as the clothes quickly dried again, it was only a pleasant refreshment. The anticipated pleasure of my husband's surprise on his return at the progress achieved sweetened my labour.

Nor was my attention devoted exclusively to the vegetable kingdom, but was shared by the animal world. I procured a herd of buffaloes, and was soon on such terms of intimacy with them that I could go among them in a white dress without fear. They supplied us with milk, butter, and veal, all delicacies only to be obtained at Mergui by keeping your own flocks. Goats of a peculiar and elegant species, from the Neilgherry Hills, gamboled on the grass before our house, and at the back was a poultry-yard peopled by domestic birds and wild fowl. The latter afforded me much amusement. A little cock, which had been caught in the wood in a snare, distinguished himself by his drollery. He was marked like our common domestic fowls, had a brilliant green neck and a finely arched tail, only he was much smaller. He soon became aware of the notice he received, and displayed a vanity which, as he was only about the size of a partridge, was quite comical. He was permitted to enter our dining-room, where he found his tit-bits, boiled rice and shrimps, perched without ceremony on a chair, and took his place as third person at table. If the servant forgot to place a chair for him, or omitted it for fun, the little fellow was quite enraged. He would run about scratching and flapping his little wings, and if that did not take effect he pecked at the servant's feet until he had placed a chair for him with the back to the table. He then triumphantly took his place, and was waited upon like a gentleman. He knew perfectly well the difference between master and servant, for he never behaved disrespectfully to Helfer or me.

Two large herons with bright steel-blue plumage strutted about among the other poultry or hovered in the air, as I would not deprive any creature of its liberty. When I called them with a whistle, which they recognised as my voice, they came down in gradually decreasing circles and took their breakfast from a basket of fish.

The rearing of poultry gave me a great deal of trouble. The chicks were always killed by red ants as soon as ever they began to break the shell, and I could not keep these enemies out of the nests. At last it occurred to me to put the nests on a table, with the legs in tubs of water. The ants cannot get over that, I thought. But they actually sacrificed their lives to make a bridge. With heroic contempt of death, the ant nearest to the water rushed into it, a second, third, and fourth followed, until the bodies of the drowned formed a bridge, which the rest could pass over dry-shod and secure their prey.

I even tried to make friends with the denizens of the forests, and collected a considerable menagerie, in which neither the graceful deer nor the dreaded tiger was wanting. The tiger was brought to me as a young cub. I gave him buffalo milk at first, and then rice, hoping to cure him of his taste for blood by a vegetable diet. It suited him very well, and he throve upon it, but his claws grew larger and sharper, and I observed that he cast suspicious glances at my little fawn, which had broken one of its slender legs on the smooth matting, and was always by my side. My servants put an end to all further observation of my dangerous nursling by putting him out of the way. They told me, one morning, that the tiger had made his escape during the night, but they had always detested him, and had probably prepared a worse fate for him.

But unbidden and very unwelcome guests also intruded into my animal kingdom. Among these, although they are harmless, and, indeed, useful to man, were the house snakes, of a greenish grey colour, and over an ell long. They like to keep under the roofs of the houses, and lie in wait for the bandicoot, a large kind of rat, which serves them for food, and thus they make themselves as useful as our domestic cats. In the evening there was generally a noisy chase going on over our heads—the snakes were fighting with the rats. We heard the bandicoot running from one corner of the roof to another, to escape the noiseless but rapid pursuit of its foe, and when overtaken it wrestled with it until a faint, final squeak indicated that it was overpowered. But these house snakes also creep into the rooms, crawl along the ledges, glide up and down the posts, and the cold reptile not seldom touched my hand when I was opening or closing the doors and windows; it used to spring up at the unexpected contact, and wind itself, quick as lightning, round my arm. Use at length overcame the shudder which it used to give me at first.

Much more repulsive to me was a kind of lizard, called the Touk-tey, and, so far as one could see, it was of no use. It happily always announced its presence by its shrill cry of Touk-tey, and I believe it is the only species of lizard that utters a sound. In size and form it resembles the perch, and it also has a dorsal fin; two round eyes stare out of its clumsy head, which, when the creature is angry, have an unearthly brilliance. Though not venomous, the Touk-tey is dreaded by the natives, for its claws terminate in a peculiar barb, and if it fixes itself to a man it can only be got rid of by cutting out the flesh. One of these charming creatures took great delight in surveying itself in the looking-glass, and was sitting nearly every evening on my dressing-table, staring at me as if preparing for a spring. It disturbed my nights until we succeeded in banishing the intruder for ever.

From time to time we were overrun by winged white ants; they darken the air like clouds of locusts, and cover the ground, wherever they fall, three or four inches deep, with their fat, maggot-like bodies. The only way of protecting yourself against them is to keep within closely curtained beds until they have passed, which is not generally very long, and then to brush away and destroy those that have fallen. These disgusting insects were welcomed by the Chinese as dainty morsels. Seizing the ants by the wings, they held them a little while to the fire, or even only to a light, and then devoured them with great relish. The Chinese taste is decidedly different from that of other people.

Human beings, of course, claimed my interest in a still higher degree. In order to make myself acquainted with their manners and customs, I assembled a circle of young Burmese women and girls around me and tried to instruct them. I may truly say that I have never found more natural understanding, humour, thirst for knowledge, or tact, even among ladies who have had the advantage of a good education, than among these children of Nature. They instituted comparisons, of which my person was even sometimes the subject, grasped ideas readily and correctly, and were never tired of asking the why and wherefore of things. In their behaviour to me they were quite self-possessed and at ease, perhaps even a little free; anyhow, there was no shyness or reserve. They were not available for servants, for they had no liking for feminine handicrafts, and their social position gave them a strong feeling of independence.

The Karen women are very different in character from the Burmese. They are not inferior in mental powers, but are distinguished by a gentler and softer character, as is evinced by their modest blushes. Then they are industrious and handy, and take a pride, for example, in ornamenting the men's shirts and the satchel which they always wear at their sides with tasteful embroidery in colours. A European pattern-drawer might envy them some of their designs. Unfortunately, I had not much opportunity of intercourse with them, for they seldom came to the town, and the few who lived there were under the strict supervision of the American missionaries.

The missionaries held undisputed sway over the converted Karens; they not only taught but ruled them. Their utterances were oracles, their wishes commands, and to serve them was a meritorious religious duty. The missionaries were jealous of their power, and not very civil to persons of a different faith; they were well off in a pecuniary sense, and were surrounded by state, not exactly a product of Christian humility. I speak only of what I observed at Mergui, for at other places I have met with much more amiable characters among the American missionaries.

Two Catholic priests were a favourable contrast—a simple Franciscan monk and a Frenchman of the name of Barbier, educated in the mission school at Rome, and sent to Mergui as pastor to the little Catholic community, consisting of the descendants of the Portuguese, who formerly lived there, and to represent in general the interests of their church among the other Christian communities. M. Barbier was a truly humane, well-educated man, and the resignation with which he filled his post at Mergui, which was almost a banishment, won for him our highest esteem. The pastoral care of his little congregation did not nearly occupy his time nor his unsuccessful attempts to convert the Burmese. His salary was so small that it barely sufficed to support life, so that he was obliged to dine by turns with the members of his flock, and he was equally destitute of the means of satisfying his intellectual cravings.

We with pleasure granted both priests access to the little social circle that assembled at our house, consisting of Mr. Corbier, the assistant-commissioner, and some officers of the small English regiment. When Mr. Blondell, our honoured governor, came to Mergui there was quite a little commotion. The finest fish and oysters were procured, the fattest capons killed, and sometimes a buffalo calf, an event of great importance, for veal was not to be had for money, and as in that climate meat would not keep, but had to be consumed at once, all our friends received a portion, and there was a general feasting. The European liking for beef could not be gratified in that country.

The Burmese men were not much better domestic servants than the women. Regular, daily recurring employment was intolerably wearisome to them. It not unfrequently happened that instead of a regular servant a stranger came and began to do his work. When asked how it was, he would say: 'My brother wants to rest, I will do his work for him.' And he would do it until he wanted to rest too, and disappeared in like manner. A Burmese servant whom we had scolded for some fault went away secretly without asking for his wages. We met him some time afterwards by chance, and asked him why he had left our service without taking his wages, and he answered: 'I have offended father and mother, how can I ask for wages?' And it was only after refusing for some time that he could be prevailed upon to take the money.

The Chinese servants, on the contrary, are real domestic treasures, if you know how to manage them, and take care to consider their feelings. They perform their duties day after day punctually and accurately, are clever in every way, and ready to do anything they are told. I must confess that a Chinese clad in loose blue trousers and a white shirt over them, with his broad closely-shorn pate, and a tail hanging down to the ground, his narrow eyes and puffy grinning lips, is not a pleasing object, but he works away as busily as an ant, and is in perpetual motion. If you tell him to fetch a carpenter, cabinet-maker, tailor, or what not, he will be sure to say, grinning from ear to ear, 'I can do it myself,' and do it he will. Only not one of my servants could make ladies' shoes. It appears to be against the notions of propriety of a Chinese to make shoes large enough for the feet of a European lady; he never makes them above half the right size.

You must, however, most carefully avoid offending these obliging people, for they never forget an insult, and will not fail to take an opportunity of revenge. Fortunately they look so excessively comic that even if a word of displeasure is on your lips, you withhold it, and are irresistibly compelled to laugh instead.

Petty theft, burglary, and robbery were almost unknown among the natives. Even during Helfer's absence, I felt quite safe, though our house was outside the town, and rather lonely, and used to leave my ornaments, some of them valuable, such as a gold watch, which might have excited the cupidity of the natives, lying openly on the table. As evidence of the rarity of crime, it may be mentioned that in these provinces, having an extent of eighty geographical miles, three courts of justice, each having but one official, were sufficient to try all the criminal cases. Most of the crimes were committed by foreigners—Shans, Thalians, and Chinese—chiefly when under the influence of opium, from motives of revenge, or actuated by religious fanaticism.

The Chinese, for instance, are divided into two sects who have a mortal hatred of each other. In manning the junks, therefore, the Lascars from Macao and Canton were kept strictly apart. But if it happened that junks from both provinces were anchored in the harbour at the same time, there were sure to be quarrels between the crews ending in bloodshed.

One day when the few gentlemen belonging to European society in Mergui, the chief magistrate, Mr. Corbier, at their head, were dining with us, a crowd of Chinese sailors came with great noise and tumult to our house, carrying a dead man on their shoulders. His legs and arms were hanging straight down, the glazed eyes staring out of his head, which was turned on one side. They laid the body down on the green before our house, and demanded justice and revenge for their murdered comrade. They said that there was a fight going on below in the harbour between them and the infidel heretics, and their party would be overpowered, and many of them murdered if they did not get help at once. Mr. Corbier, who well knew the fury of the Chinese against their religious opponents, went to the harbour, accompanied by Helfer, to try to put a stop to further bloodshed. The noisy rabble took their departure, but left the body on the grass. After all was quiet, I saw through the window that the quasi-dead man first moved his head, and put it in a more comfortable position, then looked round, drew a deep breath, and at last thinking himself unobserved, raised himself up.

The murder had been simulated by him and his party with a view of getting the authorities to interfere in their favour, knowing that in the unequal combat they were sure to get the worst of it, and they were probably well aware that amidst the confused cries in their unintelligible tongue it is very difficult to find out who is in fault, and that the investigation is mostly not over scrutinising. The Chinese generally prefer to give their opponents up to the authorities to avenging themselves, and they often mutilate themselves or even commit suicide in order to insure the conviction of their enemies. The cruel deaths inflicted on criminals in China may lead to these unnatural excesses, combined with their passionate thirst for revenge.

Even when we had taken a troop of criminals transported from Bengal from the prison at Mergui to work in the plantation, and had assigned the space under the house for them to live in, I slept as calmly and safely as ever, though only separated from them by thin planks, for there were no thieves or swindlers among them; they were mostly Thugs, so dreaded in their own country, but here, on foreign soil, and having lost caste, they were quite harmless. They were for ever removed from the horrible idol-worship which had taught them to murder hundreds of men whom they neither knew nor hated. As if the bloodthirsty tiger could all at once be content to suck milk, and assume the nature of a lamb, these men, no sooner was the bandage of religious phrensy and fanaticism removed from their eyes, were changed from cunning murderers into perfectly trustworthy people. There was among them a handsome youth, scarcely sixteen, who related to me in the coolest way, as if it was quite a matter of course, the circumstances of the many murders he had committed.

CHAPTER VII.

HELFER'S VOYAGES IN THE ARCHIPELAGO, AND HIS DEATH.

For five months from December 1838 to April 1839 Helfer voyaged in and out among the islands. During this period he only came to Mergui occasionally for a few days, to bring his collections into safety and to take in fresh supplies. Traversing the sea mostly in open boats from the most westward of the Torres Islands to the mouth of the Packchan river, the southern extremity of the British territory, he obtained most valuable knowledge about the situation and formation of the various groups, as well as of the products of sea and land.

He found the islands mostly uninhabited, but came sometimes upon remains of former settlements or temporary abodes of Malay pirates, who, before the time of British dominion, made these waters so dangerous. On the larger islands he observed scattered deserted camping-places of the scanty nomad race, the Seelongs. They are a peaceful people without settled abodes, who fly from hostile attacks into inaccessible mountains, or try to escape them in light boats, in which they glide rapidly over the water. Late one evening, on nearing a bay of one of the Blunt Islands, Helfer saw smoke rising from the shore. He conjectured that Seelongs must have pitched their camp there, and, as he wished to make acquaintance with them, he gave orders to make for the place, and found that it was as he supposed. I take the following description of the incident from his reports :—

'My arrival at night terrified the defenceless natives, as they did not know whether I might be friend or foe, and feared an attack of Malays from the south. The women and children had fled into the interior, having concealed their small possessions, rice and cockles, in the thickets. Everything was in the greatest confusion; even the animals were scared at the unwonted visit, for dogs, cats, and cocks set up a shrill chorus. But as soon as the islanders perceived that a white man, the first they had ever seen, had come to them, their fear was turned into joy, and the next day the whole community came to welcome me. There might be about sixty people, including women and children, encamped on the sandy shore. Each family had built a roof of palm leaves on piles, under which they all huddled together at night, and a dirty and wretched-looking lot they were. Some of these roofs looked like butchers' counters, for they were covered with large pieces of turtle flesh, the chief diet of the islanders, placed there to dry, and the air was contaminated with the smell. Besides these I saw shell-fish taken out of the shell and the roots of a species of *Dioscorea* and the shoots of the *Cycas circinalis*, which have an unpleasant odour, prepared for cooking.

'The Seelongs are a well-built and healthy looking race. They are darker in colour than the Burmese; partly Malay and partly Ethiopian in type, suggestive of a mixture of the two. The curly hair which occasionally occurs suggests an affinity with the negro race; perhaps a cross may have taken place with the neighbouring Andamanese. They were polite and respectful in their behaviour. They are unfortunately very much addicted to drink, and know no greater pleasure than intoxication. The Chinese and Malays, who carry on a barter trade with them, take advantage of this miserable tendency, which is common to all half-savage races, by bringing them toddy (palm wine), and robbing them when drunk of all their possessions. When come to themselves, however, they do not take their losses so very much to heart, for with their few wants they can easily replace them.

'Their scanty wants make them apathetic and lazy; only the young people work, that is, they collect everything that is to be had for little trouble. With some of Nature's richest treasures around them, they live in the greatest poverty, for they exchange valuable products—pearls, amber, and aloe wood—with the Chinese for medicines and charms. But having no knowledge of medicinal herbs and their uses, they are entirely helpless when attacked by disease. They told me that most of their children die between the ages of two and six—according to their description from dysentery, a very probable result of the indigestible food which they eat even at that early age—but that the health of those who survive this period is considered to be established.

'Medicines were the presents most highly prized by them. When they saw me drinking coffee, and heard that I drank this black liquor every day, they imagined that it must be the white man's chief medicine, and so overwhelmed me with petitions for some of it that I left them a good part of my stock.

'On the shore there were from twenty to thirty well-built boats; the bottom was formed of a single trunk, the sides of slender palm stems, strongly bound together with palm hemp. These boats, not over thirty feet long, are as light as nutshells, and are really the homes of the Seelongs. They are Ichthyophagi in the fullest sense of the word, and the earth with all its fruitfulness has so little charm for them that they do not even sow a grain of rice in its lap, and go from island to island trusting their lives and all their possessions to these slender craft. But even fishing among them is in its infancy, for they have no nets, but use only tridents, with which they spear sharks and other fish, and even turtles.

'Besides these, they have no other implements but the Burmese dah and their arms and hands. I accompanied a number of young men on their fishing, and observed how dexterously they use the trident, which is fixed to a bamboo cane about twenty feet long. In an hour they caught three large turtles, two sharks, and some other fish. They then went to collect orchids, which grow plentifully on the island.

'I stayed a whole day among them, and could make myself understood by means of their chief, who spoke Burmese. They are entirely destitute of any idea of supernatural things, of a God, or of a life after death. When questioned on such subjects, they said: "We are poor ignorant people, we don't understand it, or think anything about it."

'The endeavour to regenerate this race, which is not without gifts, would be a fine field of labour for a really benevolent missionary. If they are left long in their present condition, their name will soon disappear from among the nations.

'All attempts to persuade these roaming islanders to come to Mergui, to bring the fruits of their labours there, and to obtain a fair profit for their goods by a public sale in their presence, have hitherto failed. Like the Karens of the continent, they are afraid to come into the towns, although they must know by this time that they would be quite safe there, and would be justly dealt with.

'The recollection of the oppression they endured under the Burmese dominion is still too fresh and the present government too new to have conquered their distrust.'

The products of the islands are the same as those of the continent, with the addition of some maritime ones, such as the mangosteen, a fruit whose refreshing properties makes it invaluable in this climate. Its taste is almost like iced lemonade, and it does not produce the injurious effects of other cooling fruits. It thrives especially in the island of Kalegouk. It looks something like the pomegranate, and contains a reddish mass, in which five white juicy berries, about the size of gooseberries, are embedded, which are taken out and eaten with a spoon. Unfortunately this splendid fruit will not keep, and cannot be exported. Attempts have been made to send it to England in the rigging of a clipper, as an offering to Her Majesty, but they have always been spoilt before they arrived.

Many of the islands, especially Kisseraign, are so fertile that under rational cultivation they would be an inexhaustible storehouse of rice for the whole Archipelago, including the province of Mergui.

The sandy coasts also might bear forests of cocoa-nut trees if it were not for the want of men to cultivate them and reap the profits.

Hitherto industry has been confined to the products of the sea, which the cunning Chinese and enterprising Malays have taken from the poor islanders almost for nothing.

The coasts of Kisseraing are renowned for their swarms of fish. At spawning time millions of them come into the inner channels, but the fisheries have only been made profitable to a small extent. Formerly no one could venture out even a few miles to the south of Mergui for fear of the Malay pirates.

At the mouth of the Boukpeen river walls of piles are erected on the sandy bar, in which fish are caught in such numbers that the fishermen do not know what to do with them, and a great many are thrown back into the sea. Rapacious monsters, attracted by the feast, then come out of the depths of the sea; alligators, otters, herons, and hawks make it a rendezvous, and sea-mews sit in rows on the piles, their brilliant white plumage indicating the shore to the seafarer at a long distance.

On the Maingy Islands ngapé is made from garneels, a kind of crab; it is an indispensable seasoning in Burmese cookery. Round these islands there are extensive mudbanks, and they swarm with white garneels. The mud is taken up in closely-woven nets, and the little crabs are left after washing; they are then laid on mats, dried in the sun, pounded, put into pots, and buried in the earth, where the mass undergoes a process of fermentation, or rather putrefaction. The product is ngapé. It is sent throughout Burmah and Ava, as far as Yunnan in China, in jars or bamboo tubes. Even Europeans get accustomed to the sharp flavour and the by no means agreeable odour of this seasoning.

The various species of turtles also, with their nourishing and excellent flesh, the valuable shell, and the eggs which they lay in such astonishing numbers, would be lucrative articles of trade. Helfer saw near the Torres Islands, at a considerable depth in the clear water, turtles six feet long.

The bay of Sir Edward Owen's Island is the chief place where periwinkles are found; they exist in vast numbers in the moist rocky bays of the outer islands of the Mergui Archipelago, but not in the inner ones. They multiply at an extraordinary rate, for they are not the prey of any other creature. Even the rapacious marine animals disdain food which tickles the palate of the gourmand. Smoked or dried in the sun, they are a favourite article in the Chinese markets.

Still more in request with Chinese gourmands, and often worth their weight in gold, are the nests of the sea-swallow glued together with the mucilaginous substance of molluscs. They are suspended from rocks rising abruptly out of the sea and almost inaccessible crags, so that the collection of them is a perilous task, and can only be undertaken by the most expert climbers. The poor Seelongs are mostly hired for this purpose by the Chinese and Malay farmers, and are very badly paid.

The pearl oyster also is procured by Seelongs. The shells often lie close together; in a bay of the Gregory Islands the ground was covered with them, and the pearls were equal to those of El Bahrein in the Persian Gulf. Helfer brought me a pearl which had been fished up out of the deep before his eyes. He gave the fisher his own price—forty rupees—for it, but 80*l.* was afterwards offered for it by a London jeweller.

As in all our experience, Helfer found the small plagues the worst in his voyages in the Archipelago. He describes the attacks of two kinds of insects which, in spite of their minuteness, are dangerous, and sometimes even fatal to man. First, the red ants, of which he says:—' They build their nests on trees, mostly among the mangroves, and so that ten or more are held together by a web, something like the spider's web. They are bold, quarrelsome creatures, and, regardless of danger, attack everything that comes in their way. When they have seized anything with their powerful jaws, even if it be iron, they never let it go, though their heads may be severed from their bodies. In going about the shores you can hardly avoid coming in contact with them; they bite very severely, but the pain only lasts generally a few moments, and one becomes indifferent to it. But to-day, on penetrating into a mangrove wood, I came suddenly upon a colony of hundreds of red ants' nests. Instead of turning back I went on a few steps, and found them on every bush and tree. My entrance had made a great commotion among them, and their columns made an audible rustle on the dry leaves. Thousands covered the twigs, and thousands more issued from the nests. They not only crept in swarms up my legs, but fell down upon me from the trees. I retreated as soon as possible, but it was too late. I was literally covered with ants, and had thousands of bites. I do not remember ever to have suffered pain so severe. I threw myself into the water, but even then they did not leave go. My people had to tear off my clothes and pull out the creatures' heads one by one. Fever with slight delirium followed. They rubbed me all over with cocoa-nut oil, and after a few hours I was better.

'Far more dangerous is a kind of wasp which pursues the honey-bee and devours both bee and honey. My men, who were fond of honey, had found in a tree the nest of a small stingless bee, which they are not afraid of, and which makes the best honey. One of them climbed the tree to get at it, but came upon a wasp's nest, and jumped down when not above half-way up with a sudden cry. His companions hastened to his aid, but ran back immediately, calling to the rest of the crew to take to the boat. They took a torch, wrapped it in dry grass so as to make a great smoke, and then ventured to the spot where the groaning man lay. He had only two or three stings upon his back, but was in a high fever for eight days, with great nausea. Chunam (sesame oil) was applied to the stings. These wasps are considered the most dangerous of all, and not without reason; they are more dreaded than snakes or any other venomous reptile. Another of my men, the animal collector, even died from the stings. He had been so imprudent as to fire into a nest. The wasps pursued and overtook him before he could escape. One stung him on the lip, another in the neck, and his head swelled to such a size that on the third day he died from suffocation.'

Helfer ended his voyages this year with the navigation of the Packchan river, which forms the southern boundary between the British possessions and Siam. In his report he says:—

'On my arrival at the town of Packchan, I gave orders to land on the right-hand shore, the British side, to avoid any collision with the Siamese, and encamped in my tent. Five or six coasters were lying opposite, and a Chinese junk of about 250 tons. Several hundred men assembled on the shore, and the tom-tom was sounded in various directions, and a great noise made, as if for a martial enterprise. A Chinese, accompanied by two lads, came towards me from the crowd, and said, in a rather insolent tone, that he was deputed to ask me who I was, and to take me to the stadtholder. I answered coolly that I would come when the stadtholder sent me a polite invitation, but he had nothing to do with me, as I was a British official and on British soil. I would communicate my wishes to him through my attendants.

'My captain, Saduc, then betook himself to the stadtholder to offer my salutations and to ask for provisions, which we were quite out of. After two hours he came back, and said that my arrival had excited much surprise; the stadtholder could not understand what I could want in so wild a district, and he doubted whether the shore where I was, was British territory. He had, however, been polite, had promised provisions, and expressed a wish to see me, and intended therefore to send me a suitable invitation.

'Soon afterwards came a Siamese official, the karawoon (next in rank to the stadtholder), with a considerable retinue, and invited me to visit the myowoon, who was awaiting me, surrounded by great state, on the opposite shore. I condescended to accept the invitation, and was rowed over. I took my seat on two velvet cushions, and carried on as empty a conversation with the great dignitary as could be, carefully avoiding political topics. He took the opportunity of speaking of the friendly relations between the rulers of Siam and Great Britain, and assured me that not only the king but he himself cherished these sentiments. He added that he had only come into these wild jungles at the express wish of the king, to try to improve the circumstances of the inhabitants; he wished to make the district prosperous, meant to plant sugar-canes to a large extent, &c.

'Formerly there were but a few huts here, the place had been a mere hamlet, and had only lately been made a central station, where the royal troops assembled, and whence they sallied forth against the

Malays of Queda, who had revolted. A fortnight before, sixty elephants and a detachment of troops had been despatched to the south. The issue of the Malay revolt was now awaited with eagerness by the authorities, and with ill-concealed anxiety by the people. For this reason higher officials had been sent here from Bangkouk to conduct the business. Many of the Siamese who had been forcibly brought to the peninsula to fight against the Malays had deserted their colours, and concealed themselves in the jungle.

'The stadtholder, a Chinese, for which people the king has a great preference, did not understand Siamese; our conversation was, therefore, carried on with great circumlocution, as I spoke Burmese, which had first to be translated into Siamese, and then into Chinese. He wanted to impress me with a great opinion of himself and his dignity, and had surrounded himself with all the Asiatic pomp he could muster in this remote spot. He was clad in silk and gold, and wore the red Chinese Jacobin cap, while the national pigtail hung down in a net on one side. His zayat was adorned with spears, shields, sabres, and muskets, among which he showed me, with great satisfaction, a beautiful double-barrelled gun, of London make; how it came here, I could not understand. The attendant brought tea, betel, and tobacco in silver vessels. Immediately after our interview, a messenger was sent to Bangkouk to inform the king of my presence, my name, my business, intentions, &c.

'The inhabitants of Packchan were permitted to inspect the white foreigner. Among them were several

Burmese, who had been captured as children, and they availed themselves of the opportunity of trying to free themselves from Siamese bondage. All I could do for them was to promise to speak for them to the Governor of Mergui, who perhaps might be able to set them free.

'During the night, my captain woke me, to tell me that several Siamese boats had secretly approached our boat, under cover of the darkness, and that it was intended to stab me. The stadtholder disputed that the right shore of the Packchan was British territory; he maintained that the frontier was further north, on the Kazeingslo river. A number of fugitives, people brought here by force from distant parts, to fight the Malays, were concealed in the neighbourhood, and wished to put themselves under British protection, as the yoke of the new stadtholder was intolerable.

'Together with these communications, I received, what was for me much more important, information of the existence of very rich tin mines in the British territory. Nevertheless, under the circumstances, a long tarriance on the spot did not seem advisable.'

On April 21, as there were signs of the approaching monsoon, Helfer returned to Mergui. My delight on seeing him back safe and sound, after a separation of five months, during which time he had only paid a few flying visits home, and the prospect of being together for a longer time, was unspeakable. Knowing how adventurous he was, I had been overwhelmed with anxiety about him when left to himself, without me to warn and entreat him, and the feeling of loneliness, which even my active occupation could not always banish, had possessed me more and more.

His sudden appearance one day, sooner than I expected him, changed all my anxious thoughts into joyful excitement. Only those who have experienced such sudden revulsions of feeling can appreciate and sympathise with them.

With no little pride I showed my husband the domain which had, to a great extent, in the meanwhile been made fit for cultivation, and which was now to be planted, as the rainy season had begun. He entered into it all with the greatest interest.

He was specially interested in the attempt to fertilise the male nutmeg tree by inoculating it with a bud from the female tree; for, if the experiment succeeded, the male trees, which had usually been cut down when five or six years old, could in future be preserved. The high profits yielded by nutmeg plantations having induced the Dutch Government to make it a monopoly in Java, the cultivation and improvement of the nutmeg tree on free English soil was a matter of great importance.

The labourers now set to work to plant out the young saplings from the nursery with the same industry with which they had cut down, burnt off, and cleared the wood. The Burmese and Chinese emulated each other in skill and perseverance. The Chinese had a special liking for the cultivation of the tea plant and vegetables, which they had various methods of bringing on, while the Burmese chiefly devoted themselves to the areca palms, for chewing areca nuts is an indispensable luxury to them, above eating and drinking. The cultivation of areca or betel nuts is therefore as profitable as that of potatoes or corn with us. The furrows were laid out in straight lines, at a proper distance apart, and well manured with fish refuse. The feathery leaves soon shot up from the young palm plants, then drooped in graceful curves, not unlike the stalks of well-grown maize plants on a fat soil.

Before the end of the monsoon, 6,000 cocoa-nut plants, 30,000 areca palms, and 4,000 coffee plants were in the plantation, already beautiful to look at, and full of future promise. They were assiduously watched and tended until their further progress could be left to mother Nature.

Amidst these labours the time had come, only too quickly, which Helfer had fixed upon for another expedition to the Archipelago. His special destination this time was the Andaman Isles, although they were not among the British possessions, and it was therefore no part of his mission to explore them. Lying in the middle of the Bay of Bengal they had frequently been used as a refuge and anchoring-ground for ships that had met with some disaster; but such a surprising number of remains of vessels that had disappeared had been observed on their coasts, that it was considered probable that their crews had fallen victims to the cannibalism of the islanders. Very little was known of the formation or products of the islands, and still less of the natives, of whom fabulous stories were told —some asserting that they were not men but anthropomorphic apes, others that they were men but very much like monkeys.

All this inspired Helfer with a desire to go and see for himself; and although he had not been well for some time, and felt languid and depressed, he would not lend an ear to my entreaties that he would give up, or at least put off the voyage, for he never would alter his plans on account of passing moods. On January 13, 1840, he went to sea in the little schooner *Catharina*.

The voyage was unfortunate from the first. The monsoon storms were not quite over, and, as if unwilling to yield up their sway, squalls of great violence returned. The little vessel was caught by one of these sudden gusts of wind not far from Mergui, thrown on her side, and placed in great danger. Both the boats were lost, and they had to cast anchor till they could get another, which was afterwards found to be quite inadequate.

Struggling with storms and adverse currents, on the 18th the *Catharina* came in sight of the Barren Island, whose lofty peak Helfer calls the finest volcano he had ever seen. But its rocky, craggy coasts offered no anchoring-ground, so that they were compelled to tack the whole night on the open sea; while the anchor, which the crew could not heave, dragged after them in fifty fathoms of water.

Helfer reports in his diary:—

'We could not tack about any longer; the storm was increasing; with a heavy heart I left this interesting place, and gave orders to steer for the Andamans.

'I was so vexed not to be able to explore the volcano, that I stayed the whole day in bed. The waves ran mountain high. On the 19th, at ten o'clock, we came in sight of land, and at three we reached some flat scattered islands, and sought shelter under one of them.

'The first object that met my eyes was a black, naked, Andamanese negro, then came another, and then several. They did not seem to trouble themselves much about us, and were gathering shell-fish on the shore. They did not appear to me to be of less than the ordinary height, walked very upright, and were, so far as I could see, unarmed. I looked at them through the telescope until they disappeared behind the bushes on shore.

'The islands were flat, but the upper part of them appeared to consist of loose stones. On one side there were caves here and there in the sandstone, which probably serve the savages for dwellings.

'I was very sorry that prudence forbade landing. I should so much have liked to see these specimens of humanity near.

'On the 20th we weighed anchor again, had a very severe passage, and were near being wrecked. We had only two fathoms of water, and the sea was very rough; an unlucky squall would certainly have wrecked the *Catharina*.

'The sun showed himself again on the 21st; the wind still blew very strong, but I carried out my intention of returning to the little island on which I sought a landing-place in vain yesterday. We steered towards it, and in an hour we cast anchor about 100 fathoms from the island on the south-west side. My wet paper was taken on shore to dry, and soon after I landed myself. On one side of us cliffs of black sandstone, about 100 feet high, rose from the otherwise flat ground.

'I followed the shore in this direction. As the tide was at the highest I got into a dense jungle, and found some large trees standing singly, of a peculiar species such as I had never seen—something like our finest oaks—belonging to the family of the *Guttifiræ* (perhaps a *Calophyllum?*). The Andamanese are said to live chiefly on the fruit. I could not eat it; it exudes a white substance like caoutchouc.

' The flat portions of these islands would be admirably adapted for cocoa-nut palms.

' Burmese and Malays land here. There are caves with valuable swallows' nests. Paddy husks, cocoa-nut shells, old palm-leaf roofs, and a well, show that vessels come here sometimes. Our sailors drank water all day.'

On the following day, the 22nd, the *Catharina* ran into the Andaman Straits, which cut the large Andaman Island in two. Helfer says :—

'There are not many straits like this; the current was so strong that it flowed from eight to ten knots an hour.

' After a sharp turn we got into a whirlpool, so that the captain was alarmed and dropped anchor. The vessel whirled round and round like a feather in the wind; the current rushed past like a mill-stream;

and our situation was most critical. We therefore weighed anchor again as soon as we could, and came through a narrow passage into a broad bay, where we could see the open sea.

'In the bay we observed two boats, which were steered towards us. Our captain took the crews for Andaman negroes, and got into a boat to go and meet them, while we prepared for a possible conflict; but on coming nearer they turned out to be Malays from Penang looking for birds' nests.

'We anchored at the head of the bay, and saw some Andamanese looking at us between the projecting rocks, armed with bows and arrows and spears. Some came down to the beach to stare at us, and one called out to us at the top of his voice. It was a good voice; we listened, but could not understand what he said. The captain went on shore to endeavour to effect an understanding; he soon returned, and reported that three savages with faces painted white were squatting on the ground, but he had not been able to make himself understood by them. My people were evidently afraid to come in contact with the savages. In order to provide against an attack by night, we weighed anchor again towards evening, but could scarcely find anchoring-ground at a distance of 200 paces from shore.

'The next day no islanders were to be seen. Under the shade of some of the pine-like trees with smooth stems and a fine transparent crown, four Malay boats were lying, whose crews were looking for periwinkles.

'On the 29th we saw three canoes with islanders going straight across the bay from east to west. We neared the land to within about 600 paces, which seemed to frighten them; for with their united forces they drew two of their canoes over the sand into the jungle, while the third disappeared in a channel towards the north-west. After we had cast anchor they called out to us, and we answered; some of them sprang from rock to rock to a point where they were directly opposite to the vessel.

'Our boat was lowered to land me. My pilot, who had been looking for periwinkles, told me that the most acceptable present to the Andamanese were cocoa-nuts, and I accordingly took some with me. Only one of the savages had courage to follow our boat along the beach; he was unarmed. We called out to him; he answered with animation, but in—to us—unintelligible sounds. The others were armed with bows and arrows, but kept behind the rocks. He made signs to us to land, but we did not trust him, and rowed to a promontory of rock. He waded through the water to us. I showed him the cocoa-nuts, whereupon he came within fifteen feet of us; we then threw them to him, and he adroitly caught them.

'He was a young man, well built, of middle size, quite naked, and nearly as black as a coal, but with a tinge of brown. His hair, shorn on both sides of his head, formed a curly woolly crest. His body was neither tattooed nor painted. He chattered a great deal, grinned with his white teeth, and laughed aloud. I laughed too, when he broke out into roars of laughter.

'We made him understand that we wanted water, and he showed us where it was to be found. Our second boat brought a large earthen jar; we threw it into the water, he caught it, another islander came to help him, and they went together to get water.

'I rowed to the vessel again and forbade my people to shoot, that the confidence just beginning might not be disturbed.

'My Malay captain took the savages a bowl of rice. The young man took it, and afterwards brought back the bowl filled with fresh water. One of my Malay boatmen jostled against him, and unfortunately the bowl was broken. After that the savages would not come near the boats any more, but only peeped at us from behind the rocks.

'I wanted to land at the place where the water was, but my people were afraid. At last I succeeded in overcoming their fears; the water casks were put into the boat, and we landed armed.

'The savages, about twenty in number, all ran to a point about 1,200 paces off, pulled their canoes out of the jungle, and disappeared behind a rock.

'It was fearfully hot, my head was burning.

'In about an hour I returned to the schooner. My people drank water till sunset. The savages appeared again from time to time.

'I wished to attempt communication with them again, and landed at a spot from which, not long before, I had seen smoke rising. The savages had just been encamping there, the fire was still glimmering. The shells of the cocoa-nuts, which we had given them in the morning, and among them bows and arrows for children, were lying about. Skulls and bones of turtles strung upon threads and hung on poles diffused a pestilential smell. Not seeing anyone I wandered along the sandy shore, into the wood, botanising.

'Our watch called out: "Kaffri, Kaffri!" He thought he saw the savages lying in wait in a threatening way behind the rocks, but all remained quiet. Evening drew on, and I went back to the vessel. The captain took another bowl of rice to the island, hoping to gain the confidence of the natives, but in vain; they ran away at his approach.

'We lay at anchor for the night. These, then, are the dreaded savages! They are timid children of Nature, happy when no harm is done to *them*. With a little patience it would be easy to make friends with them.'

These are the last words in Helfer's diary. They are characteristic of him as a persevering naturalist and philanthropist. With these words his career closed for ever!

The fatal morning dawned. The gloomy forebodings which I could not shake off when my husband was engaged in his daring explorations without me by his side, were to be terribly realised.

Deceived by the retreat of the islanders, which seemed to indicate fear rather than hostile intentions on their part, he resolved to make another attempt to establish friendly intercourse. Accompanied by the captain and eight sailors, he rowed to the sandy bank where the larger number had been assembled the day before. Several were standing there together, again naked and unarmed. The sailors showed them the cocoa-nuts they had brought in the boat, and a large vessel of rice, and beckoned to them to come. But instead of coming nearer they went further and further off, till they were concealed by a wood. Not apprehending any danger, Helfer was about to go further inland. Suddenly hosts of islanders, armed with spears and bows and arrows, came forth from behind heaps of stones and bushes, where they had been lying in ambush, and rushed upon the boat's crew with frightful yells. In order to give the natives no cause for distrust they had left their guns behind; they therefore had no means of defence, and were far outnumbered by the enemy, so that they were compelled to rapid flight. The boat capsized as they were hastily getting into it, and they had to swim to the vessel, which was some way off. The savages sent a shower of arrows after them from the shore. All escaped the fatal shots, except Helfer, who was an expert swimmer, and was in advance of the rest. A poisoned arrow pierced his head, he sank, and did not again come to the surface. All the efforts of his men to recover his body were fruitless. It could not be found to be committed to earth. No mound marks his resting-place. He was engulfed in the waters of the ocean, and his young and energetic existence would long ago have been forgotten if it were not still fresh in my remembrance, and if I had not raised a monument to his memory, very imperfect, indeed, but traced by the hand of affection, in the foregoing pages.

CHAPTER VIII.

CONTINUATION OF THE PLANTATION AT MERGUI.

BEFORE proceeding with my narrative, the arrival of my brother, Otto des Granges, at Mergui, must be mentioned ; this has not been noticed before as he had no direct influence on the course of events. He joined us shortly before the fatal catastrophe, the witness of which he was destined to be.

The labours in the plantation had grown beyond my powers, for Helfer's zeal in his scientific pursuits and faithful fulfilment of engagements left him neither leisure nor inclination for looking after his own interests. If this promising undertaking was to be carried on, if our plan was to be realised of making a permanent abode for ourselves, and a second home for many of our starving country people, in this splendid climate, amidst a friendly population, it was necessary to seek help from someone like-minded with ourselves. This I hoped to find in my youngest brother.

Educated in the Cadet House at Berlin, in his seventeenth year he had joined the 24th Regiment of Infantry as lieutenant. But the strict discipline of the Cadet Corps had not sufficed to curb his youthful spirits. His light-heartedness, his gifts, his honourable sentiment of fellowship, which not seldom caused him to stand up for others, and to be made a catspaw of, made him the favourite of his comrades, and even of his superiors, and they often only gave him fatherly advice instead of punishment when his spirits had carried him beyond bounds. It may readily be imagined that such a character would not patiently submit to the discipline and monotony of garrison life. He felt this himself; and when I asked him to join us at Mergui, he was ready at once to exchange the uniform of a Prussian officer for the planter's jacket.

It was shortly after Otto's arrival at Mergui that Helfer set out on his last fatal voyage. He proposed to his brother-in-law to accompany him, to which I readily acceded, for it was a comfort to think that in case of need my husband would not be without protection and assistance, and I was quite willing meanwhile to superintend the plantation alone.

Many Europeans, when new comers, especially young and vigorous people, suffer from carbuncular boils in all parts of the body. My brother was attacked with unusual severity during this expedition. Racked with pain and unable to move, he lay upon the deck of the little vessel, and was thus prevented from joining Helfer when he last rowed over to the Andaman Islands. He had to look on, unable to render any help, when, struck by the arrow, my husband sank beneath the waves.

After an absence of four weeks, my brother returned in the deepest gloom to Mergui. He had, however, recovered his health.

News of the arrival of the vessel in the harbour quickly reached my house, and I prepared eagerly to welcome the absentees. But my household had heard what had happened, and I was struck by their dejected looks. Instead of sharing my joy at the return of their master, to whom they were much attached, they avoided me, and seemed struck dumb. When I questioned anyone I received only unintelligible answers, until at length my brother stood before me and told me the terrible truth.

Over the next few days I must be allowed to draw a veil. Not in vain do words fail those who are smitten with the deepest grief; sorrow such as this belongs not to others: it must be borne alone.

When I was aroused from the lethargy into which I had fallen, and began to reflect, my unhappy position appeared clearly before my eyes.

I saw myself involved in a costly though promising undertaking, which it would require considerable means to carry out. Up to this time Helfer had provided them, but with his death the source was dried up. I was alone and helpless, in a strange land, without the means of paying hundreds of labourers their wages. My brother stood faithfully by me, but in one way his presence increased my cares. I had induced him to abandon his career in the Prussian army, and what recompense could I now offer him? And what was I to do, for with the then slow rate of communication a considerable time must elapse before I could even receive the necessary money from home to return to Europe?

But the very desperation of my situation, the imperative necessity to act, came to my aid.

It aroused my energies anew, and left me no time to dwell upon my grief. I was compelled to think and act. He only succumbs to sorrow on whom it imposes no necessity for action.

My thoughts were directed exclusively to the keeping up of the plantation which I wished to leave to my brother as a legacy from my husband. I acquainted Mr. Blondell, governor of the Tenasserim provinces, with this wish, for on hearing of Helfer's death he had hastened to Mergui, and proved himself an honourable and helpful friend. He arranged what was immediately necessary, and provided the sum needed to prevent the plantation from going down, but represented to me that I must at once exert myself to find capital to go on with, and this he thought could only be found in Calcutta.

After a hard struggle, therefore, I resolved upon a long absence from the spot endeared to me by the memory of many happy days and the brightest hopes. But no choice was left me.

Leaving the plantation in my brother's hands, I went first to Moulmein, to wait for a vessel bound for Calcutta. I met there with all the kindness shown us before, now mingled with the warmest sympathy; indeed, the compassionate looks bestowed upon me pierced me to the heart, for they perpetually recalled my great loss, and I could sometimes scarcely maintain my composure even in the presence of strangers.

The stormy season, during which the passage between Moulmein and Calcutta was almost entirely interrupted, had set in, and after waiting for weeks there was nothing to be done but to take passage in a coasting vessel for Rangoon. The voyage happily was not long, but I suffered extremely. The little vessel was so crammed with goods that there was scarcely room to sit down; and when, during rough weather, the only air-hole between decks was closed, the air was almost suffocating.

Rangoon, the capital of the former kingdom of Pegu, and now of the English province of that name, presents a curious aspect as seen from the sea. Immediately behind the town is a high hill; on this stands one of the largest and handsomest pagodas in India, and near it the wooden scaffolding with a powerful gong, whose silver tones, heard far and wide, accompany religious processions. The level ground between this hill and the sea is covered with bamboo houses on piles which sway to and fro in the breeze. At high tide the piles are under water, and the town appears to float on the sea. When it retreats, pools of salt water are left in the mud beneath the houses exhaling noxious vapours. All the refuse from the houses is thrown down between the wide spaces in the floors, and, worse than all, great quantities of fish refuse after preparing fish for exportation. No one unacquainted with the odour of decaying fish can form an idea of the smells here during low tide. Notwithstanding all this, however, and the fearful heat in the dry season, Rangoon is not unhealthy, nor the neighbourhood a hotbed of epidemics, while at Aracan, a few degrees farther north on the same coast, malignant fevers are constantly raging, so that the English garrison has to be relieved every month, and Europeans, who cultivate the tea-plant in the neighbouring province of Assam, often succumb to climatic influences. Even foreigners enjoy good health at Rangoon. The American Consul, in whose house Mr. Blondell's introduction secured me a most kind reception, told me that he had lived there twenty years, and had had no reason to complain of the climate. These are climatic enigmas which science has not yet succeeded in solving.

Rangoon is the chief place of export for goods from the interior of Burmah, the seat of a brisk trade, and therefore of several European Consulates.

A week passed before any opportunity occurred for proceeding to Calcutta. The vessel afforded rather more space and air than the coaster, but all comfort had to be dispensed with. Physical discomfort, however, formed a wholesome corrective to mental suffering. On landing at Calcutta, I for the first time experienced a sensation of pleasure, and thankfully turned my eyes to heaven.

Many of my former friends had in the meantime left Calcutta. Some had returned to Europe; but I did not fail to find sympathy and hospitality. Lord Auckland, the Governor-General, received me with special kindness; he assured me that he would do all in his power to relieve my anxieties, a promise which he honestly fulfilled, but even the power of a Governor-General had its limits imposed by the Court of Directors in Downing Street.

The great Anglo-Indian Empire having been founded as a commercial speculation, commercial interests continued to be the mainspring with the Directors of the East India Company so long as their monopoly lasted. They only undertook and promoted schemes which promised immediate return or good interest.

Helfer and I had appropriated the land at Mergui, and begun a costly plantation on it without considering it necessary to obtain any kind of title to the property. There was unowned land in abundance on the coast of Malacca, and its cultivation, the improvement of native methods, and the introduction of useful products, appeared to us a praiseworthy object. Anyone who chose could then, for instance, sow a plot of land that was lying fallow with rice, and his possession was seldom or never disputed. Now that Moulmein rice is a valuable article of English commerce, this state of things may be materially altered.

Lord Auckland promised to exert all his influence with the Directors in London to obtain for me a grant whereby the area of 4,000 acres should be secured to me and my heirs for ninety-nine years. Further than this his influence did not extend, however much he was himself convinced of the importance and future profitableness of the undertaking, and of the advantage it might be in increasing the productiveness of the province in the future. He had no funds at his disposal for a loan for carrying on the undertaking.

As, therefore, no pecuniary aid was to be had from the Government for my plans, I had to try to find private capital. I succeeded in interesting the husband of one of my friends, Mr. Theodore Dickens, partner in the banking-house of Ferguson and Co., in the enterprise. Having made precise calculation as to the prospect of a good return, he was willing to become a partner in the property and in carrying on the plantation.

I immediately sent for my brother, and on his arrival we entered into partnership on the following terms :—

Mr. Dickens undertook to advance all the money necessary for the cultivation and development of the plantation. To supply my brother, who was to remain at Mergui, as manager and overseer, with suitable means of living, and to pay me a not inconsiderable sum per annum. On the other hand, a proportionate share of the future returns was secured to him.

Thus, as I supposed, the prosperity of the plantation and my brother's support were well provided for.

CHAPTER IX.

THE HEALTH RESORT, DARJEELING.

Up to this time I had been in a state of continual excitement, which had lent extraordinary elasticity to my bodily powers.

But now a reaction set in; my strength diminished day by day, and my friends were seriously alarmed. Several physicians were consulted, and all agreed that I must leave Calcutta without delay, for recovery was only to be hoped for from a change of climate.

The nearest health resort to Calcutta, is Darjeeling, 400 miles to the north. It lies on the boundaries of Nepaul and Bhootan, on the western slopes of the Himalayahs, on an isolated ridge 8,000 feet high. The English bought it, in 1835, from the Rajah of Sikim, for a sanitary station. It is reached by way of Moorshedabad, 125 miles from Calcutta, the former capital of the Nabob of Bengal, where Lord Clive, after the victory of Plassey, found such vast treasures of gold, silver, and jewels, that he not only sent vast sums to the Company, but enriched himself and his friends. The succeeding Nabob was deposed, but received from England an annual pension of six lacs of rupees. I saw his heir, who was under English guardianship, at the races at Calcutta, by the side of Lord Auckland, who showed him princely honours. He was then a youth of from fourteen to sixteen years of age, and his property was increasing enormously during his minority.

There was a posting route between Calcutta and Darjeeling by means of palanquins; that is, the authorities provided the necessary number of bearers for the whole route from station to station. The traveller had nothing to do but to make himself as comfortable as he could. Ladies who had often made the journey gave me a satisfactory account of travelling 'per dack,' and I knew from experience that English travelling arrangements might be relied on. When, therefore, Mrs. Lloyd, a friend of mine, informed me of her safe arrival at Darjeeling, and invited me to be her guest, my last scruples were overcome. On a sultry afternoon, in August 1840, I entered my palanquin, four black bearers took it on their shoulders, and carried it off at a short trot.

The traveller cannot have any luggage with him, except a few trifling things, among which is a Chinese sunshade of oiled paper on a long bamboo handle, used for shelter in getting in and out. All other effects were packed in square boxes in tin frames carried by special bearers.

You generally set out between four and five p.m., when the sun has begun to sink, and travel through the night until eight or nine a.m., resting in some cool spot during the day. Invalids, however, generally only make half a day's or rather night's journey.

At many of the places which I passed civil or

military government officers were stationed. These Europeans, living among a native population, live very monotonous lives, so that the arrival of a stranger with a white skin is a most welcome variety. Most of them were apprised of my coming through the orders for relays, so that when the bearers set me down before the elegant and comfortable villas, the inmates met me, though a total stranger, with a hearty welcome.

The thing the traveller most longs for, after having been exposed to the burning heat of the plains of Bengal, is a bath. And a bath, justly placed by Homer among the first duties of hospitality, was always prepared for me, and then a fragrant and elegant breakfast. Thus refreshed, I endeavoured to show my gratitude by telling the news from Calcutta, giving an account of myself, and answering all inquiries with hearty good-will. Then, after an hour's repose, we met round the well-furnished dinner table, to which the rich fruit of the tropics lent a special charm. Quite contrary to usual English manners, a friendly and confidential tone was quickly assumed, and when the fresh bearers came, towards evening, for the start, I could see that my new friends would willingly have kept the parting guest for several days, who had relieved the monotony of their lives for a few hours.

The plains of Bengal have little in the way of the picturesque to offer. As far as the eye can reach you see nothing but fields of rice, cotton, or indigo plantations. I lost nothing therefore by travelling mostly by night. But the recumbent position, which I had found comfortable enough for short distances in Calcutta, became almost intolerable for a continuance from the peculiar gait of the bearers. They make within a given time two short and one long step, and continually shift the pole on which the palanquin rests from one shoulder to the other. The person inside is thereby kept in a perpetual rocking and jolting motion; there is no pause even at the stations, for the fresh bearers stand ready bent to take the palanquin, without even putting it to the ground, and on they go in the same short trot. A week's journey in a palanquin, without halt, is said to be dangerous, not only to patients suffering from nervous irritation, but even to healthy persons.

On the morning of the fourth day halt was made at a place where no English official was stationed. The residence of the district governor was some distance off, so that the palanquin was set down in the open air, under the shade of palm trees and bananas. I was soon surrounded by a host of black men, women, and children, the various marks on their foreheads and breasts indicating their caste. As they spoke only the dialect of the Bengal common people, I had no means of making myself understood by them. And what aid could I expect from people who shunned all contact with me as pollution? In vain I made signs to the women nearest me that I wanted something to eat and to drink. They only shook their heads and did not stir. I offered money, but no one would take it from my hand; when I threw it on the ground, however, it was picked up by some of the children.

My appetite was becoming more and more importunate, when a young woman drew near carrying a little child. Her slender form, covered only with an apron about the hips, was faultless, but her small hands and feet were not adorned with the rings which the Indian women wear. I made signs of eating, when she nodded and disappeared, but returned in a little while followed by a young man, probably her husband. He laid a kid at my feet, while she pointed to the cooking utensils she had brought with her. Before I could look round, the man had cut the animal's throat and begun to skin it. From this I saw that these two well made people, with their soft velvet skins, must be pariahs, for no Hindoo belonging to either of the other four castes would have thought it compatible with his dignity to prepare food for a white person; I believe they would sooner have let me starve. It is a melancholy truth that nothing so hardens the heart as religious fanaticism.

Some hours had passed by this time without a sign of the fresh bearers, and I began to be very anxious. They took no more heed of my desire to go on than of my need of food. But on my making signs of writing, a man drew near in a flowing white muslin robe, bound round with a girdle, in which an ink bottle was placed; he was probably the schoolmaster. Drawing a sheet of paper and a pointed reed out of his bosom, he handed them to me, and I wrote as well as I could a few lines to the English district governor to acquaint him with my situation. Happily, for good pay a lad undertook to carry the note.

The pariah had meanwhile cut the kid in pieces, and his wife had improvised a fireplace with stones, in which a bright fire was soon burning. She put the best pieces, with a good portion of rice, into the pot; and the other ingredients of an Indian curry—cocoanut oil, coriander seeds, ginger, and spices—were not wanting. It was a pleasure to watch the graceful movements of her naked form; and her eagerness to refresh a hungry stranger, compared with the proud callousness of the Hindoos, made her seem like a good Samaritan.

But before the curry was ready a troop of horsemen came trotting up. It was the district governor in person, accompanied by his underlings and servants. After making I know not what apologies for this unfortunate and unheard of incident, he invited me to his house, where a meal fit for a European awaited me. Even in his eyes the pariah was an unclean being, from whose hands you could not take food; at any rate, his servants would have refused me their services if they had seen me take food prepared by her. So I had to forego partaking of the fragrant curry, and to re-enter my palanquin; not, of course, without nodding thanks and adieux to the merciful pariah pair. After another hour I was compensated for my anxiety by a refreshing bath, cool rooms, and a tempting repast in the district governor's house.

I was now only separated from the Himalayahs by the jungle at their base. The jungle here, watered by mountain streams not dry even during the hot season, is an almost impenetrable mass of tangled vegetation, from the lofty bamboo to the most elegant climbing plants; and it is therefore the favourite haunt of wild beasts, who lurk for their prey in the thickets. They serve the Bengal tiger especially as a capital hunting-ground.

At table the gentlemen recounted numerous stories of encounters with the dreaded monarch of the jungle; the master of the house boasted that he killed one almost every Sunday. There was no church in the neighbourhood, and he thought that he could not keep Sunday better than by fighting these dangerous beasts.

As before, I set out between four and five; I preferred traversing even the jungle in the night, to being exposed all day to the stifling heat. Besides the bearers, two men were given me as a convoy—each carrying a lantern at the end of a long pole—one going before, and the other behind the palanquin, to scare away the tigers by the light as well as by loud cries uttered from time to time. In spite of all these precautions, as may be supposed, I was uneasy enough; sleep fled from my eyes, and I thanked God when in the morning we reached the end of the jungle without any disaster, and were soon at the station.

From this point the path up the mountain on which Darjeeling stands begins to rise; the palanquin travelling comes to an end, and I was glad enough to be relieved from the six days' torture, and to mount a horse.

The narrow mountain path wound under the shade of thick and ever varying foliage. The air became more and more cool and invigorating. At a height of about 4,000 feet there was a vista, through which the plain could be seen stretching as far as the eye could reach, glowing in tropical hues, with its palm forests, plantations, and settlements. Looking upwards, the eye ranged over the slopes, clothed with white, lilac, and rose-coloured rhododendrons, which grow here to large trees, to the mountain tops veiled in blue mist beyond. It was a most enjoyable ride.

Further up, vegetation gradually loses its tropical character and approaches that of the temperate zone. Here and there a stunted oak grows in layers of humus, and round Darjeeling itself, peaches, apricots, pears, and even some European vegetables, thrive.

Darjeeling, at that time, consisted of a military hospital with the barracks belonging to it, round which a few English families, attracted by the climate, had built bungalows and laid out gardens. The temperature falls so low in winter that now and then a few flakes of snow float in the air and fall as raindrops. It has since grown to a considerable place, with churches, schools, theatre, and assembly rooms, and the Governor-General has a residence there. Round about there are 12,000 acres of tea plantations, yielding annually 2,600,000 lbs. of tea.

I met with a cordial reception in Mrs. Lloyd's house, and enjoyed intercourse with a small circle of amiable people, consisting—besides my hostess—of Mrs. Napier, her husband, the military governor, and Mr. Campbell, commissioner at Darjeeling, afterwards Governor of Bengal.

In the enjoyment of the repose of which I had so long been deprived, and in this salubrious climate, my health of body and mind visibly improved. My new friends, observing this, tried to induce me to remain there; Mr. Campbell even gave me a lot on which to build a house, at that time granted to anyone, gratuitously, who would engage to cultivate it within two years. Thus, for the second time, and now without my own seeking, I became a landowner on the furthest verge of the Anglo-Indian Empire.

But not all the advantages which combined to induce me to live a quiet life here, far from the world, could extinguish my longing to see my native land and my mother once more. Moreover, I had engaged to negotiate in person with the directors in London for the grant of the plantation at Mergui.

With a divided heart, therefore, and with the intention of returning and bringing my relations with me, I resolved to return to Europe for about a year.

Up to this time I had never seen the Himalayan snows unveiled. But shortly before I left, this rare and splendid sight was vouchsafed to me. On a height above Darjeeling there was a ruined Buddhist convent, from which there was an unobstructed, distant view, and I had therefore often visited the spot. But the mountain chain, which closed in the panorama towards north and east, was always veiled in mist. On one of the last days of my stay, I climbed up once more to take leave of my favourite point. At first there was a little rain, but just as I reached the top, the mist parted, as if a curtain had been drawn aside, and the snow and ice-clad peaks stood clearly defined before my eyes, in the roseate hues of the setting sun, Kinchin

Junga, 28,176 feet high, towering majestically in their midst. The unbroken series of lower ranges, partly clothed with sombre foliage, partly with flowering trees, formed a charming contrast of colour. I lingered long over this sublime scene, and never will it fade from my memory.

The day fixed for my departure had arrived. Rain clouds were gathering in the sky, but I could not delay it, because the bearers were bespoken for the whole journey to Calcutta. To my surprise, Mr. Campbell offered to accompany me as far as the first station. I protested, pointing to the threatening clouds; but he insisted on showing me this chivalrous attention, and I could but be glad of his escort. It was getting dusk when we reached the station. Mr. Campbell took tea with me, but then ordered his horse, to return to Darjeeling, in spite of the rain and darkness. My remonstrances were vain; although there was a separate bungalow, he considered that it would have been a breach of decorum to pass the night at the station. When we parted, I expressed a hope that we should meet again, but had, even then, a presentiment that it would not be fulfilled. And it was not so. I have only followed from a distance the career of this distinguished man.

The next morning I had again to enter the uncomfortable palanquin, and proceeded as before, only more quickly, as it was down hill. I found the relays of bearers waiting at the stations, so that I hoped to perform the journey without any difficulty. But not far from Boglipoor, I was awakened, in the middle of the night, by a rough jolt of the palanquin. On opening the door, I found that I must be close to the Ganges, for I could hear the rush of the waters. I looked round for the bearers. They were standing, a little apart, talking eagerly to each other in a low voice. On seeing me, they pretended to be quite exhausted, and gave me to understand that we were at the station, where they were to be relieved. But no fresh bearers were there, and, knowing that the posting arrangements were to be relied on, I at once saw that they were deceiving me, and that it was a trick to extort money. Perhaps it might have succeeded, had I not remembered the oft-repeated warning, that the traveller should never let money be seen on the journey. I jumped out of the palanquin, drew the long bamboo staff out of the sunshade, waved it over the heads of the rebels, and ordered them, in English, in a loud voice, to carry me on. They looked at each other in amazement. They had, obviously, not expected this coolness from a woman. I got quietly in again, and with hastened steps, in order that I might not report them, they carried me on to the real station, where the relays were punctually waiting. I am convinced that, under the circumstances, my mode of proceeding was the right one, because it alone would have saved me. Whether it was unwomanly, whether true womanliness suffers detriment when a woman grasps the stick in self-defence, I must leave to others.

I reached Calcutta, restored to health, and much invigorated. Having arranged my affairs to my satisfaction, nothing stood in the way of my voyage to

Europe. There was then no regular steam communication *viâ* Suez, and sailing vessels seldom took this course. I could not make up my mind to a three months' voyage round the Cape, and, fortunately, I found a party of the same mind, and we, eighteen persons in all, hired a sailing vessel for the voyage to Suez for 3,600*l.*

It was in October 1841, that I went on board, sad in the presentiment that I was perhaps leaving India for ever, where I had enjoyed much happiness, and to which many bonds of friendship endeared me; but, on the other hand, there was the pleasurable excitement of the prospect of seeing my native land, and once more embracing my loved ones there. The motion of the vessel, however, soon put an end to all reflections, and sent me to my cabin, which, thanks to the kindness of friends, was on deck, and afforded me fresh air and a look out.

CHAPTER X.

IN EGYPT.

AFTER a favourable voyage of six weeks we saw land, the shores of Arabia Felix. A short halt was made at Aden, whence, driven by the south-east monsoon, we entered the Red Sea. On account of gales from the north-west from June to October, and from the south-east from October to May, it is most difficult, almost impossible, for sailing vessels to enter the Red Sea during the first period, or to get out during the second. We were in the south-east period, and our ship entered with difficulty. She tacked about between the Arabian and African coast, and enabled me to see how different these countries must be from that which I had just left.

I had an ardent desire to continue the journey by land and down the Nile, and to see the monuments of Egypt, which had occupied my imagination from childhood. This wish was echoed by Mr. and Mrs. Prinsep, who, tired of India, were returning from Calcutta with two children, and we resolved to land at Kosseir, and to go thence through the desert to Kenneh, the nearest point on the Nile, and then down the river to Cairo.

In very early times Kosseir was a considerable seat of commerce. Later, the pilgrims to Mecca from all parts of Africa used to congregate here to cross over to the grave of the Prophet. Curiously enough, it is here also that the Ghawazi, the notorious dancing women of the East, carry on their wildest and most immoral orgies.

We had fortunately taken the precaution of asking the captain to let us have our share of the provisions, or we should have fared badly in the desert, for the wants of Europeans were not at that time to be met at Kosseir. All the help we could get from the English consul, a native, was that he procured donkeys for us, and a tachterdervan for the Prinsep's children. This is a box with a shade over it, long enough for two children to lie down in. It is suspended between two camels, one following the other, and as they step together with the right or left feet, it is kept in a perpetual jolt. Our asses were of the smallest and weakest sort, so that Mr. Prinsep's feet reached the ground.

Immediately on leaving Kosseir, the stony path led into a valley of rocks with numerous branches, the walls of which, consisting of porphyry of various colours, glittered like jewels in the sun. There was the red kind, of which the obelisk of Sixtus V. and other monuments at Rome are built, the black with veins of white spar, not less valuable, the violet, brown, grey, and emerald green, producing a charming play of colour, like the palace of diamonds in the story of Haroun-al-Raschid.

The children did not seem very comfortable in their jolting tachterdervan; we soon heard them sighing and groaning and crying out for water. We, too, were glad when we could alight from our asses, and proceed on foot. During the whole of the second day the air had been very sultry, making our march most fatiguing. Towards evening we saw our guide, who was a few steps in advance, fall on his knees, exclaiming, 'Allah! Allah!' and raising his hands in prayer. Just then one of the camel drivers pointed to his brown hand moistened by a drop of rain. The heavens had opened after a three years' drought, and moistened the parched earth, though with but a few large drops. What a contrast to the happier regions I had left, where rain and sunshine alternate at longer or shorter intervals, and lend inexhaustible fertility to the soil.

On the evening of the fourth day's march we reached Kenneh, and the green shores of the Nile. As Mr. Prinsep did not wish to miss the sailing of the *Oriental* from Alexandria to England, very little time was unfortunately left us for inspecting the Egyptian antiquities. Even of Thebes we could take but a superficial view.

It would be presumptuous of me to attempt any description of the monuments of Egypt after the cursory view which was all I could take of them. I must refer the reader to the numerous works based on thorough investigation of them.

The extensive tombs of the kings in Bab-el-Meluk, the Valley of Death, extending northwards from Thebes in weird desolation, between bare, yellowish brown rocks, impressed me deeply. Not a sound breaks the solemn silence, not a blade of grass springs up on the stony soil; sky, earth, and air seem to be of one monotonous hue, and everything as if petrified into one gigantic tomb. About two miles from the entrance the valley is closed in by circling cliffs 1,000 feet high, and in this perpendicular wall the kings of Egypt built their labyrinthine tombs thousands of years ago. Here the body was to be preserved from corruption till the purified soul was to be reunited to it for everlasting life. Do not these costly works, the sole object of which was to preserve intact the dwelling place of the soul, tell us how deeply the hope of personal life after death is rooted in the mind of man?

From the third century after Christ pious Christian hermits began to retire into the Egyptian tombs, and from this, as is well known, monasticism took its rise. With my cheerful and sociable disposition I never could understand before how men could voluntarily renounce the world and all communion with their fellows, but I now began to comprehend it. Amidst these stern and lifeless aspects of nature, where no events attract the attention, the mind is necessarily turned in upon itself. A longing came over me to end my days here given up to meditation. I was, however, roused from these dreams by my companion, but left the spot with reluctance.

We began the voyage on the Nile in two dahabeeyahs, one for the Prinsep family, the other for myself and my servant. From a distance the river looks blue, but near, the waters are thick and yellowish.

The boats flew quickly down the stream, too quickly for my desire to see more of the numerous monuments than can be seen from the river. The beautiful green of the sycamores, acacias, and date palms gave the shores a very pleasant aspect. The latter, however, had no charm for my eye, accustomed to tropical growths; compared with the lofty and slender growth of the cocoa-nut palm they looked like stunted dwarfs. The Nile crocodile, on the contrary, which we often saw lying stretched on the sand, holding two of his short paws in the air and sunning his thick, whitish body, is much larger than the Indian alligator. In this position he looks like a fat pig, if you can fancy one from twenty to thirty feet long. In spite of his long, thick body the crocodile is very agile, and his senses are so acute that, when apparently asleep, he hears the least noise of anyone approaching, and escapes danger by plunging into the water. No ball will pierce his skin, so that he can only be killed by a shot in the eye.

The rafts made of pots and jugs which one sees on the Nile are very peculiar. The manufacture of pottery is an important branch of industry in Upper Egypt. When a quantity of articles are ready for export, thousands of pots and jugs of all sizes, with their openings closed over, and fastened together by their handles, are floated down the stream with the help of people on the shore.

We landed in the harbour of Siout, the most important city of Upper Egypt, which we had seen long before, at intervals, peeping out from its green gardens.

Its minarets and cupolas, its mosques and houses of stone, give it a stately appearance. The lively streets, the gates adorned with marbles of various colours, the curiously carved window gratings and balconies of the wealthy bazaar, give a foretaste of the Arabian quarter in Cairo. All the races of Upper and Lower Egypt meet at Siout: Nubians, known by their curious way of wearing their hair, which they wind into stiff little spiral tails, just like the ancient Egyptians, hanging in rows round the head; Arabians, Copts, Bedouins, the lords of the desert, a few Turks and gipsies, who, as in Europe, are travelling tinkers. Among them all rides the richly clad official upon a handsomely caparisoned horse, making way for himself among the crowd.

In the midst of this throng march long rows of heavily laden camels; and on the bales of goods sits enthroned a man with fine features and sparkling eyes, clad in a white burnoose, a figure who always seemed to me to wear a strange and mystic aspect, as if he came out of the Thousand and One Nights.

The situation of Siout must be remarkably healthy, for the plague which often desolates Lower Egypt had never entered the walls. Many people from Cairo, therefore, and other infected places, take refuge here when an outbreak occurs, and escape quarantine, which to a faithful Mussulman is peculiarly repulsive, as a precaution of man's taking.

Among all the races mingling here, the Copts interested me the most. Clad in long black robes, they wander through the streets with downcast looks, as if lost in thought, apparently taking no account of the external world, though really nothing escapes their watchful black eyes. They are descendants of the ancient Egyptian population of Caucasian race, with strongly marked, intelligent-looking features, unmistakably indicating their origin, although they have not kept distinct from the immigrated races. They have remained true to the Christian faith, notwithstanding the humiliations to which they have been subjected by fanatical Mohammedans. Their Christianity consists, however, rather in form than in any deep recognition of Christian truth and doctrine, for their ideas and practices are scarcely less superstitious than those of the non-Christian inhabitants. The Coptic language, with slight deviations, identical with the ancient Egyptian, is no longer spoken, but is exclusively used in divine worship, particularly by the priests in the temples. The number of Coptic Christians is much diminished by cruel persecutions, but the numerous ruins of Coptic churches and convents in the desert, show that their number must have been much greater, and that they must at one time have practised their worship unmolested. Two convents remain to this day on the borders of the desert, the white convent, Deir-el-Abiad, and the red, Deir-el-Achmar, which both enjoy the odour of sanctity.

The Copts now mostly live in the villages of Upper and Central Egypt. Some devote themselves to learning, but in a very limited and one-sided way; they are the scribes of the country, and are often employed as clerks and officials. In recent times the attention of

Christian missions has been much directed to the Copts. May success attend their efforts!

The most dangerous spot on the Nile, where the wall of rock, Gebel-Abu-Fodd, rises perpendicularly out of the river, was safely passed by our boats. Sudden squalls often arise here, which are dangerous to larger vessels, and have wrecked many dahabeeyahs. Thousands of vultures, eagles, black geese, ducks, &c., build in the clefts of the rock, and when startled by a shot, with its thundering echoes, they swarm like a cloud round the top. The caves and fissures at the base of the cliff are the haunts of crocodiles, and they take their siesta, or as the Orientals call it, their 'kef,' on the burning rocks.

At Memphis I admired most the colossal statue of Ramesis II., sixty feet high, the great Sesostris, the same which was seen by Herodotus, Diodorus, and Strabo, standing before the temple of Hephæstos—Ptah, and of which the father of history relates, that when Darius wanted to set up his statue before it, the priests of Ptah would not permit it, because Darius 'had not performed any deeds like Sesostris.' The colossus consists of one block of fine-grained limestone; the features are wanting, but it is otherwise well preserved. On the legs there are figures of a prince and princess in bas-relief. On the shield and girdle of the otherwise naked figure are the shields of Ramesis II.

Before leaving Memphis we were surprised by a curious sight, which I describe with some hesitation, as I have not found it mentioned in any work on Egypt that I have seen. Two Arabs, observing us wandering about the ruins, told us through our guides that for a suitable backsheesh they would show us much more wonderful things. We accepted the offer, and the men, having procured torches, led us to a mass of stone buried to a considerable height in sand; but whether it was an isolated rock, or a mass of ancient masonry, I could not make out. A small opening was half choked with sand. Through this the Arabs crept, lying flat on the ground, and told us to follow in the same way. But this was easier said than done. I could not succeed in making any progress on the loose yielding sand, until one of the Arabs seized me by the shoulders and pulled me in. Mr. Prinsep had to submit to the same process. When within, the torches were lighted, and we could see a narrow passage close to us leading into the depths below.

Supported by the Arabs, and carefully placing one foot after another on stones projecting from the walls we climbed down. We were in the catacombs of the Ibis, the sacred bird of Egypt. There were piles of Ibis mummies, heaped up on both sides of long passages, here preserved from corruption for ages. We could not of course stay long in the close air of these subterranean passages. For an addition to the pay, I was allowed to take away a number of these embalmed birds, and two of them are in my possession to this day.

The great sphinx of Gizeh belongs undoubtedly to the most remarkable monuments of the world. The face, turned towards the East, deprived of the nose, has rather the Ethiopian cast of countenance, but if you imagine it with the nose restored, the pure Egyptian type is unmistakable.

We again floated down the stream in our dahabeeyahs, and soon caught sight of the pyramids, which we had been eagerly looking for. Seen from a distance they neither appeared so high nor so large as I had imagined. Standing as they do alone in the sandy waste there is nothing with which to compare them. It was not till I stood at the base of the pyramid of Cheops, and beheld the length of the sides, the massive blocks, and raised my eyes to the top, where men looked like specks, that I realised its immensity, and felt the solemnity of these monuments of history. Far as our thoughts carry us back into antiquity, the pyramids are always in the background as seen by Moses a thousand years after the foundation of the Pyramid of Cheops.

I was looking with longing eyes, yet with some hesitation, at the top. Who would not wish to have been there? Our officious Arab guides tried to persuade me by pantomimic gestures that the ascent was easy, and without waiting for my consent, two of them seized me and lifted me up the first step, while a third pushed behind, something as masons hand tiles to one another in building. It would be almost impossible for a woman to climb the crumbling steps, mostly three or four feet high, alone, but with the help of the Arabs I did not find it such a very great exertion. It required some stoicism to see certain insects creeping out of the dirty shirts of these people, crawling up their tawny arms, and finding a resting place in my sleeves, but the thought that I was ascending the pyramid reconciled me even to this.

Mr. Prinsep thought it beneath his dignity to accept

the help of a guide, but was scarcely half way up when he called out for assistance. Arab girls, however, sprang up the steps by our sides like gazelles, gracefully holding a pitcher of water on their heads with one hand, in order to earn a bit of money for the draught which the thirsty strangers would want on the top.

At length the plateau was reached. The magnificent panorama defies description. Language fails and man must be silent when the world's history, with its vast changes, revolutions, and races, passes as it were in review before his eyes. In this frame of mind it appeared most contemptible to me to see the name of Prince Pückler-Muskau cut upon a vast block of stone, thirty feet long. I am told that this then isolated desecration has since become common.

Although very tired, I could not forego going into the interior of the pyramid, but found it not less difficult than the ascent, for from the lowness of the passages you have to stoop, and to avoid slipping on the sloping stone you must hold fast the arm of the guide, who treads much more firmly with his naked feet. Nor does the interior reward you for your labour, interesting as it is to the archæologist.

Exhausted by the exertions and new and powerful impressions of the last few days, I needed repose; this I enjoyed in the house of the Austrian Consul, Baron Laurin, and his wife, who was a Levantine lady. The Baron was one of the circle of friends with whom, years before, Dr. Helfer had spent many happy hours in Sicily, and recurring to the pleasures of that time he invited me to be his guest during my stay at Cairo. A peculiar combination of European solidity with Oriental luxury, made this house one of the pleasantest and most comfortable which I have met with in my travels.

My servant had only accompanied me from Calcutta on condition that she should be sent back from Cairo. She was, therefore, now dismissed, and an Abyssinian slave was given me for a waiting maid. I shall never forget the fine features, the gentle expression, the dark eyes and long lashes of this girl. Although we could not communicate by words, there was soon a good understanding between us. I incidentally said to Baron Laurin how much I liked her, when he at once proposed to give her to me. He called her in and introduced me as her new mistress, whom she would have to accompany over the sea to Europe. The lovely creature sadly bent her head, crossed her arms over her breast, and murmured: 'The master's will is law to me.' But tears began to flow, and deep grief was reflected in her countenance. Fond as I had become of her, of course I could not think of taking her with me against her will. I begged the Baron, if he was willing to grant her her liberty, to send her home to her people.

Before I had had time to devote proper attention to the sights of Cairo, the bell of the *Oriental* sounded for the departure for England, and the coasts of Egypt soon vanished from view.

CHAPTER XI.

IN LONDON.

THE numerous passengers by the *Oriental*, although nearly all English, divided themselves into sundry well-defined groups, according to their standing, culture, or family connections, and these distinctions became more apparent as we neared old England. In the far East, when people are limited for social intercourse to but few of their countrymen, the only whites perhaps within a circuit of a hundred miles, where people are drawn together by similar aims, joys, sorrows, and privations, the finer shades of respectability, so called, are not so precisely observed. Now, on returning to the land of rigid propriety and manifold social restraints, it was necessary to loosen the ties formed in India, when they did not accord with the position of the parties in the English social hierarchy. To observe the way in which this was done within the narrow bounds of shipboard, how, without transgressing the forms of good society, people contrived to withdraw from their former friends, was to me, who had no part in it, very diverting, and afforded me ample material for the study of human weakness and vanity.

In one feeling all were agreed, in the pleasure of

nearing their native land, and impatience hourly increased. Here was a man who had not seen his wife and children for ten years or more, and had borne for their sakes the perils of the climate, and often deprivation of all social intercourse. Here a mother who had sent her daughter to England years before, counting the minutes till she should clasp her, no longer a child, in her arms. Here a young man who went to India with a beloved image in his heart, returning with the fruits of his labours to claim her as his bride; there another in joyful anticipation of greeting the parents whom he had scarcely hoped to see again. Here is a veteran, grown grey in the service of forty years, at last returning to enjoy his wealth in the home of his youth. These people are mostly bitterly disappointed; long unused to the English climate, mode of life, and social habits, irritable from illness and climatic effects, accustomed to be surrounded by obsequious servants, they are become quite impracticable for English life, and have acquired the nickname of 'Tigers.'

Among all these people, full of hope and expectation, I stood alone, with a bitter feeling of isolation. It must have been depicted in my countenance, for all showed sympathy and pity, and various recommendations were given me for suitable accommodation in London, most of which, however, were not suitable at all.

A small packet boat was sent from London with letters for the passengers on board the steamer, the approach of which had been signalled. No sooner was the letter bag brought on board than all streamed down into the cabin, where its contents were to be distributed. I followed, although reflecting that there could be no letter for me, for who was there to write to me? We assembled round the large table, Sir Edward Rayne at the head, a worthy old gentleman who had long held the office of chief judge in India, and had retired with a high reputation. He deliberately opened the bag, and calling out the address in a loud voice, handed each letter to its owner. The distribution lasted nearly an hour; many had withdrawn to the deck or their cabins to read their letters undisturbed. Sir Edward then called out in a loud voice, holding up a letter, 'Mrs. Helfer.' I thought there must be some mistake; the letter was handed to me, it really bore my correct address, and to my still greater astonishment, the seal of the Prussian embassy in London. I hastily tore open the envelope, and found an autograph letter from my patroness, the Princess William of Prussia, accompanied by a cordial invitation from Baron Bunsen to take up my quarters at the Prussian Embassy, in Carlton House Terrace. How shall I describe the change wrought all at once by this letter? The lonely compassionated widow was transplanted, as if by magic, into London high life, was to reside in the best part of St. James's Park, to be entertained by the Prussian Ambassador, was honoured by an autograph letter from a Princess, and was to be presented at the English Court. I rose, all at once, many degrees in the scale of respectability with the English, who prize high connection above all things. Those who had regarded me only with pity, or ignored me altogether before, now came to offer their congratulations, and felt honoured by my acquaintance. I thought of the shoemaker's boy, who found himself Khaliph one fine morning, and was ready to ask, as he did: 'Am I myself or not?' I no longer dreaded my arrival in the great city.

The house of Baron Bunsen and his excellent wife not only offered all the material comforts that could be desired, but an intellectual treat of the rarest kind. Attracted by Bunsen's extensive and various learning, his incomparable powers of conversation and fine social tact, the most eminent men of learning and letters frequented his house. I made their acquaintance and was permitted to listen to their intellectual discourse.

Thanks to the introduction of the Princess William, the Court circle, and the houses of the first nobility were opened to me. I was received by the Duchess of Kent, honoured by a call from the Duke and Duchess of Sutherland, and invited to attend a drawing room of Her Majesty the Queen. This is, perhaps, the most splendid court ceremony that can be witnessed. The Queen stood under a canopy in front of the throne, on her right the royal princes and princesses, on her left the ladies of the ministers and ambassadors. I made a profound obeisance to the Queen, taking hold of the edge of her robe, and, with a graceful bend, she gave me her hand to kiss. As one of those presented by the Prussian Ambassador, I was privileged to enter the ranks of ladies belonging to the diplomatic circles to the left of the throne. Otherwise it requires great skill to retire without turning your back on the Queen, or entangling your feet in the long train. From my post

I could see all the ladies pass close by, and admire their toilettes, sparkling with diamonds. All seemed to have carefully studied the prescribed ceremonies, except one young lady from the country, who so lost her self-possession, that she hurried past the Queen without bowing, stumbled over her train, and sank almost fainting into the arms of a chamberlain, who came to the rescue.

I had afterwards the honour of being introduced to the Prince Consort at a court ball. He was interested in hearing the opinion of a German on Indian affairs, and we should probably have had a longer conversation, had not the Prince been just then summoned to the Queen.

But neither the pleasure of the select society in Bunsen's house, nor social entertainments, could make me forget the objects of my visit to London. These were to obtain the grant which would secure the land to me at Mergui, and, by the advice of my friends, to present a claim for a widow's pension from the directors of the E. I. C. It was a very tedious business. As to the grant, negotiations had to be carried on between the directors in Downing Street and the Indian Government, as well as between the latter and the local authorities in Malacca, and the colony not being then, as now, connected by a line of steamers, the time occupied was incalculable. The secretary of the Company, Mr. Melville, therefore, though very friendly to my interests, could do very little to advance them.

The attempt to get a pension met with still greater obstacles. For though Dr. Helfer had lost his life in an expedition in the service of the Indian government, he did not belong to the special class of officials entitled to pensions, and it was therefore a question whether his widow had any legal claim. Even the zealous efforts of Baron Bunsen and the Austrian ambassador, Neumann, were of no avail; there was evidently a fear of creating a precedent. My hopes diminished day by day. I was, therefore, the more agreeably surprised, when Mr. Melville wrote to me that the Company had granted me a pension of £100 a year. As I afterwards heard, the Queen had said that, in her opinion, the directors were, at all events, morally bound to give pecuniary compensation to the widow of an explorer who had lost his life in the service of the Company. And even in constitutional and parliamentary England such expression of opinion from royal lips is seldom without effect.

Spring had meanwhile approached, and renewed my longings for home. I made up my mind to leave London, and was not shaken in my resolution even when honoured by an invitation to a costume ball at the palace, great as was the attraction to be present on one of those rare occasions, when the cream of London society is to be seen in all its glory. Some ladies of my acquaintance, who were disappointed at not having received invitations, thought it quite incomprehensible that any consideration should induce me to decline. I had, however, a slight foretaste of it, for the Duchess of Sutherland, then one of the most beautiful women in England, consulted me about the costume of a German lady of noble birth in the olden time. The black velvet robe, the bodice, the girdle, the cap adorned with costly jewels, in short, the whole costume became her admirably.

With a thankful heart I took leave of the Bunsens and other kind friends whose acquaintance I had made in London. With my departure from the great city, where I had hoped for but little, expected nothing, and yet had found so much, ended another chapter of my changeful life.

CHAPTER XII.

AT THE COURT OF PRUSSIA.

THE Hamburg steamer, which was to take me to my own land, was to leave the mouth of the Thames during the night. I therefore went on board the evening before, and being tired, at once retired to my cabin, so that it was not till the next morning, when I went into the saloon to breakfast, that I heard the fearful news which had arrived during the night, that all Hamburg was on fire, and that many thousands of the inhabitants were deprived of their homes. I was at first engrossed with sympathy for these unfortunate people, but then the thought fell heavy on my heart, where should I find shelter in the burning city? The captain, whose advice I asked, only shrugged his shoulders; he was full of anxieties of his own.

I had a letter of introduction from Baron Bunsen to his friend, Senator Sieveking in Hamburg, but how could I expect a man who took so active an interest in the welfare of his native city to concern himself with my small affairs, at a moment of general distress? Still, as soon as we had cast anchor, I got one of the porters to take the letter, to which I had added a few lines, and awaited the answer on board. After some hours, an elderly man, with a most benevolent expression of countenance, introduced himself to me as Senator Sieveking. He was glad to say that his house was one of the few spared by the flames, which enabled him to offer me hospitality. I at once accepted the invitation.

After an absence of seven years, I once more set foot on my native soil, on June 8, 1842. It was covered with ashes and rubbish as far as the eye could reach. The great rich city, so proud of her commerce with all the world, was in ruins. It was enveloped in thick clouds of smoke; innumerable tongues of flame shot up from the ruins, as if the devouring element was not yet satisfied. This harrowing sight was the greeting that awaited me. The cries of distress cut me to the heart. But it was not this alone that depressed me; to my eyes, accustomed to the verdure of the tropics, the hues of northern vegetation looked pale and chill, as if a sickly character was impressed on the whole landscape. It chilled me more than the temperature itself, and the joy of my return was damped by a tear.

We had to make our way through rubbish, and over smouldering ruins, till we reached a short row of houses spared by the fire, of which the Sievekings' was one. I was most kindly received, and rejoiced in the comforts of a Hamburg patrician home, to which I was just then doubly susceptible.

The next day the Senator took me to his villa, a little way from the town, where he had an extensive dairy. The sleek, well-fed cows had had to make way for human beings. The stalls were all cleared for some poor burnt out family. With fresh straw to lie upon, and bread given them gratis, cut up by a straw cutter, they made themselves very comfortable in these clean and healthy, though narrow abodes. Many of them had not, perhaps for a long time, had so good a resting place, nor enjoyed provision so abundant. It was plain that it would not be easy to get rid of these visitors, and it did cost the Senator much trouble to become master of his own house again.

I did not stay more than a few days at Hamburg. I was especially desirous to offer my respects and thanks to the Princess William of Prussia, for her great kindness and many proofs of goodwill to me during many years, and I therefore went first to Berlin.

I dreaded a night journey in the diligence, and preferred taking the Elbe steamer to Magdeburg, thinking that I should have a good night's rest in the cabin, and be protected from the cool night air, to which I was very susceptible. In order not to be disturbed in passing the Prussian frontier at Wittenberg in the night, I gave my passport and the keys of my trunks, which contained nothing subject to duty, to the captain, and went to sleep, secure, as I thought, from disturbance.

I was awakened by the stopping of the wheels. The ship's bell sounded midnight; we must be at Wittenberg; I wrapped the coverlet closer around me for it was very cold. I heard the sound of boxes being shoved hither and thither, and loud voices as well. Then all was quiet again. Suddenly there was a knock at my door, and I was requested to come up. I replied that the captain had my keys and papers, and would do all that was necessary. Another pause, and another knocking, and a renewed request that I would come up. I answered as before, but the knocks grew louder and louder; I must come at once to the customs office; they would not allow the vessel to pass unless I appeared in person. I wrapped up as warmly as I could, went on deck, and asked the captain for an explanation. All he could say was, that I must obey the summons and cross the landing-bridge to the office. As I entered, the officers all looked at me with curiosity, as if I were some strange animal. My passport was in the commissioner's hands, and he looked first at it, and then at me.

'What is the matter?' I asked, 'and why do you oblige me to expose myself to the night air, and to come here?'

With some embarrassment the gentleman answered: 'This is such an extraordinary passport, it has been beyond all Christian lands, where you have disappeared among Turks and Mohammedans, and now after several years you have come back here. I wanted to know what you looked like, and whether the description was correct?' 'Ah,' I said, 'you wanted to see whether I was black or white. Anything else, if you please?' 'No,' he replied in still greater confusion, handing me back the passport. It had been made out at Prague seven years before, and had been last *visé* by Colonel Taylor, the English Resident at Baghdad. Since then it had never been asked for, but the German customs officer thought it his duty to convince himself of the identity of the owner of so singular a document. Having compared the description with my person, he put his *visé* immediately under that at Baghdad.

In spite of this cold nocturnal adventure I reached Berlin in safety. On inquiring for the Princess William I learnt that she was at Potsdam, so I went there, and wrote to inform her of my arrival. I was told that she was at the royal table in the marble palace, so that I could not expect an audience that day. But his Majesty, who had heard of my adventures through my letters to the Princess, took much interest in them, and had had some extracts published in the court journal, expressed a wish to see me at once, and Fräulein von Obstfelder was sent to bring me to the palace. She, however, did not find me at the hotel, but her orders had been so strict to bring me to the royal party that she did not venture to return without me. At last she found me with a friend, and asked me to accompany her at once to the palace.

'Impossible,' I answered, 'in this toilette,' a black woollen travelling dress. 'Never mind—the King told me to bring you at once, and I cannot go back without you.' I saw that the King's pleasure must not be contradicted, and gave in.

The royal party was assembled at tea. As I entered the room, the King said, giving me his hand, 'Ah! here is our traveller,' and introduced me to the Queen and the Grand Duchess of Mecklenburg. The Princess William greeted me with her usual kindness and courtesy, and I gratefully kissed her hand. All this transpired in so short a time that I felt almost giddy. I had no time to collect my thoughts, for the King had already said to Tieck, who was reading one of his tales aloud—'Leave off now, Tieck; we want to hear something else,' and went on, as he handed me a chair, 'sit down and tell us about your travels; I am very much interested in them.' Flattering as this was it was painfully embarrassing. How could I begin a discourse *impromptu* in this august assembly, and without knowing what they wanted to hear? But the King kindly came to my aid, and by putting various questions encouraged me to go on from one thing to another, and kept up the thread of the conversation. By degrees the other members of the royal family joined in, and it was kept up with great animation during supper. Seeing the King in such good humour, I ventured to tell him of my latest adventure at Wittenberg, at which he laughed heartily, and said it must be prevented in future.

The next day the Princess William gave me a private audience of several hours. She inquired most kindly about the particulars of my experiences, and what prospect the plantation at Mergui offered for my future support. She graciously accepted a gold bracelet from Delhi, which was afterwards greatly admired at the royal table for the fineness of the gold and beauty of the workmanship. It had on it a representation of the Taj Mahal at Agra, surrounded by a wreath of leaves in gold and emeralds.

During my stay at Potsdam I had often the honour

of being asked to drive with the royal family, and then to remain to tea and supper. On one of these occasions I met Alexander von Humboldt, whose acquaintance I had much wished to make, and who astonished me by the flow of his eloquence and his vast knowledge.

One evening the supper, at which there were but few present besides Humboldt and myself, was served at a small table, on one side of which the royal family were seated, and by the King's orders Humboldt and I were placed opposite to him. With a friendly nod he invited us to talk. I was abashed at being put into the same category as this learned man, and should have begged off if there had been time, but Humboldt at once began a discourse. He talked, as usual, much and well, until he was interrupted by the King with: 'Now Humboldt, you stop a bit, and let your neighbour talk; she can tell us something new.'

I was ready to fall off my chair. Humboldt was to be silent for me to talk! That was too much, and I looked down at my plate in speechless confusion. The King, observing this, put questions about tropical countries, and thus opened the way for me; but I was happily soon released, for Humboldt, who of course knew it all far better than I did, joined in, and continued the conversation until he was again interrupted by the King.

The next Sunday I was summoned to a farewell audience in the King's apartments at 12 o'clock. His Majesty, who was alone, received me very graciously, and said, 'I want to-day circumstantial information about those countries in which you have resided some time; I am much interested in them; tell me all you know about them.' The Queen then came in, seated herself in a window recess, and made me sit opposite; and though there was but little space left, the King shoved a chair in between us, on which he took his seat, and spread out on our laps a map of the peninsula of Malacca, in which he was as much at home as a general with his charts. He then said, 'I have long had a scheme of founding a German settlement in those countries. I have therefore informed myself as well as possible about their geography, and want you to give me your experience about the climate, soil, and capabilities of the country.'

It was a very pleasant surprise to find my favourite scheme, of preparing for some of my poor fellow-countrypeople a profitable field for their labours in those favoured lands, supported in so influential a quarter, and I told the story of my plantation from the beginning to the entrance into partnership with Mr. Dickens at Calcutta; I told him about my brother, who was making great efforts to carry on the plantation, and gave it as my opinion that, at Mergui, the finest harbour in the Bay of Bengal, with its splendid climate, varied products, and the friendly character of the natives, a German settlement would be sure to succeed.

The King listened with great attention. When I had finished, he said, 'It would certainly not be an easy matter to carry out the scheme. Prussia has no fleet to protect so distant a colony. I have therefore thought of interesting Austria in it, of inducing her to share in the undertaking.'

To this I ventured to reply, that the participation of Austria, even if she would agree to it, would, so far as I could see, only increase the difficulties; for though the English would offer no opposition to a settlement of peaceful agricultural colonists from Prussia on the borders of their Indian Empire, and would willingly take them under their protection, a colonisation scheme, undertaken jointly by Austria and Prussia, might excite their suspicion and even hostility.

The Queen several times nodded approval, and then said to her husband, 'I think she is right.'

The King replied, 'It may be so, but still I should like to know what Metternich would say to the plan.' Then turning to me, he continued, 'You are an Austrian, and, as I hear, a citizen of Prague, and are intending to go to Bohemia; Metternich is now staying there at his country-seat at Marienbad; go and see him.'

I was frightened at the idea of having to speak of such matters to the great statesman. The King, observing this, continued with a smile: 'Do not be afraid. Give my compliments to him; he will be sure to receive you kindly; tell him what you have told me, and what I have been thinking of, and say that I want to know his opinion of it;' adding, with special emphasis, 'I am really interested in your plantation, and charge you to keep me informed of its progress and prosperity.' With every mark of favour I was then dismissed.

It may here be mentioned that in consequence of my reception at Court I was induced by friends to get permission to resume my family nobility. By a royal letter of September 13, 1843, I was permitted to assume the name of Helfer-Desgranges, of which, however, I did not much avail myself.

CHAPTER XIII.

MY PARENTAL HOME.

There was nothing now to detain me at Potsdam or Berlin, and I hastened to my dear mother at Dresden. My travelling companions were two very pretty girls and their father, a stately man with a military bearing. His dialect and sociability betrayed him to be an Austrian, and he at once attracted me, for since my marriage with Dr. Helfer I had reckoned myself as one of this cheerful and light-hearted people. We were speaking of the pleasures of travelling, when I remarked that I was acquainted not only with comfortable travelling in Europe, but with the toils and hardships of Eastern travel. My opposite neighbour started from his seat, and taking both my hands, exclaimed, 'Are you the brave lady who accompanied her husband in all the dangers of travelling through the wilds and in primeval forests?' 'Do you mean the wife of Dr. Helfer?' I asked. 'Yes, I am Madame Helfer!'

His pleasure at the meeting was unfeigned, and there was no end to his questions, until I expressed a wish for nearer acquaintance, when he introduced himself to me as Count Schlick, who played a great part in the subsequent wars. We separated at Dresden with the hope on both sides that we might meet again, and I had to promise to visit them when I came to Prague. This accidental meeting was not without result on my future life. It helped to bridge over the gulf which could but exist between the conservative old Bohemian nobility and the widow of Dr. Helfer, and opened the way for a future *rapprochement* between me and the liberal section of the ancient noble families.

Inexpressibly great was the joy of reunion with my beloved mother, though her pleasure was damped by the pain of seeing me return alone, instead of by the side of him whom she had loved as a son, whose mental powers and love of research had filled her with pride, and to whom she had willingly given her daughter to travel in strange lands. But it was only now and then for a moment that she lost her equanimity at the sight of me, or that the classic repose was disturbed, which, combined with her great beauty, made her appearance so remarkable.

Her simplicity and modesty, for she was without a trace of feminine vanity, won universal love and esteem. When she appeared at the ladies' parties in the neighbourhood the place of honour was always given her as a matter of course. Here she sat with that distinguished and gracious bearing which only the minuet school of our grandmothers could impart. With her large dark eyes wide open she would sit composedly knitting row after row of her stocking, taking no heed of the ladies around her, whose talk was mostly of domestic matters or the nursery. She would sit thus perhaps a whole afternoon, for a coffee party on a Sunday in the country is not a short occasion. But when the gentlemen came in in the evening her face lighted up, and she would listen, with eager interest, to their conversation on the news in the 'Spener'sche Zeitung,' remarkable natural occurrences, or discoveries in foreign lands.

Her daughters revered and loved her as perhaps few mothers are revered and loved, though our relations with her were more like those of younger sisters. Her habit of getting lost in thought gave rise to many a joke. Sometimes when she was going out we engaged her in some earnest conversation, which took up her attention, when one of us would arrange her head-dress, another array her in shawl or mantle, and then take her to see herself in the glass, when she would say, half in jest, and half in earnest, 'You silly girls!' or, although she did not place the least value on her beauty, 'It is a pity that not one of my daughters is fit to hold a candle to me.'

These peculiarities must have had a special origin, and are not to be traced to education alone, but rather to native qualities, and they explain many of my own peculiarities; for if I am asked how I came to be as I am, a woman without fear—though it must be added, not without reproach—it cannot be answered by a word, but involves a story in which I must go back to previous generations.

On the father's side I am, as the name betrays, of French descent. My great-grandfather, president of the parliament of Bordeaux, was exiled from France on account of his Protestantism, and took refuge in Switzerland. There my grandfather was born. He chose the career of a soldier, and fought against Prussia as an officer of Jägers. In spite of his valour he was taken prisoner by the Prussians. His bravery and extraordinary height, for he was nearly seven feet high, attracted the attention of Frederick II. When peace was concluded he made him an advantageous offer of entering his service, and of forming a Jäger regiment, the first, I believe, in the Prussian army. He rose to the rank of general, married a Fräulein von Schichtling, from Silesia, and bought the estate of Zinnitz, in Lower Lusatia, where he died universally beloved and honoured, covered with thirty-two wounds. His bones rest in the park, which was laid out by himself.

My father, also a tall and handsome man, united in himself the different nationalities of his parents. His appearance, and lively excitable temperament, were French, his mind and character and love of scientific pursuits were German. But the two tendencies did not form a harmonious whole; they seemed to exist independently, side by side; sometimes he was all French, sometimes all German—a discord which in the subsequent Franco-German wars often brought him into conflict with himself, but, on the other hand, enabled him to perform great services to his country.

My mother's ancestors belonged to the noble race of von Bülow, which goes back to the thirteenth century. During this long period it has furnished many dignitaries both to Church and State, most of whom were distinguished by their mental powers, but some also by singularity. Among the last was my mother's grandfather. He had, it was said, suffered some rebuke from his king, Frederick William I., and lived ever after, until his death twenty-five years later, in sullen seclusion from the world, on his estate of Falkenberg, in the Altmark. He only left his room when compelled to do so, and even his wife, whom he otherwise treated with great esteem, was not allowed to enter it. If anyone caught sight of him through the window, his tall form, with a white beard down to his breast, was seen pacing up and down the same boards, so that at last they were quite worn through; or standing in the middle of the room, surrounded by a circle of chairs, and talking aloud, as if to one or another of them. Each chair represented some department of knowledge, and the conversations with these spirits were said to have been of deep meaning and logical connection. One morning he was found dead without previous illness, leaning against the back of a chair.

He left five sons, all gifted men, though not free from eccentricities. Dietrich, the fourth son, published, at the beginning of 1806, a work called 'A History of the Campaign of 1805,' in which the faults of the military Prussian system, as it then was, were severely criticised; and, Cassandra like, he foretold the subsequent Napoleonic wars, so fatal to Prussia and Germany; he also unsparingly attacked the Russian government, and was therefore imprisoned at Berlin, at the instigation of the Russian ambassador, Alopeus. He was afterwards sent to Kolberg and Riga. A mystery hangs over his subsequent fate. It is conjectured that he was dragged into the interior of Russia, and there died.

The third son, Wilhelm, was the celebrated general, who, in recognition of his victories in 1813, was made a count, with the addition of von Dennewitz to his name. His deeds are recorded in Prussian history, and many biographical works speak of the gifts and culture which made him the companion and friend of Prince Louis Ferdinand of Prussia.

My mother was the daughter of the second son, August. He married young, but the union was unhappy, and was soon dissolved. The grandmother took charge of the child. Thus it happened that my mother spent her early youth with her father and his brothers. As a child, she heard their conversation on politics, philosophy, religion, natural science, and all sorts of serious subjects, and it had a decided influence on her tastes. She could never afterwards be engrossed with little domestic cares, but was, up to old age, enthusiastic for everything true, great, and good. Her patriotic spirit and her admiration for the heroism and statesmanship of the great Frederick, gave her courage to meet, with fortitude, the sad times in store for our house in 1813, and made her the protector of the family during my father's frequent absences.

My father, more French than German, held the ideas of liberty and equality of the French Realists, and adhered to them as long as he lived, although, when necessary, he sacrificed his sympathies to his duty to his Prussian fatherland, and served for a short time as captain in the army.

Soon after their marriage my parents took to the paternal grandfather's estate of Zinnitz. This was the birthplace of myself and my brothers and sisters, and the scene of our happy childhood and youth.

With my father's French republican sentiments, it is not surprising that his ideal in the education of his children was Rousseau's doctrine of 'Natural development.' Practically, however, the 'Emile' method was only pursued to a certain extent. The liberty which we were allowed was combined with strict obedience, not springing from fear of punishment, but from profound reverence for our parents. Above all things, the strictest love of truth was impressed upon our minds. There was to be no lying on any account, and voluntary confession was an atonement for faults.

After my brothers entered the cadet corps at Dresden, no tutor was kept for us girls. My parents thought they could themselves impart the very modest amount of learning then considered necessary for them. They certainly did not give us any regular lessons; my father was no friend to 'drumming things into people's heads,' or to loading the memory at the cost of the thinking faculties, but he often took occasion to exercise our judgment in a peculiar fashion. He would state some proposition, only apparently or partially correct, and set us to find out or refute the errors. This often gave rise to long conflicts, which sometimes lasted into the night, for even when children feel what the truth is, they find argument very difficult. We were thus early accustomed to systematic thought and correct expression. When we were right we were rewarded, but well laughed at when wrong.

We children were seldom left to ourselves, but were allowed to be present when visitors came, and during the winter evenings, when my father read the papers, or a book aloud, while my mother sat at her spinning wheel, weaving the fabrics of which we still treasure some pieces as relics.

As my father was lord of the manor and magistrate, causes were tried in our house, and these had a special interest for me. As a little child, right or wrong, I used to sit for hours at the chink of the door, listening to the arguments and the decisions of the judge. No play could entice me away. There was once a criminal case which interested me greatly.

A miller, in the village, had shot a shepherd of my father's, because he had pastured his sheep on the miller's winter seed, which he had a legal right to do. It gave rise to a long trial, and in the end the delinquent was found guilty. Although much grieved about the shepherd, who used to give me the prettiest lambs to play with, my pity for the criminal was no less sincere. I could not help feeling that the miller was right, that he was only defending his own property, and thought that I should have done the same. Happily the execution was forestalled by the death of the criminal in prison.

My father was passionately fond of growing fruit and flowers, and busied himself much in the garden; in this also he liked us to join him, and carefully fostered the taste for all rural occupations, during which botany and other sciences were practically studied. He was of opinion that no one can direct labour without having practised it himself, and therefore liked us to perform, for a time, all the work of garden and field as if we had been labourers. We thereby not only learnt it thoroughly, but greatly strengthened our bodily powers, for it was a matter of honour with us not to be outdone.

We were also inured to heat and cold; our sleeping rooms were never warmed, not even when the frozen breath, during the night, made the bed-head a wall of ice in the morning. According to regulation, our special sitting room was not warmed till November 1; but as the elements did not respect these domestic laws, we children hit upon a plan of warming ourselves on homœopathic principles, of curing cold by cold. We used to bathe in the neighbouring brook, even during snow storms, not caring if they half-blinded us. It answered the purpose; there is no more effectual defence against cold.

When I was ten years old, and had acquired the elements of learning, my father took me one day into his library, and said; 'You have learnt enough now, if you want to learn more you can read; here are the books.' He might well say this, for in his select library there were none of those exciting romances too often to be found in ladies' boudoirs. I stood irresolute amidst all this learning, gazing at the volumes placed at my disposal; I knew not where to begin. My eye fell, accidentally, on the pretty binding of Voss's translation of Homer. I seized the Odyssey, read it over and over again, perhaps five times running, without getting tired of it; it laid the foundation of my liking for the classics, and became the standard by which I judged other books. I afterwards read Lessing and Herder, and their humane views made a great impression on me.

Meanwhile, the time had arrived when French arrogance and Napoleon's tyranny had exceeded all bounds, and the German nation arose to throw off its fetters. The year 1813 came with its triumphs, but also with the horrors of a desperate struggle, in the very midst of which we lived, for Lusatia suffered more in this war than any other part of Germany. Day by day we heard the roar of cannon, and saw the glow of devastating fires. Prussian, French, and Russian troops, among the latter Cossacks and Baschkirs, passed through our estate, which was on the high road, between Luckau and Kalau, and we were often doubtful whether our visitors were friends or foes.

My father's fluency in French on the one hand, and his relationship to the Prussian general on the other, often served him in good stead. The Saxon government at Lübben entrusted him with the office of mediator between the two head quarters, and of providing for the troops, so that arbitrary requisitions and plunder should, as far as possible, be prevented. He was often able to provide our house with a guard, sometimes French, sometimes German, and often both at once.

My mother, of course, was not to be persuaded to leave the estate and take refuge, like our neighbours, in a town. The plate and other valuables were packed in water-tight chests, and sunk in the village pond. Nothing but indispensable articles of furniture, bedding and linen were kept in the house. The only thing stolen by the soldiers was a polished copper water can, which a son of the Russian steppes fell in love with and carried off.

At first we had plenty of provisions; but they were soon exhausted, and there were no more to be had; for weeks we had no bread in the house, and had to live on potatoes and garden produce. When soldiers were quartered upon us, my mother used to give them the keys of the cellar and store room, that they might see the state of things for themselves. But insolent demands she met with dignified composure.

In spite of our scanty fare, we children delighted in soldier life, which brought novelty and excitement every day. Nobody did any work, not even the peasants. Of what use would it have been, when the fields would only have been trodden down! Neither did we do any, and I was glad to escape sewing and knitting stockings, for which I had but small taste. We wandered about, like the rest of the villagers, listening to the thunder of the guns in hope and fear. Spies used to be sent out to learn news of the troops and of our father. One of these, the village weaver, distinguished himself by his cunning and devotion. He had been a wandering artisan, but had been induced to settle down by my father, who had discovered that his head and heart were in the right place. A brother of his rose to be a learned professor.

A Wendish woman also, called, on account of her immense height, the great Christiana, was very useful to us in those evil days. She was the factotum of the house, loved us as if we had been her own children, and protected us like a Cerberus. When her work was done, she told us pretty stories, and sang us Wendish songs. By her knowledge of the Wendish language she could make herself pretty well understood by the Russians, which was often a great help.

Once, when my father was at home for a few days, we were sitting with him outside the door, when a woman came running down the road and begged for protection from some marauding Frenchmen, who had taken from her a sack of corn she was carrying to the mill. Ever ready to help, my father went in to exchange his civil dress for the Saxon uniform, which was known and respected by the French, and was just about to go with the woman, when a troop of Cossacks dashed into the premises. On seeing this uniform, which was strange to them, they seized the wearer, and would have carried him off as prisoner. The news of this spread quickly in the village, and the peasants, headed by Tillich, the weaver, hastened to us with pitchforks, scythes, and flails to defend their laird. Their zeal, however, nearly cost him his life, for the Cossacks were pointing their pistols at his head, and would have fired, had not my mother interposed and persuaded our people to retreat. Tillich, alone, followed at some distance to the Prussian head quarters, unobserved by the Cossacks, and when my father was released he rushed back, post haste, to bring us the joyful news.

Another character in our household was Gottlob, the coachman, called, because he was rarely sober, 'drunken Gottlob,' but, nevertheless, he always had his wits about him. Faithful and trustworthy, wary and taciturn, he was extremely useful to my father in all these vicissitudes, and he took him with him on all his difficult missions.

Apprised of the advance of Bülow's army corps, my father drove to Kalau, the town a few miles off, to make provision for the troops. He had scarcely entered the town when some of the French, who knew him, got hold of him and demanded where the Prussians were. Not having found them at Kalau, as he had expected, he could answer truly that he did not know; but they did not believe him, and he was detained as a hostage until their whereabouts should be discovered. They mounted the church tower with him to look round, and seeing clouds of dust in the distance, they thought they had discovered the Prussian troops, and my father agreed, although he knew that it could not be Bülow's corps coming in that direction.

The French commander at once sent a strong detachment to attack the enemy and prevent his advance. It was Marshal Oudinot's purpose to push on to Berlin, and General Bülow's to prevent it, and each was trying to forestall the other in investing Luckau, as the vanguard of Berlin. The French, on their advance from Kalau, instead of the bulk of Bülow's corps, found only a small detachment under General Oppen, who retreated fighting, but they thereby lost precious time, and were prevented from taking possession of Luckau, only sixteen miles off, which was only held by a weak detachment of Prussians.

My father, rightly surmising where Bülow might now be, saw the great importance of informing him of the unexpected advance of the French to Kalau, and their delayed march to Luckau, which might enable him, in spite of the progress the French had made towards Luckau, by a forced march to overtake them, and get there first, though he knew well enough that if this communication became known to the French, he should lose his head. In this difficult and perilous mission he availed himself of the services of drunken Gottlob, knowing that he would sooner be hanged than betray his master. Gottlob reached Bülow's headquarters, through byways, at a stretch gallop, and himself handed the important missive to him, whereupon Bülow immediately set out with all his corps to get into the road between Kalau and Luckau, and, guided through bypaths well known to Gottlob, he reached it near Zinnitz by four p.m.

We knew nothing of all this, but were enjoying the few days quiet, and sitting peacefully outside the door. Some villagers hastened to tell us that a great army—whether friend or foe they did not know—was encamped not far from the village, on the banks of the stream. My youngest brother, who was too young to join the army, went to learn more about it, and was not a little surprised to find Bülow's corps encamped there. He introduced himself to his great-uncle, and asked if he had any commands for him.

'What!' he exclaimed, 'you here? I had quite forgotten that this village belongs to you, and that Fieken (short for Sophiechen) lives here. That is unfortunate. My troops are exhausted with a forced march. To-morrow the French will come up and give battle, and my position on the further side of this stream is favourable. But then your village will inevitably be burnt!—Let us go to your mother.'

I shall never forget the look of this famous man, so revered by us, as he entered our house, somewhat bent and covered with dust. As he lifted the blue field cap, his hair, which was nearly white, fell over his temples, and the cap, from the great heat, had made a strong blue mark all across his forehead. Taking my mother by the hand, he said, in a tone of pity, 'I bring bad news. There will inevitably be an engagement here to-morrow, you will be without any protection, and the village will be given over to the flames and plunder.'

After considering a little while, he added, 'I will see what can be done,' whereupon he called his generals and all the staff, who had followed him, into an adjoining room. What passed in this council of war I do not know.

While this was going on, my mother's brother, a colonel in the army, asked for refreshments, and said, 'Sister, bring out whatever you have in kitchen and cellar.' Never did my mother feel the want of everything so keenly as at that moment. She confessed, with shame, to these gentlemen that she had nothing, absolutely nothing, to offer them. 'Convince yourself of it,' she said, giving the key of the store-room to her brother. He hastened away, but soon returned, with shouts of laughter, bringing an old cheese on a plate. This, his only booty, was placed in the middle of the long table. They were going to draw lots for it, when my uncle, in fun, brandishing his sword over the heads of the other officers, stuck it into the cheese, and carried it round in triumph as his own. The fun had reached its climax, when the door opened, and Bülow, with stern voice, ordered a march on to Luckau.

How quickly the merriment ceased! The officers rushed every one to his post to order the start. We had scarcely time to milk a couple of cows to give our great-uncle a little refreshment. At the head of his corps, my mother and the rest of us by his side, he began the march, just as the sun was setting blood-red in the west, foretelling a hot day for the morrow, which indeed it was, in more senses than one. The band struck up a hymn tune; my great-uncle bared his head. Struck by the sight, the soldiers followed his example, and accompanied it with their voices. It was an inspiriting moment, to see the great army going forth thus courageously to a great battle on the morrow, and to hear words of gratitude and praise from thousands of voices. Could such an episode ever be forgotten!

On the boundary of the estate we took leave of our uncle, and did not see him again. He was confident of victory. His star, as he said, had preserved him from taking part in a lost battle. Before leaving us he provided for our safety as far as it lay in his power. He left my mother's brother behind, with orders not to leave the house until it was entered by the French, and as this might happen at any moment, nobody went to bed.

My uncle's horse was kept standing before the open window, that he might spring upon it the moment the French should appear at the door. He was just devouring, with excellent appetite, some potatoes and sour milk, when three French Uhlans suddenly appeared. They were recognised at once as a guard by a white handkerchief round the arm. As such they permitted my uncle to depart through the door. My father, who had been compelled by Marshal Oudinot to stay with him, said that he would only consent in case his family and estate were protected during the march of the French troops through it, on which a guard was sent to Zinnitz.

Day had scarcely dawned when the advanced guard of Oudinot's corps arrived, and they went on in uninterrupted march, hour after hour, towards Luckau.

These troops looked very different from the Prussians. Many lagged behind, exhausted and famished. We saw soldiers, after asking in vain for bread, crawl on, throwing away their arms and knapsacks. One fell down dead in our courtyard. Whether it was that the Prussians, having their own country behind them, were better provided for, even in famished Lusatia, or whether it depended on their respective commanders, the French were in a pitiful condition. My father came with them, and was permitted to remain. About nine o'clock the thunder of cannon announced that the battle at Luckau had begun. The roar became louder and louder, and very soon a great column of smoke told us that the town was in flames. In order the better to witness the spectacle, which had a magic attraction for us children as well as for grown up people, we mounted to the thatched roof of a lofty barn by means of a fire ladder, whence we could see every movement of the troops, every flash of the guns, and the flames as they devoured the town.

It was not till late, when the French were entirely defeated, and had left the field in wild confusion, that we came down from our watch tower, and announced to our parents the glorious and fruitful victory won by Bülow on June 4, 1813, on the field of Luckau. Tired and exhausted by the excitement we went early to rest.

Whether the above events are related in the annals of the memorable year 1813, I do not know, but I can assure the reader that they are strictly true. No one need wonder now that dauntlessness and fearlessness are among the chief features of my character.

That a just estimate may be formed of my father's self-sacrificing spirit, I must add that after Lusatia was freed from troops, another and greater danger set in.

Hospital fever broke out in the lazarettos, which were over-crowded and not properly superintended. Many of the doctors had succumbed to the disease, and there was danger of a wide-spread epidemic. It was an urgent necessity to inspect and clean the hospitals, and make provision for better medical attendance and nursing. A Government commission was to be appointed, but no one, whose place it was, was willing to be upon it. My father, however, who held no office, undertook the task, and, with two medical men from Dresden, made the round through the province. The danger to health and life was very great. In one of the hospitals one of the doctors fell dead at his side, but my father was able to complete his mission. Just, however, when he was making his report to the president at Lübben, the seat of the provincial government, and the president was congratulating him, and handing him a glass of wine, he felt a cold shudder pass through him, a sure sign of having taken the infection. He at once desired to be taken home. He reached it with every symptom of the dreaded malady. After an illness of eight weeks, he got over it, but the after effects undermined his previously strong health, and were the cause of his early death.

I have permitted myself in this chapter to give a little account of my parentage and childhood, although it does not properly belong either to the travels or the sequel, and the book is not intended for an autobiography. I thought, however, that even a fugitive sketch of my early years, when the foundations of my character were laid, might conduce to the better understanding of the events described.

Hoping that the reader will pardon the digression, I now return to the special subject of the book.

CHAPTER XIV.

IN BOHEMIA.

My husband's will had made me his heir, and therefore a citizen of Prague, so that business matters required my presence there. Besides this, I was still more strongly attracted thither by the desire to carry out the wishes of the deceased by the presentation of the natural history collections, made in Asia Minor and Burmah, to the museum at Prague. Part of them were already deposited in the city, but the greater part I had with me. The collection was of great value, on account of the many rarities it contained, especially in *Coleoptera*, and it was my desire, by this gift to the national museum, to raise a lasting monument to Dr. Helfer's name. I wished that it should be exhibited in a room named after him, and that the authorities of the museum should have a work written descriptive of the objects.

Before going to Prague, however, my health required that I should take the waters at Marienbad. I suffered more from the changes of temperature on my return from the torrid zone, than I had ever done from tropical heat, and, strange as it may appear, the summer heat in Europe was intolerable to me. I still remember a drive, at mid-day, in a fir wood, when the air seemed so close that I could scarcely breathe, so great is the difference between our heavy northern atmosphere, and the pure, clear air of the tropics.

At Marienbad, I had to deliver the message of King Frederick William to Prince Metternich, who was at his seat of Königswart; for though I was fully convinced that he would decline any participation in the King's projected colonisation in Malacca, I felt bound to execute his commission. I, therefore, one day drove to Königswart, and sent in my name to the prince, adding that I had a message from the King of Prussia, otherwise my insignificance would hardly have been admitted to an audience by the great and busy statesman. He was a tall, imposing looking, and very handsome man, even in advanced life, with an agreeable expression of countenance. He received me with great condescension, took a seat beside me on the sofa, and asked me to mention the subject of my commission. But he looked so high and lofty, that I felt far more embarrassed under his searching gaze than in the King's sociable presence at Potsdam. My alarm then may be imagined when, after a little while, I observed that his countenance had changed, that he was making the greatest effort to attend, that his replies, at first clear and to the point, began to wander from the subject, and at last became incoherent and unintelligible. I saw plainly that he was making a great effort to overcome this absence of mind, and was in the greatest perplexity what to do. After a struggle he mastered it, himself recurred to the subject, and asked me to proceed. But it did not last long; he relapsed into the same state, and, seeing the effort it cost him to attend, I thought it most suitable to relieve him of my presence. At a moment when he was scarcely aware of it, I slipped out of the room, and breathed freely again, for to see the great man in this condition was most painful.

When, on my return to Marienbad, I told my physician of this strange occurrence, he said, 'If you had told me that you intended to visit the prince I could have prepared you for it, for I have known for some time that he suffers from these attacks.' As I afterwards heard, however, he entirely got over them.

Estranged by years of absence from the circles in which I had been intimate, still more so, perhaps, by the changes that had taken place in them and myself, I felt very lonely in Prague, of which I had before been so fond. The house in which I had passed the first happy months of my married life was now occupied by strangers.

I was, therefore, all the more desirous to finish my business, and to arrange for the presentation to the museum. This took longer than I anticipated. The authorities of the museum feared whether the pecuniary resources or mental qualifications at their disposal would enable them to have the work written and published, which I desired as an equivalent for the gift.

The president of the museum was Count Joseph Nostitz, Count Franz Thun-Hohenstein was managing director, and Dr. Franz Palacky, secretary. The latter, who had just published his 'History of Bohemia' in

German, did not disdain to take part in the management of the museum, then a national German one, nor to associate with German-speaking people. Times were changed!

Count Franz Thun, a man of high culture, and an enthusiast for art and science, was for accepting the collection, and Dr. Palacky, although more interested in the historical than the natural history department, fully agreed with him. Count Joseph Nostitz, however, had grave scruples about it, urging that, although the museum would certainly be enriched by the gift, it would bind itself to an obligation which it was scarcely in a position to fulfil. He, therefore, conscientiously opposed its acceptance.

These gentlemen were all strangers to me, but Count Thun soon introduced himself in the name of the president. Count Joseph I knew only from hearsay as an oddity. It was said that he lived like a recluse in the house of his aged father, to whom he devoted the greater part of his time and care, finding his recreation in books, particularly astronomical ones. He avoided all intercourse with ladies, and—so it was whispered to me—he did not wish personally to have anything to do with me, although he was not insensible to the enrichment of the museum; I, no doubt, belonged to the class of learned ladies, the most intolerable of all. After this I did not of course feel any great desire to make the singular Count's acquaintance. The negotiations, therefore, were carried on between me and Count Thun. He thought the conditions might easily be fulfilled, and finally persuaded the president out of his scruples. When the time came for drawing up the contract, the president felt obliged to lay it before me for signature, and to offer his thanks in person. Curious to behold this woman-hater, who had so shunned my acquaintance, face to face, when he was led, or rather dragged in by Count Thun, I turned my eyes anxiously towards the door, expecting to see a morose looking personage. With obvious embarrassment he apologised for the delay, but his excuses were little to the purpose, and ill accorded with the honourable and open expression of his face, from which it was evident that untruth was unknown to him, even the so-called necessary falsehoods of social life. This was the man then, with this benignant countenance, who had been described to me as a misanthrope. There must surely be some misunderstanding I thought, and the idea awakened my sympathy.

Wishing to put an end to the painful situation, I said, as I offered my hand, 'You have brought me the contract to sign; perhaps you will kindly read it over to me, that the business may be concluded as soon as possible.' He expected all sorts of difficulties and objections on my part, so that it was a great effort to him to read it. When he had finished, I said, 'Very good,' and taking the pen signed at once. I heard a sound like the breathing of a person relieved from oppression on the chest, and saw the count draw a long breath with a look of great satisfaction. By this stroke of the pen he was relieved from all unpleasant discussion, and perhaps he no longer regarded me as a captious, intolerable blue-stocking. Surprised by my complaisance he vouchsafed me a friendly look, the first, I believe, that a woman ever received from Count Joseph.

The ice was broken. The dread of tiresome negotiations with a disagreeable woman was supplanted by a feeling of obligation. He felt that he had done me injustice, and, as president of the museum to which I had just presented a valuable gift, he felt bound to do the honours of it. Too much of a gentleman to omit a duty of politeness he invited me to inspect the rooms of the museum, which I had not seen, and to select with him a suitable place for the Helfer collection.

Ten o'clock next morning was the hour appointed. Just as I was preparing for the long walk from the lower part of the city to the Hadschrin, where the museum then was, Count Joseph presented himself and offered his escort. I could not decline this polite attention, though I should have preferred the walk through the ancient streets and over the Nepomuk bridge alone, to having an eccentric man by my side to whom my companionship was doubtless unpleasant. Our conversation would probably have been scanty enough were it not that Prague offers objects of interest at every step.

At the museum a ceremonious reception awaited me. All the custodians had been invited by the president to meet me, and to show me their various departments. This afforded me an opportunity of making the acquaintance of some of the professors of Prague University, and other learned and interesting men, who, from the retirement in which they lived, were rarely to be met with. The morning passed quickly away in agreeable intercourse. When the business part of my visit, the choice of a suitable place for the collection, was concluded, with many thanks to these gentlemen, I prepared to leave. Count Joseph again begged permission to accompany me. I really should have preferred being left to my own reflections, and therefore politely declined, assuring him that every obligation on his part had been amply fulfilled. He persisted, however; and, seeing that he was in earnest, I submitted to the inevitable, and prepared myself as best I could for an effort at conversation. This, however, was spared me, for very soon Count Joseph began to speak with surprising openness of his mode of life. With visible emotion he told me of his intimate relations with his late mother ; how she had formed the link between him and other people ; how he had withdrawn from all social intercourse after her death, and given himself up entirely to his studies and his aged father. He said that his views on politics, mankind, and the equal rights of men were entirely opposed to those of his own class, and only led to unpleasant discussions, so that he avoided society and lived in great isolation. I saw that the communication of thoughts and feelings, so long shut up in his own breast, especially as they found sympathy with me, did him good. I related some of my travelling adventures, and happened to mention that, in order to arrange my affairs at Prague as soon as possible, I had interrupted a course of the waters at Marienbad, and was going to finish it here, taking my walks on the fine promenade on the bastion.

We parted with assurances of mutual esteem, as I supposed for ever, as there was nothing further to bring us into contact.

The next morning I set out very early for my promenade on the bastion. I was scarcely there when Count Joseph met me, and joined me without ceremony. I could scarcely believe my eyes, and was in great perplexity how to construe his behaviour. To be walking at this early hour with a gentleman with whom I had so slight an acquaintance, was, to say the least, peculiar. I could not refrain from expressing my surprise at his appearance, when he said, with perfect simplicity, 'I thought, when you told me of your morning walk, that it implied an invitation to accompany you.'

I started at these words. How could they be taken in any but an offensive sense from the lips of a modern cavalier, for which I had no reason for *not* taking the count?

I turned quickly, intending to give expression to my annoyance. But I met his gaze, a look so entirely honourable and true-hearted, that it was plain that he was totally unconscious of the meaning that might be put on his words, and, abashed before the pure and childlike spirit of this man, I cast my eyes on the ground.

'Will you not allow me to accompany you?' he continued; 'it really gives me pleasure.'

'Most willingly,' I replied. 'Although what I said

was by no means intended as an invitation, your company will always be agreeable to me, if you think it worth while to rise so early.'

'Early!' he said. 'The sun has been up some hours, and I am always ashamed when I oversleep myself. It seems to me unworthy to be behind him.'

I looked at him with increasing wonder. A cavalier so simple that he did not perceive the double meaning of his words, and rose with the sun! What a singular personage. It was something quite new and surprising.

After this the count and I regularly took our early morning walk on the bastion. The place was calculated to enhance the elevated frame of mind produced by a walk in the fresh morning air, when all things are glorified by the beams of the rising sun. For before us was spread the venerable and picturesque city, with its palaces, churches, and convents, the silver thread of the Moldau running through it, crossed by the bridge with its statues, and on the other side the imposing pile of the Hadschrin and the cathedral. Both of us were disposed to be communicative, and much did we enjoy the interchange of ideas and opinions. It was, however, a pleasure of short duration, for, after a week's stay at Prague, I returned to Dresden to meet my mother, who had a great liking for the German Florence, to make arrangements for a long stay there. But I was not long to enjoy reunion with her. Before we could remove to Dresden she was suddenly snatched from me by death.

Once more I was left alone. But as if fate would allow me no time to give way to sorrow, almost at the same time I received news of the failure of the house of Ferguson & Co., and therewith of my partner, at Calcutta, Mr. Theodore Dickens. He informed me that he was not in a position to advance any more money for the plantation, and must withdraw from it altogether. At the same time my brother wrote to me that funds for the most pressing expenses were exhausted, and that it was imperative to find new sources of help. This bad news aroused me from my grief. I saw at once that I should scarcely find the partner I required in Germany, and resolved to go to London. I arrived there with my sister in January 1843.

I had previously been kindly received in the house of the Prussian ambassador, through the kind offices of the Princess William of Prussia, but this time I was welcomed from real friendship by the amiable family of Baron Bunsen. The Baroness was distinguished by goodness of heart and sterling worth, and I shall ever recur, with special gratitude, to her kindness, during a stay of several months in her house. Her society, as well as intercourse with people of eminence in London, was as great a pleasure as it was an advantage to me.

In business matters, too, I was fortunate enough to attain my purpose. A gentleman in a high position having examined the prospect of future revenue from the plantation, resolved to put two of his sons into it. They were to go out to Mergui, on condition that my brother should retain his post as manager.

Once more relieved of a great anxiety I returned

with lightened heart to Germany, and went first to Carlsbad to restore my shattered health.

I was recalled thence to Prague, by the transactions with the Museum. Great difficulties had arisen about a work descriptive of the Helfer collection. It consisted, as before stated, of *Coleoptera*, the minutest species, scarcely visible to the naked eye. In order to determine their species it was necessary to compare them with those in the collections at Paris and the Hague. But the authorities at the Prague Museum had no means at their disposal for this. The consultations were, necessarily, carried on between the president and myself. With his high sense of honour, it was in the highest degree repugnant to him not to be able to fulfil the engagements made in the name of the Museum. He could not bear, as he said, 'to pocket' a valuable collection without any return. His mind was only set at rest by my assurance that, in accordance with Dr. Helfer's will, I wished, at all events, to see it incorporated with the museum in his native city. Repeated consultations on the subject led to a renewal of the intercourse which had been so agreeable to us both during my previous visit to Prague.

With the count's open character, it could not long remain a secret to me that a stronger impulse than the need of social intercourse led him to seek my society, neither could I long be in doubt about my own warmer interest in him, and I resolved, for the sake of both, to leave Prague as soon as possible. No sooner did he hear of this than he decidedly opposed it, declared his sincere attachment, and his desire to enter into a union with me, in which he hoped to find a happiness he had little dreamt of.

His proposals made me both proud and happy. Not because he was a count, but because he was a man of rare uprightness of character, nobility of sentiment, and goodness of heart. But I had great scruples on the subject, for I knew only too well that the widow of Dr. Helfer, and a Protestant, could not be a welcome daughter-in-law to his rigidly Catholic father, with his deeply-rooted traditional ideas on the subject of rank. I therefore declined his proposals. He persevered, however, and, although in all other respects he consulted his father's wishes, in this he stood firm. He followed me to Berlin, where I had gone to visit a friend. When I found how deeply he was wounded by my refusal, and how much he suffered in contending with the obstacles in the way, I yielded to his wishes. His mother had said to him, in her last days, as if it were her testament, 'I wish you a good wife, who will make you happy'; and a good wife to him I promised to be.

CHAPTER XV.

THE END OF THE PLANTATION.

SHORTLY after my betrothal with Count Nostitz, I heard from my partner in London of the severe illness of my brother at Mergui, with the remark, that nothing but a return to Europe could restore his health, which was confirmed by my brother himself. My partner, at the same time, signified that, having only agreed to the partnership of his two sons in the plantation, on condition that my brother should remain there, they could not undertake it under these altered circumstances, and he therefore must dissolve the contract. Family circumstances which had occurred may, perhaps, have formed the chief motive for this decision, and consideration for his family deterred me from taking legal proceedings against it, although my brother's recovery, and continuance at the plantation, would have given me ample ground for doing so.

Remembering that the King of Prussia had charged me to keep him informed of the progress of the plantation, I went to Berlin, and addressed myself to the Princess William, begging her kindly to inform his Majesty of the state of affairs, and was very soon informed by her that the King would like to see me.

He listened attentively while I told him of the unfortunate failure of the banking house at Calcutta, as well as the recent withdrawal of my partner in London, and described the bad results which must follow to the plantation.

'What are you going to do now?' he said, at last. 'You know I am interested in it; will you sell the property to me?'

'No, your Majesty,' I replied, 'for two reasons. First, in its present state the plantation has no absolute value, since it produces no revenue, but will, on the contrary, require considerable outlay for several years before it can be profitable; by what standard, therefore, could it be valued for sale now? And secondly, to carry it on successfully it requires to be managed by a man thoroughly acquainted with it, like my brother.'

'You are right,' said the King, adding, with a laugh, 'you want a moneyed partner. Well, I cannot be that in my own person, but I will find a representative. You need not fear, the plantation *shall* be kept up.'

These words were to me a sure pledge of the maintenance of my property. Overwhelmed with joy, I expressed my gratitude in the words, 'I lay the plantation, in full confidence, at your Majesty's feet.'

I now considered that the enterprise, which had cost so many sacrifices and so many anxious nights, was safe by royal favour, and that my brother's future was secure, in a career which suited him so well. Much more was said by the King, from which I could but conclude that he was going to take a share in the plantation from personal interest as his private property. The very next day Count Anton Stolberg came to tell me that the King had put the business into the hands of Herr Rother, the Minister of Marine, and had ordered a not inconsiderable sum of money to be sent to my brother to meet the most pressing expenses.

I feel it to be necessary to take this opportunity of refuting an idea, which has gained wide credence, that in the transactions about the plantation, I was seeking, and actually derived, pecuniary advantage myself; I did not claim any payment to myself, either directly or indirectly, nor did I receive any such whatever. All the money advanced by the marine department went direct to Mergui, and was lost both to myself and the department.

The plantation at that time consisted of 2,000 acres, and contained 150,000 young areca palms, 6,000 nutmeg trees, 6,000 coffee plants, and 50,000 cocoa-nut palms; 2,000 acres more were promised me by the Indian government. The Minister Rother, in accordance with his orders, entered into a preliminary contract with me as to the joint possession of the plantation, on March 16, 1844, in which he reserved to himself unlimited powers, and liberty of withdrawal, while no power was granted to me until the uncertain period when the definitive treaty should be concluded. My culpable carelessness in this business is only to be excused by my firm belief that the maintenance of the plantation was fully resolved upon by the King, that this contract was a mere business-like form, and I thought that it would be unsuitable to confront the minister, whom I regarded simply as the King's representative, with a legal adviser, to guard my interests. I thought it proper, under the circumstances, to hand over my property to the minister unconditionally, and took care to acquaint him with my reasons for doing so, and my full confidence in the King's intentions.

The minister sent two commissioners to India to value the plantation, and take part in the management. They set out at an unfavourable time of year; contrary winds delayed their arrival. Irritated by sickness and a bad passage, they arrived during the worst period, that of the tropical rains. Just as the rain was coming down in torrents, and making the land a swamp, they had to inspect some thousand fields, and value the young trees smothered in briars and thorns. Suddenly transplanted into this strange land, without any knowledge or experience of the country, they were to form an estimate of the value of the plantation. No wonder that they were not ready with it at the end of seven months, and it probably was not very favourable. But neither this, nor the other reports of the commissioners, were ever communicated to me, and I was thus deprived of any opportunity of discussing them.

Other accounts of the property reached me, which described its condition as prosperous. These were laid before the banking house of F. M. Magnus, of Berlin, and they made a very favourable report as to the prospect of revenue.

At this time, the Minister Rother had a tedious and

painful illness, which left him in a state of great irritability and weakness; he never entirely recovered from it, and it hastened his end. It was no wonder that this gentleman, oppressed with sickness and business, found this novel task, which could not fail to occasion him much trouble, a great burden, and that he tried to get rid of it. His aversion to it may have been the greater because, although the grant of the 4,000 acres was promised to me by the East India Company, the act was not completed by the directors, for the negotiations took a very long time, having to be carried on between the directors in London, the government in Calcutta, and the local authorities in Malacca. This served the minister as a pretext for dissolving the partnership, and the resolution to do so was made known to me on December 15, 1845, with the remark that 'circumstances did not admit of the government or the marine department taking part in the plantation.' Further reasons, like the report of the commissioners, were withheld.

A year and three quarters of painful uncertainty had passed while these negotiations had been going on, and the decay of the plantation, through want of cultivation, was inevitable. It is quite conceivable that the King, with his numerous interests, may, in the space of two years, have quite forgotten so insignificant a circumstance.

This third failure cut me to the heart. My last hopes had vanished. All the care and trouble, all the effort, and all the capital, which was not inconsiderable, were lost, and my brother was deprived of the property for which he had laboured and endured so much. Although people acquainted with the subject, in Calcutta, London, and Berlin, considered that, at the end of five years, after a gradual expenditure of 150,000 rupees, an income of 130,000 rupees per annum might be derived from it, I had no hope of being able to find a partner, willing to advance so large a sum for an undertaking in the remote peninsula of Malacca, which would not yield a return for five years, high as it might then be.

The country, then a wilderness without an owner, is now a valued possession of the English crown, and is celebrated for the quality of its Moulmein rice. It was Dr. Helfer's knowledge of the great fertility of the soil, and its favourable situation for commerce by means of water communication, which made him form a true estimate of the value of the land, and induced him to lay out the plantation. It had now lain uncultivated for over two years, in which time underwood springs up with such rapidity in the loosened soil in the tropics, that it is more laborious to clear it than to cut down and cultivate a portion of the primeval forest, and the natives often desert their fields after two or three years, and prefer to take a fresh piece of forest into cultivation.

The circumstance, therefore, that I should have had almost to make a fresh beginning, and the conviction that further attempts to obtain capital would be in vain, compelled me to give up the further cultivation and possession of the land as impracticable. There could be no thought of disposing of it in a country where everybody was allowed to appropriate land for nothing.

My brother returned from India, and, having become alienated from European life, is now a planter in California, where the climate permits him and his family to cultivate the ground themselves.

CHAPTER XVI.

PRAGUE AND VIENNA.

My marriage with Count Nostitz had taken place, in July 1844, at Dresden. My brothers and sisters, and my husband's attached friend Count Franz Thun, accompanied us to the altar; we were also particularly gratified by the presence of his sister, the Countess Salm-Reifer-Scheid, who, from early childhood, had lived in close intimacy with her brother, and desired nothing so much as to see him permanently happy. With winning kindness she welcomed me as a sister, and to her I owe many of the happy hours I afterwards spent at Prague.

My husband's father, accustomed to daily intercourse with his son, desired that we should live at Prague; and his son, equally accustomed to gratify his every wish, readily acceded to it, although the place was not congenial to him, and could not be so, on account of the great differences of opinion between him and his equals in station. His only passion was an ardent patriotism for Austria, his ruling idea a desire for her restoration to her former power and glory. Curiously enough he hated the nobles and the clergy, because he regarded them as the impediments to the progress of Austria, and considered the selfish adhesion of the old nobility to their feudal privileges, and the ambition of the clergy, to be the beginning and end of all Austria's misfortunes.

As a friend and patron of learning, my husband—for our own edification, and to supply a want felt at Prague—set up a reading-room in our house, having a separate entrance, so that it could be entered by any one without disturbing us. Modern learned periodicals, in German, French, English, and Italian, lay on the table; and the professors of the university, as well as other literary and cultivated men, were invited to avail themselves of it. They were also invited to take tea with us every Thursday evening for mutual interchange of ideas. These occasions became very interesting and instructive. Many of the gentlemen gave lectures on novelties in their special departments, experiments in chemistry and physics were even made, and new things read by authors present. These evenings were a source of high enjoyment to my husband and myself, but our pleasure was to be of short duration.

The year 1848 arrived, and its baneful breath spread over Europe like a pestilence. It fell like lightning into the combustible material of an antiquated and corrupt state of things, inflamed the minds of peaceful citizens, and transformed them all at once into red Jacobins ready to murder each other.

The evil spread to the usually peaceful and pleasure-loving city of Vienna. The news of it had scarcely reached Prague, when an arch-politician—a tavernkeeper of the name of Faster, known by the nickname of the Duke of Bohemia—hastened thither to see what was going on for himself, to report it to his own city, and take his measures accordingly.

One evening our party had just assembled, and an interesting conversation was going on. Everyone seemed happy and content, when an absent member rushed into the room, and, scarcely able to speak from excitement, told us the news brought by Faster of the revolution at Vienna and the bombardment of the city. A spark in a powder-barrel could hardly produce a more startling effect than these words did in our social circle. The men who up to this time had been so united and friendly blazed up, and, as if they had long agreed upon it, separated into two hostile camps. A professor who was sitting by me on the sofa, who was known as a gentle and peace-loving man, raised his arm and exclaimed repeatedly, as he let it fall upon the end of the sofa, 'I must see blood! I must see blood!'

When the revolt broke out in Prague, and the youths—who were great politicians—went about the streets with swords too long for them rattling by their sides, threatening their native city and terrifying their families; and when these, who might have been punished like boys, were joined by men of standing, when even men of learning succumbed to this spirit of discord, and the boyish nonsense became a really dangerous revolt, it made my husband's heart bleed. He was a humane and peace-loving man, and when brought into contact with coarseness and ignoble things he shut up like a sensitive plant, and would a thousand times rather suffer wrong than do the least wrong himself. Benignity was so stamped upon his countenance that, in later years, when his hair and beard were white, though his complexion still had the freshness of youth, and his blue eyes beamed with benevolence, strangers not seldom respectfully raised their hats and turned to look at him, for his mien and bearing bore the stamp of true nobility. The revolt at Prague made him still more dislike it as a residence.

When he had faithfully performed his filial duties to his aged father, had devoted all his time to him during his last illness, and finally followed him to his final resting-place, at the close of 1849 we removed to Vienna.

We looked forward to enjoying the many advantages of the city in peace; but destiny, which has so often interfered imperiously with my plans, ordered otherwise.

The Revolution, although put down, had inflicted severe wounds on the population of Vienna; many a citizen and father of a family had fallen, and others were so reduced in circumstances as to be unable to provide for their wives and children. It was said, though this was an exaggeration, that there were 6,000 children, particularly girls, running about the streets, promising a ruinous increase in the future of the already numerous proletariat. I accidentally met with two ladies who, like myself, were childless, and had a desire to care for these neglected children. We consulted some experienced men about forming a Ladies' Society for their benefit, and resolved at once to make a beginning. I was elected president, and accepted the office in order to forward the business, but only provisionally, as the work of societies was new to me, and I was besides but little known in Vienna.

The liberality of the Viennese was, as it had often proved itself before, splendid. No sooner was the object of the society known, than the greatest sympathy was manifested. This object was to found schools for neglected girls, in which they were to be taught all kinds of useful work, and thus be enabled to support themselves. The ladies of the highest aristocracy took an active part with the wives of citizens in the work of the society, large sums were given for establishing the schools, as well as hundreds of gulden as annual subscriptions. The merchants gave materials, and artizans their labour, gratuitously; a carpenter, for instance, gave all the fittings for a large school. Neither did art refuse to aid. The dancer, Fanny Elsler, who had retired from the stage, and had refused pressing invitations to reappear, granted my petition. When I described to her the condition of the poor children, and asked her to give a performance for their benefit, she exclaimed, 'For the poor children of the city, my former companions? Most certainly I will.' In a few days she appeared at the Opera House as Yelva, supported by the first artists of the Burg Theatre, and though it was a morning performance every box and every ticket was taken; no inhabitant of Vienna would miss the opportunity of seeing her once more. This was her final leave-taking of the theatre.

The task of finding sites for the schools where they were most needed fell of course to the president. In order to economise funds I had to ask the authorities to give them gratuitously. The officials, who had grown grey in their time-honoured ideas, were mostly averse to innovations, and not seldom bluntly refused my requests. But I was not to be repulsed, and renewed them again and again; one of the burgomasters, when I saw him for the first time, said, 'I am not in favour of your schools, but I know you will not take a refusal, so I may as well say yes at once.' This good man was afterwards one of our most active coadjutors.

Some of the parish priests, whom I wished to ask for their co-operation, would not even grant me an interview. I was simply shown the door. These gentlemen feared that their influence on education would be diminished by the instruction we gave in feminine handiworks.

The most difficult task was to get the poor people to send their children. They were accustomed to get money by letting them beg, and were very averse to giving it up. But this also was overcome, as the children before long were paid for their work, and clever and industrious girls could earn from ten to fifteen gulden a month.

Her Imperial Highness the Archduchess Marie took the society under her protection; Baron Welden, the Commandant of Vienna, allotted to it the fines levied by the police, and it increased so rapidly in dimensions that in one year sixteen schools were established for 2,000 children, and a capital collected of 54,000 gulden.

In the course of two years my strength was nearly exhausted in the manifold labours of the society, and I longed for rest. Besides this, I had long felt it to be unsuitable that a Protestant should be at the head of an association in the midst of a population so predominantly Catholic; an association for founding institutions which, though only intended to teach feminine handicrafts, bore the name of schools, and where the children were brought into contact with many Protestant ladies, so that the Catholic clergy feared the spread of religious error. I therefore resolved to give up the office, which, as before stated, I had only accepted provisionally. But in spite of all my efforts I could not find any lady willing to undertake it, and should probably have borne the burden longer, had not Catholic organs, even from a distance, as, for instance, a Rhenish paper, lifted up their voices against the office of president of the society being held by a Protestant. Induced perhaps by this and other considerations, his Eminence Archbishop Milde asked me to call upon him, when he, in the most considerate manner, requested me to give up my office, adding: 'I am unable to protect you from the attacks of my clergy.'

But even after this no lady could be found to take it. I therefore saw that the only way was to absent myself, and withdraw from the society altogether.

Having succeeded in inducing the Princess Marie Liechtenstein to undertake the presidentship, I withdrew, with a feeling of gratitude for the many proofs of attachment I had received from high and low.

CHAPTER XVII.

CONCLUSION.

FOR some time both my husband and I had wished for a permanent residence in the country. The pleasures of the great city, and the entertainments of the *salons* were not to his taste, nor could they satisfy me, accustomed as I was to active employment and life in the open air.

Our attention had been directed to Hungary, a country of great promise, whose productiveness offers a hopeful field of labour, and reminded me more than any other of tropical regions.

The idea of acquiring a property there grew into a resolve, and, in 1852, my husband bought the estate of Schöndorf, very advantageously situated in the Banat, the corn-producing district. Here I spent seventeen years with the noblest and most loveable of husbands, in almost entire seclusion from the world, and even from our nearest neighbours. We were Germans, and Germans we desired to remain, and this fixed an impassable gulf between us and the Magyar inhabitants. A few of our neighbours understood and respected our sentiments, and received us with the amiable hospitality peculiar to the Hungarians, and of this I shall always retain a grateful remembrance. With these few we were on the most friendly terms, but the great distances prevented us from keeping up much intercourse, and we lived, therefore, in almost complete isolation.

While my husband, who had never had anything to do with farming, and had neither taste nor talent for it, gave himself up to his favourite pursuit of science, continued his astronomical observations, and felt a lively interest in what was going on in the world, I took, with great zest and energy, to the management of the estate, partly from a liking for farming, partly from a wish to justify my husband's confidence by brilliant results, for he had given the estate entirely over to my care, and finally in the hope of introducing improvements in the very imperfect methods of agriculture in Hungary.

My exertions were unceasing. I was often in the fields by four o'clock in the morning to supervise the culture of tobacco, one of the most valuable products in the district. This, at any rate, brought its reward, for in 1866 I received the silver agricultural medal from the Austrian Government, and the diploma and medal for the best tobacco from the Paris Exhibition of 1867. But of having attained the higher objects of advancing civilisation, and improving the methods of agriculture, I cannot boast. Custom, prejudice, sometimes designed obstruction, and other untoward circumstances, frustrated my best endeavours.

The months not occupied in farming, I employed, by my husband's wish, in writing the narrative of Dr. Helfer's travels. He took great pleasure in these notes, and urged their publication, which however he did not live to see.

I have neither the wish nor the power to enter on any description of the affairs of Hungary. They have been the subject of so many polemics, and in recent times of so much bitterness, that I do not wish to add a grain to it by any experiences of my own. The future will show whether the cherished idea of the Magyars will be realised, that they are a privileged nation destined to rule over others, and to found a great Magyar empire. It would not be advisable to pass any opinion now on what may or may not be realised, for many things more incredible have come to pass. One thing is certain, that they will not fail of the mission, to which they think themselves destined by Providence, by undervaluing themselves.

The unhealthy climate of the Banat, the notorious Hungarian intermittent fever, affected even me. I thought myself steeled by my travels against all climatic influences, and that, having borne the heat of the tropics, I could certainly bear the climate of the forty-sixth degree of latitude. But the sudden changes of temperature, the alternations of icy cold blasts with great heat, and the miasma from the rich soil of the Banat after rain, followed by sunshine, are so injurious to the health that a stranger rarely escapes attacks of fever.

In my case, the malady assumed its most dangerous form, that of continued but outwardly scarcely perceptible feverishness. After I had struggled with it for years, my husband insisted on leaving the country, as change of climate is the only remedy.

I the more willingly consented as my strength was no longer equal to my task, and I had arrived at the humiliating conclusion, that all my labours would, at the best, only result in advantage to myself, and that no efforts to raise the community would ever succeed. This painful conclusion alleviated the parting from Schöndorf. Having let the land in separate lots to the villagers, in 1869 we left for Switzerland. My husband had a great liking for that country, and had long wished to introduce me to its beauties. We traversed it in all directions, and then settled down at Zürich, where we enjoyed pleasant social intercourse, and entire freedom from care.

But in 1871, I was assailed by the hardest fate that could befall me—my most beloved and revered husband was taken from me.

He died after a short and painless illness, in his seventy-sixth year. His last hours, like his whole life, bore witness to his unruffled peace of mind.

Here I crave permission to lay down the pen, and to close the narrative of the various vicissitudes of my life.

THE END.

LONDON: PRINTED BY
SPOTTISWOODE AND CO., NEW-STREET SQUARE
AND PARLIAMENT STREET

www.ingramcontent.com/pod-product-compliance
Lightning Source LLC
Chambersburg PA
CBHW030305240426
43673CB00040B/1066